PRAISE FOR
FASCISM: A WARNING

"Why, as Madeleine Albright asks early in her new book, 'are we once again talking about fascism?' Who better to address these questions than Albright, whose life was shaped by fascism and whose contribution to the cultivation of democracy as a stateswoman and private citizen is unparalleled?"

—*New York Times*

"Albright [has] serious credibility on the subject. She witnessed the evils of fascism firsthand, as her book movingly chronicles. And she effectively makes the case: pay more attention to the signals, subtle and strong. A lot more." —*The New Yorker*

"*Fascism: A Warning* is dedicated to victims of fascism, but also to 'all who fight fascism in others and in themselves.' Ms. Albright has earned the right to that ambitious mission statement. At a moment when the question 'Is this how it begins?' haunts Western democracies, she writes with rare authority. . . . [Yet] if her learning is to be expected, her way with words is a happy surprise, as is her wisdom about human nature. Free of geopolitical jargon, her deceptively simple prose is sprinkled with shrewd observations about the emotions that underpin bad or wicked political decisions." —*The Economist*

FASCISM

A WARNING

FASCISM

A WARNING

MADELEINE ALBRIGHT

WITH BILL WOODWARD

HARPER PERENNIAL

NEW YORK • LONDON • TORONTO • SYDNEY • NEW DELHI • AUCKLAND

To the victims of Fascism

Then and now

And to all who fight Fascism

In others

And in themselves

Every age has its own Fascism.

—PRIMO LEVI

CONTENTS

PREFACE

I AM AT MY FARM NEAR THE BORDER THAT SEPARATES VIRGINIA from West Virginia. This morning, upon awakening, I poured a cup of coffee, put on a jacket, and walked outside to greet the cows who replied with a hearty chorus of moos. Having exhausted their vocabulary, I returned to the house, took a deep breath, switched on the television, and began writing this.

My desktop calendar is turned to December 2018. Last month, I was among the tens of millions of Americans who went to the polls, thus participating in democracy's signature rite. The balloting in the midterm election was described by many—including the president—as a referendum on the leadership of Donald Trump. As such, the results were inconclusive, but to me, mildly encouraging. The Democrats regained control of the House of Representatives although the Republicans, as expected, increased their majority in the Senate. Maneuvering for the next big election has already commenced. I pray the campaign will be uplifting—but confess to harboring doubts.

This book, *Fascism: A Warning*, rose from the wreckage of 2016, for many of us a year of bewilderment. First the British were lured into Brexit by the false promise of a new relationship with the European Union, one they mistakenly thought would enable them to retain their rights while shedding their responsibilities. Then, in November, Donald Trump won a majority in the American electoral college despite violating every precept of conventional political wisdom (aside from remaining in the public eye) from the beginning of his campaign until the end. Few believed that could happen, but it did.

Even before the 2016 balloting, I had decided to write about the toils and snares confronting democracies around the world. My idea was to make support for free governments a foreign policy priority in Hillary Clinton's first term. The political upheaval following the election added urgency to the task, and partially shifted the focus to include Trump's take-no-prisoners approach to governing. Where in the past I could assume that the U.S. government would put its foot down on the side of democratic institutions and values, Trump's foot has been fully engaged in kicking America's allies, the independent press, federal prosecutors, immigrant families, and the notion—stressed to most children at an early age—that facts matter.

The resulting book was published originally in hardcover in April 2018. I dared hope then that the fears I express in its pages would quickly prove exaggerated. Alas, that has not been the case.

During the interval between then and now, heads of government with an autocratic bent have won reelection in Russia, Hungary, Egypt, Venezuela, Turkey, Azerbaijan, and Cambodia. In each case, the field of competition was tilted heavily in favor of the incumbent. These were not fair elections. In Brazil, voters fed up with corruption, crime, and recession turned to an openly misogynistic right-wing candidate who promises quick solutions based, in part, on a full-scale retreat from environmental stewardship. In Europe and elsewhere, extreme nationalist movements continue to scale the ramparts—shifting the terms of debate, moving into legislatures, and grabbing for themselves a thicker slice of power. Italy's new leaders boast of their refusal to knuckle under to regional norms. In Syria, the brutal dictator Bashar al-Assad still flaunts his ability to dominate seven years after an American president urged his removal. In the Middle East, more fissures are opening due to such shocks as the cold-blooded murder and dismemberment of a reporter in the Saudi Arabian consulate in Istanbul. Worldwide, there are more refugees huddled in camps than there have been since the Nazi surrender almost three-quarters of a century ago, and the United States is less welcoming to the international homeless now than at any time in modern memory.

According to an old Czech saying, it's no trick to make soup from a fish, but making a fish out of soup is a challenge. In the chapters to come, I argue that ambitious, often arrogant leaders are intentionally undermining the institutions and democratic principles that have held the world together through much of my life. Without offering anything real or better, they ask us to abandon the ideals of international cooperation, political pluralism, civil discourse, critical thinking, and truth. The longer these false prophets have their way, the more damage they will wreak and the more difficult it will be to heal the wounds they are opening. The trend is worldwide, and among those most directly affected are Americans.

In traveling around the United States to discuss this book, I have shared my thoughts with thousands of people from every region. The experience was bracing—and a little odd. In Las Vegas, my appearance coincided with a convention of the wine and spirits industry. Behind the table at which I signed books for both the sober and the tipsy, a banner read: MAKE WHISKEY GREAT AGAIN. Despite all the attention given to the "me too" movement, a gentleman in Miami rose to his feet and said, "I'm ninety years old, but I haven't lost my eyesight, and you're a good-looking gal." An article in the *Washington Post* referred to me as "a lovable feminist granny." By contrast, a man in Brooklyn who heard me speak told a reporter later that I was a "war mongering ghoul," this according to a Russian newspaper. At every stop, when I opened the floor to questions, a hundred hands flew up.

Overall, I found the national mood to be cranky; and it's no wonder we're on edge. Our political parties are at war with one another and fracturing internally at the same time. We have a president who considers it good politics to drive our citizens apart and whose approach to world affairs prompts many among us to cringe while others stick out their chests. Common ground is hard to find; instead, we are at each other's throats. Even now, with the volume on my television turned low, I can hear the yelling.

In this book, I offer both a historical perspective and a global one. Many of the trends we now see were also evident in much earlier decades. This leads to some important questions: What lessons can we derive for the future from the horrors perpetrated long ago by the followers of Mussolini and Hitler? Where do we draw the line between the simple abuse of authority and the gross misrule we call Fascism? How can we explain the alarming rise and contagious spread of anti-democratic trends? Is the hitherto unshakable bond between Europe and the United States unraveling and, if so, can it still be mended? What must we do to ensure the preservation of freedom for our children and those who will come after?

My farm provides a good vantage point from which to ponder such topics. Like a democracy at work, the property is vulnerable both to sudden storms and to the encroachment of termites, pests, viruses, and weeds. There are predators in the woods, reptiles on the ground, and—overhead—occasional bolts of lightning. Survival depends on adherence to a rigorous schedule of maintenance. Yet the farm is also resilient, having endured for generations, its evergreens still majestic and its foundation, though set in the rock of an earlier era, satisfyingly firm.

In recent years, we have all become familiar with the counter-terrorism mantra: "See something, say something." In the pages that follow, I propose an added exhortation—*do* something. What that something might be is for each of us to decide in accordance with our opportunities and talents, but it begins by pushing back harder against the debilitating cancer of cynicism.

Fascist attitudes take hold when there are no social anchors and when the perception grows that everybody lies, steals, and cares only about him- or herself. That is when the yearning is felt for a strong hand to protect against the evil "other"—whether Jew, Muslim, black, so-called redneck, or so-called elite. Flawed though our institutions may be, they are the best that four thousand years of civilization have produced and cannot be cast aside without opening the door to something far worse. The wise response to intolerance is not more intolerance or self-righteousness; it is a coming together across the ideological spectrum of people who want to make democracies more effective. We should remember that the heroes we cherish—Lincoln, King, Gandhi, Mandela—spoke to the best within us. The crops we'll harvest depend on the seeds we sow.

I look once more through the window and can see that the winter sun is now high in the sky. The air outside is warming and it has occurred to me that there might be value in taking a long walk, gathering my thoughts, then initiating a discussion on the herd instinct with my four-legged friends.

Thank you in advance for your interest in this book.

MADELEINE ALBRIGHT
LOUDOUN COUNTY, VIRGINIA
DECEMBER 2018

FASCISM

A WARNING

ONE

A DOCTRINE OF
ANGER AND FEAR

O N THE DAY FASCISTS FIRST ALTERED THE DIRECTION OF my life, I had barely mastered the art of walking. The date was March 15, 1939. Battalions of German storm troopers invaded my native Czechoslovakia, escorted Adolf Hitler to Prague Castle, and pushed Europe to the threshold of a second world war. After ten days in hiding, my parents and I escaped to London. There we joined exiles from all across Europe in aiding the Allied war effort while waiting anxiously for the ordeal to end.

When, after six grueling years, the Nazis surrendered, we returned home with high hopes, eager to build a new life in a free land. My father continued his career in the Czechoslovak Foreign Service and, for a brief time, all was well. Then, in 1948, our country fell under the control of Communists. Democracy was shut down and once more my family was driven into exile. That Armistice Day, we arrived in the United States, where, under the watchful eyes of the Statue of Liberty, we were welcomed as refugees. To protect us, and to make my life and those of my sister, Kathy, and brother, John, seem as normal as possible, my parents did not tell us what we would learn only decades later: that three of our grandparents and numerous aunts, uncles, and cousins were among the millions of Jews who had died in the ultimate act of Fascism—the Holocaust.

I was eleven when I came to the United States with no goal more ambitious than to become a typical American teenager. I ditched my European accent, read stacks of comic books, glued my ear to a transistor radio, and became stuck on bubble gum. I did everything I could to fit in, but I could not escape knowing that, in our times, even decisions made far away could spell the difference between death and life. On entering high school, I started an international affairs club, named myself president, and provoked discussions about everything from Titoism to Gandhi's concept of *satyagraha* ("The Force which is born of Truth and Love").

My parents cherished the freedoms we found in our adopted country. My father, who quickly established himself as a professor at the University of Denver, wrote books about the perils of tyranny and worried that Americans were so accustomed to liberty—so "very, very free," he wrote—that they might take democracy for granted. After I began a family of my own, my mother called each Fourth of July to confirm that her grandchildren were singing patriotic songs and had been to the parade.

There is a tendency among many in the United States to romanticize the years just after World War II—to imagine a time of sky-blue innocence when everyone agreed that America was great and each family had a reliable breadwinner, the latest appliances, children who were above average, and a rosy outlook on life. In fact, the Cold War was a period of unceasing anxiety in which the lingering shadow of Fascism was darkened by another kind of cloud. In my teenage years, due to atomic tests, the radioactive element strontium 90 was found in babies' teeth at fifty times the natural level. Virtually every town had a civil defense warden urging the construction of backyard fallout shelters stocked with canned vegetables, Monopoly boards, and cigarettes. Children in big cities were issued metal tags, embossed with their names, for identification should the worst happen.

Growing older, I followed in my father's footsteps and became a professor. Among my specialties was Eastern Europe, where countries were dismissed as satellites orbiting a totalitarian sun, and where it was widely thought that nothing interesting ever happened and nothing of importance would ever change. Marx's dream of a workers' paradise had degenerated into an Orwellian nightmare; conformity was the highest good, informants kept watch on every block, whole countries lived behind barbed wire, and governments insisted that down was up and black was white.

Then, when change did come, it was with a velocity that amazed. In June 1989, the decade-old demands of dockworkers and the inspiration of a pope born in Wadowice brought democratic governance to Poland. That October, Hungary became a democratic republic, and in early November the Berlin Wall was breached. In those miraculous days, our televisions brought news each morning of what had long seemed impossible. I can still picture the decisive moments of my native Czechoslovakia's Velvet Revolution, so called because it was secured without the widespread cracking of heads or gunfire. The time was a frosty afternoon in late November. In Prague's historic Wenceslas Square, a crowd of 300,000 joyously rattled keys to emulate bells tolling the end of Communist rule. On a balcony overlooking the throng stood Václav Havel, the valiant playwright who six months earlier had been a prisoner of conscience and five weeks later would be sworn in as president of a free Czechoslovakia.

In that instant, I was among the many who felt that democracy had aced its severest test. The once mighty USSR, made fragile by economic weakness and ideological weariness, shattered like a dropped vase on a stone floor, liberating Ukraine, the Caucasus, the Baltics, and Central Asia. The nuclear arms race subsided without blowing any of us to bits. In the East, South Korea, the Philippines, and Indonesia cast off longtime dictators. In the West, Latin America's military rulers made way for elected presidents. In Africa, the freeing of Nelson Mandela—another prisoner who became president—engendered hopes of a regional renaissance. Around the globe, countries meriting the label "democracy" expanded from thirty-five to more than one hundred.

In January 1991, George H. W. Bush told Congress that "the end of the Cold War has been a victory for all humanity . . . and America's leadership was instrumental in making it possible." Across the Atlantic, Havel added, "Europe is attempting to create a historically new kind of order through the process of unification . . . a Europe in which no one more powerful will be able to suppress anyone less powerful, in which it will no longer be possible to settle disputes with force."

Today, more than a quarter century later, we must ask what has happened to that uplifting vision; why does it seem to be fading instead of becoming more clear? Why, per Freedom House, is democracy now "under assault and in retreat"? Why are many people in positions of power seeking to undermine public confidence in elections, the courts, the media, and—on the fundamental question of earth's future—science? Why have such dangerous splits been allowed to develop between rich and poor, urban and rural, those with a higher education and those without? Why has the United States—at least temporarily—abdicated its leadership in world affairs? And why, this far into the twenty-first century, are we once again talking about Fascism?

ONE REASON, FRANKLY, IS DONALD TRUMP. IF WE THINK OF FAScism as a wound from the past that had almost healed, putting

Trump in the White House was like ripping off the bandage and picking at the scab.

To the political class of Washington, D.C.—Republican, Democrat, and independent alike—the election of Trump was so startling it would have caused an old-time silent film comedian to clench his hat with both hands, yank it over his ears, leap in the air, and land flat on his back. The United States has had flawed presidents before; in fact, we have never had any other kind, but we have not had a chief executive in the modern era whose statements and actions are so at odds with democratic ideals.

From the early stages of his campaign and right into the Oval Office, Donald Trump has spoken harshly about the institutions and principles that make up the foundation of open government. In the process, he has systematically degraded political discourse in the United States, shown an astonishing disregard for facts, libeled his predecessors, threatened to "lock up" political rivals, referred to mainstream journalists as "the enemy of the American people," spread falsehoods about the integrity of the U.S. electoral process, touted mindlessly nationalistic economic and trade policies, vilified immigrants and the countries from which they come, and nurtured a paranoid bigotry toward the followers of one of the world's foremost religions.

To officials overseas who have autocratic tendencies, these outbursts are catnip. Instead of challenging anti-democratic forces, Trump is a comfort to them—a provider of excuses. In my travels, I hear the same questions all the time: If the president of the United States says the press always lies, how can Vladimir Putin be faulted for making the same claim? If Trump insists that judges are biased and calls the American criminal system a "laughing-stock," what is to stop an autocratic leader like Duterte of the Philippines from discrediting his own judiciary? If Trump accuses opposition politicians of treason merely for failing to applaud his words, what standing will America have to protest the jailing of prisoners of conscience in other lands? If the leader of the world's most powerful country views life as a dog-eat-dog struggle in which no country can gain except at another's cost, who will carry the banner for international teamwork when the most intractable problems cannot be solved in any other way?

National leaders have a duty to serve the best interests of their countries; that is a truism. When Donald Trump talks about "putting America first," he is stating the obvious. No serious politician has proposed putting America second. The goal is not the issue. What separates Trump from every president since the dismal trio of Harding, Coolidge, and Hoover is his conception of how America's interests are best advanced. He conceives of the world as a battlefield in which every country is intent on dominating every other; where nations compete like real estate developers to ruin rivals and squeeze every penny of profit out of deals.

Given his life experience, one can see how Trump might think that way, and there are certainly cases in international diplomacy and commerce where a clear separation between winner and loser is evident. However, at least since the end of World War II, the United States has championed the view that victories are more readily won and easier to sustain through cooperative action than by nations acting alone.

The generation of Franklin Roosevelt and Harry Truman argued that states would do best by promoting shared security, prosperity, and freedom. The 1947 Marshall Plan, for example, was grounded in a recognition that the American economy would stagnate without European markets able to buy what U.S. farmers and manufacturers had to sell. This meant that the way to put America first was to help our European (and Asian) partners rebuild and develop dynamic economies of their own. The same thinking led to Truman's Point Four Program, which made U.S. technical assistance available in Latin America, Africa, and the Middle East. A comparable approach has served us well in the security realm. Presidents from Roosevelt to Obama have sought to help allies protect themselves and to engage in collective defense against common dangers. We did this not in a spirit of charity but because we had learned the hard way that problems abroad, if unaddressed, could, before long, imperil us.

This job of international leadership is not the kind of assignment one ever finishes. Old dangers rarely go away completely, and new ones appear as regularly as dawn. Dealing with them effectively has never been a matter of just money and might. Countries and people must join forces, and that doesn't happen naturally. Though the United States has made many mistakes in its eventful history, it has retained the ability to mobilize others because of its commitment to lead in the direction most want to go—toward liberty, justice, and peace. The issue before us now is whether America can continue to exhibit that brand of leadership under a president who doesn't appear to attach much weight to either international cooperation or democratic values.

The answer matters because, although nature abhors a vacuum, Fascism welcomes one.

NOT LONG AGO, WHEN I TOLD A FRIEND I WAS WORKING ON A NEW book, he asked, "What is it about?" "Fascism," I said. He looked puzzled. "Fashion?" he queried. My friend was less mistaken than it might have seemed, because Fascism has indeed become fashionable, insinuating its way into social and political conversation like a renegade vine. Disagree with someone? Call him a Fascist and thereby relieve yourself of the need to support your argument with facts. In 2016, "Fascism" was searched on the Merriam-Webster dictionary website more often than any other word in English except "surreal," which experienced a sudden spike after the November presidential election.

To use the term "Fascist" is to reveal oneself. For those on the far left, virtually any corporate bigwig fits the bill. To some on the not-so-far right, Barack Obama is a Fascist—in addition to being a Socialist and a closet Muslim. To a rebellious teen, Fascism may apply to any parentally imposed cell phone restriction. As people vent their daily frustrations, the word escapes a million mouths: teachers are called Fascists, and so, too, are feminists, chauvinists, yoga instructors, police, dieters, bureaucrats, bloggers, bicyclists, copy editors, people who have just quit smoking, and the makers of childproof packaging. If we continue to indulge this reflex, we may soon feel entitled to label as Fascist anyone or anything we find annoying—draining potency from what should be a powerful term.

What, then, is real Fascism, and how does one recognize a practitioner? I put these questions to the graduate class I teach at Georgetown—two dozen students sitting in a circle around my living room balancing lasagna-leaking paper plates on their laps. The queries were harder to answer than might be expected, because there are no fully agreed-upon or satisfactory definitions, though academic writers have spilled oceans of ink in the attempt. It seems that whenever some expert shouts "Eureka!" and claims to have identified a consensus, indignant colleagues disagree.

Despite the complexity, my students were eager to have a go. They began from the ground up, naming the characteristics that were, to their minds, most closely associated with the word. "A mentality of 'us against them,'" offered one. Another ticked off "nationalist, authoritarian, anti-democratic." A third emphasized the violent aspect. A fourth wondered why Fascism was almost always considered right-wing, arguing, "Stalin was as much a Fascist as Hitler."

Still another noted that Fascism is often linked to people who are part of a distinct ethnic or racial group, who are under economic stress, and who feel that they are being denied rewards to which they are entitled. "It's not so much what people have," she said, "but what they think they *should* have—and what they fear." Fear is why Fascism's emotional reach can extend to all levels of society. No political movement can flourish without popular support, but Fascism is as dependent on the wealthy and powerful as it is on the man or woman in the street—on those who have much to lose and those who have nothing at all.

This insight made us think that Fascism should perhaps be viewed less as a political ideology than as a means for seizing and holding power. For example, Italy in the 1920s included self-described Fascists of the left (who advocated a dictatorship of the dispossessed), of the right (who argued for an authoritarian corporatist state), and of the center (who sought a return to absolute monarchy). The German National Socialist Party (the Nazis) originally came together around a list of demands that catered to anti-Semites, anti-immigrants, and anti-capitalists but also advocated for higher old-age pensions, more educational opportunities for the poor, an end to child labor, and improved maternal health care. The Nazis were racists and, in their own minds, reformers at the same time.

If Fascism concerns itself less with specific policies than with finding a pathway to power, what about the tactics of leadership? My students remarked that the Fascist chiefs we remember best were charismatic. Through one method or another, each established an emotional link to the crowd and, like the central figure in a cult, brought deep and often ugly feelings to the surface. This is how the tentacles of Fascism spread inside a democracy. Unlike a monarchy or a military dictatorship imposed on society from above, Fascism draws energy from men and women who are upset because of a lost war, a lost job, a memory of humiliation, or a sense that their country is in steep decline. The more painful the grounds for resentment, the easier it is for a Fascist leader to gain followers by dangling the prospect of renewal or by vowing to take back what has been stolen.

Like the mobilizers of more benign movements, these secular evangelists exploit the near-universal human desire to be part of a meaningful quest. The more gifted among them have an aptitude for spectacle—for orchestrating mass gatherings complete with martial music, incendiary rhetoric, loud cheers, and arm-lifting salutes. To loyalists, they offer the prize of membership in a club from which others, often the objects of ridicule, are kept out. To build fervor, Fascists tend to be aggressive, militaristic, and—when circumstances allow—expansionist. To secure the future, they turn schools into seminaries for true believers, striving to produce "new men" and "new women" who will obey without question or pause. And, as one of my students observed, "a Fascist who launches his career by being voted into office will have a claim to legitimacy that others do not."

After climbing into a position of power, what comes next: How does a Fascist consolidate authority? Here several students piped up: "By controlling information." Added another, "And that's one reason we have so much cause to worry today." Most of us have thought of the technological revolution primarily as a means for people from different walks of life to connect with one another, trade ideas, and develop a keener understanding of why men and women act as they do—in other words, to sharpen our perceptions of truth. That's still the case, but now we are not so sure. There is a troubling "Big Brother" angle because of the mountain of personal data being uploaded into social media. If an advertiser can use that information to home in on a consumer because of his or her individual interests, what's to stop a Fascist government from doing the same? "Suppose I go to a demonstration like the Women's March," said a student, "and post a photo on social media. My name gets added to a list and that list can end up anywhere. How do we protect ourselves against that?"

Even more disturbing is the ability shown by rogue regimes and their agents to spread lies on phony websites and Facebook.

Further, technology has made it possible for extremist organizations to construct echo chambers of support for conspiracy theories, false narratives, and ignorant views on religion and race. This is the first rule of deception: repeated often enough, almost any statement, story, or smear can start to sound plausible. The Internet should be an ally of freedom and a gateway to knowledge; in some cases, it is neither.

Historian Robert Paxton begins one of his books by asserting: "Fascism was the major political innovation of the twentieth century, and the source of much of its pain." Over the years, he and other scholars have developed lists of the many moving parts that Fascism entails. Toward the end of our discussion, my class sought to articulate a comparable list.

Fascism, most of the students agreed, is an extreme form of authoritarian rule. Citizens are required to do exactly what leaders say they must do, nothing more, nothing less. The doctrine is linked to rabid nationalism. It also turns the traditional social contract upside down. Instead of citizens giving power to the state in exchange for the protection of their rights, power begins with the leader, and the people have no rights. Under Fascism, the mission of citizens is to serve; the government's job is to rule.

When one talks about this subject, confusion often arises about the difference between Fascism and such related concepts as totalitarianism, dictatorship, despotism, tyranny, autocracy, and so on. As an academic, I might be tempted to wander into that thicket, but as a former diplomat, I am primarily concerned with actions, not labels. To my mind, a Fascist is someone who identifies strongly with and claims to speak for a whole nation or group, is unconcerned with the rights of others, and is willing to use whatever means are necessary—including violence—to achieve his or her goals. In that conception, a Fascist will likely be a tyrant, but a tyrant need not be a Fascist.

Often the difference can be seen in who is trusted with the

guns. In seventeenth-century Europe, when Catholic aristocrats did battle with Protestant aristocrats, they fought over scripture but agreed not to distribute weapons to their peasants, thinking it safer to wage war with mercenary armies. Modern dictators also tend to be wary of their citizens, which is why they create royal guards and other elite security units to ensure their personal safety. A Fascist, however, expects the crowd to have his back. Where kings try to settle people down, Fascists stir them up so that when the fighting begins, their foot soldiers have the will and the firepower to strike first.

FASCISM CAME INTO BEING EARLY IN THE TWENTIETH CENTURY, A time of intellectual liveliness and resurgent nationalism coupled with widespread disappointment at the failure of representative parliaments to keep pace with a technology-driven Industrial Revolution. In previous decades, scholars such as Thomas Malthus, Herbert Spencer, Charles Darwin, and Darwin's half cousin Francis Galton had propagated the idea that life is a constant struggle to adapt, with little room for sentiment, and no assurance of progress. Influential thinkers from Nietzsche to Freud pondered the implications of a world that had seemingly broken free of its traditional moorings. Suffragettes introduced the revolutionary notion that women, too, have rights. Opinion leaders in politics and the arts spoke openly about the possibility of bettering the human species through selective breeding.

Meanwhile, astonishing inventions such as electricity, the telephone, the horseless carriage, and steamships were bringing the world closer together, yet those same innovations put millions of farmers and skilled craftsmen out of their jobs. Everywhere, people were on the move as rural families crowded into cities and millions of Europeans pulled up stakes and headed across the ocean.

To many of those who remained, the promises inherent in the Enlightenment and the French and American Revolutions had become hollow. Large numbers of people could not find work; those who did were often exploited or later sacrificed in the bloody chess game played out on the battlefields of World War I. Winston Churchill wrote of that tragedy, "Injuries were wrought to the structure of human society which a century will not efface." But with the aristocracy discredited, religion under scrutiny, and old political structures, such as the Ottoman and Austro-Hungarian Empires, breaking up, the search for answers could not wait.

The democratic idealism put forward by President Woodrow Wilson was first to seize the public's imagination. Even before the United States entered the war, he proclaimed the principle that "every people has a right to choose the sovereignty under which they shall live." This doctrine of self-determination helped secure postwar independence for a handful of mostly smallish European countries, and his plan for a world organization blossomed into the League of Nations. Wilson, though, was politically naïve and physically frail; America's global vision did not survive his presidency. The United States rejected the League and, under Wilson's successors, washed its hands of European affairs at a time when the continent's recovery from conflict was not going well.

Many governments that started out liberal after the war were confronted by explosive social tensions that seemed to demand more repressive policies. From Poland and Austria to Romania and Greece, fledgling democracies took wing, then plunged back to earth. In the East, fierce Soviet ideologues were purporting to speak for workers everywhere, thus haunting the sleep of British bankers, French ministers, and Spanish priests. In Europe's center, an embittered Germany struggled to regain its footing. And in Italy a rough beast, its hour come round at last, was striding forth for the first time.

TWO

THE GREATEST
SHOW ON EARTH

THOMAS EDISON HAILED HIM AS THE "GENIUS OF THE MOD-
ern age"; Gandhi, as a "superman." Winston Churchill
pledged to stand by him in his "struggle against the bestial
appetites of Leninism." Newspapers in Rome, host to the Vatican,
referred to him as "the incarnation of God." In the end, people
who had worshipped his every move hung his corpse upside down
next to his mistress's near a gas station in Milan.

Benito Mussolini was ushered into the world in Predappio, a
small farming town forty miles northeast of Florence, in 1883. His
father was a blacksmith and a Socialist, his mother a teacher and
devout. He grew up in a two-room cottage attached to the one-
room school where his mother taught. His family was comfortable but unable to afford full tuition at the priest-run boarding
academy that he began attending at age nine. There, during meals,
the wealthier students were assigned to one table, Benito and his
companions to another—an indignity that kindled in Mussolini

a lifelong rage against injustice (to him). The boy was full of mis-
chief, often pilfering fruit from farmers and getting into fights. At
eleven he was expelled for stabbing a fellow pupil in the hand, and
at fifteen he was suspended for knifing a second classmate in the
buttocks.

But Benito was also a reader. He loved to sit alone with the
daily newspapers and the thousand-plus pages of *Les Misérables*.
From his father he inherited a liking for bold action; his mother
taught him patience—the twig bent his father's way. In college,
when other students griped to each other about the staleness of
the bread they were supposed to eat, Mussolini confronted the rector one on one, causing his classmates to cheer, the rector to back
down, and the bread to come freshly baked.

School days behind him, Mussolini earned a teacher's certif-
icate but lacked discipline in the classroom and was quickly cut
loose. At nineteen, he headed to Switzerland, where he worked
as a laborer, slept on a packing crate, and was jailed—the first
of many arrests—for vagrancy. Out of prison, he got a job as a
bricklayer and soon became active in the local union. This was a
period in Europe when labor politics tilted sharply to the left and
Socialist firebrands preached anger toward the government, contempt for the Church, and militancy on behalf of workers' rights.
Mussolini was not an original thinker, but he was a gifted actor
who could play a role. Though neatly dressed in private, he often
refrained from shaving or combing his hair before appearing in
public. Prior to a speech, he rehearsed diligently so that he might
sound spontaneous. He knew the value of the popular touch and
usually succeeded in eliciting whoops of approval from his audience. Before long, he had come to consider himself a man of
destiny—the next Napoleon, perhaps, or Augustus Caesar.

Swiss authorities, however, were unimpressed by the bud-
ding emperor. They viewed him as an irritant and kicked him
out. Undaunted, he returned to Italy, where he penned a popu-

lar magazine serial about a lecherous cardinal,* edited Socialist newspapers, and began to develop a following. Speaking in
smoke-filled halls, Mussolini warned workers that the elite classes
would never relinquish their privileges without a fight and that no
parliament would take their side against the bourgeoisie. The old
answers, provided by religion or embodied in a sense of patriotic
duty, had been exposed as false and should be abandoned. Justice,
he said, could be obtained only through violent struggle. Revolution was essential.

Then, suddenly, it wasn't. In the summer of 1914, with war in
Europe imminent, Mussolini transformed himself without warning from a Socialist caterpillar into a patriotic butterfly. Rather
than join his leftist comrades, who wanted nothing to do with a
calamity generated, as they saw it, by upper-class imbeciles, he
founded an independent newspaper, *Il Popolo d'Italia*, and urged
Italy to enter the war. The turnabout may have stemmed from a
sincere change of heart, because Mussolini's ideological commitments were never deep, and pacifism was alien to his nature,
but there are other possibilities. French business interests asked
his help in pushing Italy into the struggle against Germany and
Austria-Hungary and promised to reward him should that happen. Also, running a newspaper is expensive; weapons manufacturers were generous in financing *Popolo d'Italia*.

On May 24, 1915, Italy waded into war on the side of England
and France. Mussolini was conscripted by the army and served
honorably for seventeen months while writing weekly dispatches
for his paper. He was promoted to corporal, then almost killed

---

* Years later, when Mussolini's serial *The Cardinal's Mistress* was published in
English translation, Dorothy Parker wrote: "This is not a book to be set aside
lightly; it should be thrown, with great force." Sample dialogue: "I will build you
a secret altar in the depths of my conscience. You will be the Madonna of the
temple within me. I will be your slave. Strike me, despise me, beat me, open my
veins with a subtle dagger, but grant me the revelation of yourself."

when a howitzer exploded during a training exercise, the shrapnel ripping dozens of holes in his guts. He was recuperating when, in October 1917, Italian forces suffered their most humiliating defeat. At the Battle of Caporetto, ten thousand were killed, thirty thousand were injured, and, in the face of enemy artillery, more than a quarter million surrendered.

Though the Italians were part of the eventual winning alliance, the fruits of their victory soon spoiled. The heavy casualties were difficult to absorb, but the pain became even worse when the country's partners in Paris and London failed to deliver on secretly promised territorial concessions. They neglected even to invite Italy's head of state, King Victor Emmanuel III, to the peace conference. These rebuffs strengthened the hand of Mussolini's former leftist colleagues, who argued persuasively that they had been right to oppose the war. Membership in the Socialist Party swelled, and, in the 1919 parliamentary elections, it garnered more votes than any other.

Buoyed by their showing, but still excluded from the governing coalition, the Socialists were not content to sit quietly and vote on legislation. Democracy had instilled in labor ranks a deeper consciousness of rights than had existed in earlier times. The advance of technology had brought industrial workers together in large factories, making it easier for organizers to solicit support and for agitators to stir anger. Pressure built as the Socialists, inspired by Russia's Bolshevik Revolution, began an armed struggle to empower the proletariat and exterminate the bourgeoisie. The party hired gunmen to intimidate strikebreakers, assumed control of numerous municipal governments, and hoisted the red flag above manufacturing plants in Milan, Naples, Turin, and Genoa. In the countryside, Socialist peasants claimed the land they had long been tilling, sometimes murdering estate owners to spread terror and settle personal scores.

To the industrial and agricultural establishment, the protests were deeply unsettling. It was one thing for workers to demand a few more cents an hour, or fewer hours to earn the same weekly wage; it was another when they asserted the right to do away with bosses altogether, take and operate factories, and seize and redistribute land. The extremity of the tensions, the high stakes that were involved, and the blood already shed put barriers in the way of those trying to identify a middle ground. Politicians who sought to calm both sides were trusted by neither.

The rash of strikes and the strife over land played havoc with the Italian economy, causing prices to soar while food shortages grew, basic public services broke down, and railroads—hindered by labor disputes—ran hours, and sometimes days or weeks, behind schedule. Meanwhile, tens of thousands of discharged combat veterans returned home only to be heckled instead of honored and frozen out of jobs that the trade unions had already locked up.

Italy was on the verge of falling apart. Parliament was regarded even by its members as a corrupt bazaar where favors were divvied out to those with political and social connections. As for Victor Emmanuel, he was tiny, timid, and indecisive. In twenty-two years as monarch, he had received the credentials of no fewer than twenty prime ministers. Mainstream political leaders quarreled incessantly among themselves but made almost no effort to communicate with the public at large. The times were ripe for a real leader, a duce, who could bring Italy together and make it once again the center of the world.

IN MILAN ON A RAINY SUNDAY MORNING, MARCH 23, 1919, A FEW dozen angry men crowded into a muggy meeting room of the Industrial and Commercial Alliance in Piazza San Sepolcro. After hours of talk, they stood, clasped hands, and pledged their readiness "to kill or die" in defense of Italy against all enemies. To dramatize their unity, they chose for their emblem the *fasces*, a bundle of elm rods coupled with an ax that in ancient times had represented the power wielded by a Roman consul. The manifesto they signed bore just fifty-four names, and their foray into electoral politics that autumn was barely noticed, but within a couple of years the Fascist movement had more than two thousand chapters, and Benito Mussolini was their leader.

The Fascists grew because millions of Italians hated what they were seeing in their country and were afraid of what the world was witnessing in Bolshevik Russia. In speech after speech, Mussolini offered an alternative. He urged his countrymen to reject the capitalists who wanted to exploit them, the Socialists who were bent on disrupting their lives, and the crooked and spineless politicians who talked and talked while their beloved homeland sank further into the abyss. Instead of pitting class against class, he proposed that Italians unite—workers, students, soldiers, and businesspeople—and form a common front against the world. He asked his supporters to contemplate a future in which those who belonged to his movement would always look out for one another, while the parasites who had been holding the country back—the foreign, the weak, the politically unreliable—would be left to fend for themselves. He called on his followers to believe in an Italy that would be prosperous because it was self-sufficient, and respected because it was feared. This was how twentieth-century Fascism began: with a magnetic leader exploiting widespread dissatisfaction by promising all things.

When the new decade arrived, the Socialists still enjoyed the most favorable position in parliament and had a substantial presence throughout the country. To counter them, the Fascists drew on the vast pool of jobless veterans to organize their own squads of armed men, Fasci di Combattimento (Combat Leagues), to shoot labor leaders, trash newspaper offices, and beat up workers and peasants. The gangs thrived because many in the police viewed them sympathetically and pretended not to be aware of the mayhem they were inflicting on leftist foes. Within months the Fascists were driving the Socialists out of cities and towns, especially in Italy's northern provinces. To advertise their identity, they wore makeshift uniforms—a black shirt, green-gray pants, and a dark fez-like cap with tassel. The Socialists had them outnumbered, but the Fascists were gaining quickly and were even more ruthless in applying force.

Mussolini had no playbook from which to guide this burgeoning insurrection. He was the undisputed leader of a movement whose direction was not yet defined. The Fascists had developed long lists of goals, but they possessed no single bible or manifesto. To some of its enthusiasts, the fledgling party was a way to rescue capitalism and Roman Catholicism from the Leninist hordes; to others it meant defending tradition and the monarchy. For many it was a chance to bring glory back to Italy; and to quite a few it meant a paycheck and a green light to bash heads.

Mussolini's own course was marked by zigs and zags. He took money from big corporations and banks, but he spoke the language of veterans and workers. He tried several times to patch relations with the Socialists, only to discover that his former colleagues didn't trust him and the more extreme Fascists were furious at the attempt. As the political environment continued to worsen, he had to become ever more militant just to keep pace with the forces he purported to command. Asked by a reporter to summarize his program, Mussolini replied, "It is to break the bones of the democrats . . . and the sooner the better." In October 1922, he decided to challenge the government directly by mobilizing Fascists from around the country. "Either we are allowed to govern," he exclaimed to the party conference, "or we will seize power by marching on Rome."

Given that centrist politicians were divided to the point of paralysis, the responsibility for countering Mussolini's bold move rested on the narrow shoulders of King Victor Emmanuel. He had to choose between the Socialists who wanted to destroy the monarchy and the roughneck Fascists who might, he hoped, still prove malleable; the middle ground had collapsed. The army and the prime minister advised the king to block the Fascists' proposed march, arrest Mussolini, and deal with the Socialists separately. The king refused at first, but changed his mind when Fascists began to occupy media sites and government buildings. At 2 a.m. on October 28, he ordered that the Fascists be stopped. Seven hours later, he reversed course again, apparently believing the Fascists could defeat the army, which at that point was almost certainly untrue.

With the military ordered to stand down and tens of thousands of Blackshirts gathering on the edge of the capital, Victor chose what he thought was the safest path. He sent a cable to Mussolini, who was waiting warily in Milan, asking him to Rome to replace the prime minister, who had lost his majority and was serving in the capacity of caretaker. So it was that Mussolini's gamble paid off. In the space of a weekend, he leapt to the top of the political ladder, and achieved his aim without winning an election or violating the constitution.

On October 31, the five-hour March on Rome took place more as a celebratory parade than the putsch it signified. The event attracted a mixed group and defied any narrow stereotype about what a Fascist should look like or be. Among the marchers were fishermen from Naples striding alongside clerks and shopkeepers while wearing dark jerseys and pilot caps. Farmers from Tuscany wore hunting jackets. A sixteen-year-old high school student, Giovanni Ruzzini, lacked money to buy a new shirt and so dyed an old one black; he also salvaged a military helmet from the local dump. A fair number of those present were barefoot because they couldn't afford shoes. One man brought along fifty hammer-and-sickle badges, taken, he insisted, from the bodies of dead Communists. The contingent from Grosseto was led by an eighty-year-old blind man who, a half century earlier, had stood with Italy's greatest general, Garibaldi. Members of the boisterous crowd came equipped with antique muskets, pistols, old safari guns, golf clubs, scythes, table legs, daggers; one man carried an ox's jawbone, and others lugged potentially lethal hunks of dried salt cod. Most walked, but a wealthy young man from Ascoli Piceno drove up with a machine gun mounted on his Fiat. From Foggia came fifty cavalrymen perched on plow horses. Among those welcoming Fascism and shouting "Viva Mussolini" that day were two hundred Jews.

Despite the impressive spectacle, the party's political footing was not yet firm. Mussolini's swift rise had left him vulnerable to an equally rapid fall. The parliament was still dominated by Socialists and liberals, and the conservatives saw the Fascist leader as someone they could hide behind, manipulate, and, when convenient, replace. But Mussolini, soon to be known as Il Duce, had a talent for theater and little respect for the courage of his adversaries. Two weeks after taking office, he made his first address to the legislature. He began by striding into the hall and raising his arm in a Roman salute.* Silently, he scanned the edges of the room, where well-muscled security guards from his own party were lined up on benches, fondling their daggers. Hands on his hips, Mussolini declared, "I could have turned this drab grey hall into a bivouac for my Blackshirts and made an end of parliament. It was in my power to do so, but it was not my wish—at least not yet."

---

* Beginning in the eighteenth century, the outstretched-arm, palm-down salute was attributed by European artists to classical Rome, but there is no evidence that ancient Romans used it. Mussolini's Fascists formally adopted the salute in 1923. Thirty years earlier, an identical gesture had come into common use by American schoolchildren when reciting the Pledge of Allegiance. Once World War II began, that form of salute was phased out, and civilians were instead encouraged to place the right hand over the heart.

With this warning, Mussolini demanded and was given authority to do just about whatever he wanted; but his initial priority, surprisingly, was good government. He knew that citizens were fed up with a bureaucracy that seemed to grow bigger and less efficient each year, so he insisted on daily roll calls in ministry offices and berated employees for arriving late to work or taking long lunches. He initiated a campaign to *drenare la palude* ("drain the swamp") by firing more than 35,000 civil servants. He repurposed Fascist gangs to safeguard rail cargo from thieves. He allocated money to build bridges, roads, telephone exchanges, and giant aqueducts that brought water to arid regions. He gave Italy an eight-hour workday, codified insurance benefits for the elderly and disabled, funded prenatal health care clinics, established seventeen hundred summer camps for children, and dealt the Mafia a blow by suspending the jury system and short-circuiting due process. With no jury members to threaten and judges answerable directly to the state, the courts were as incorruptible as they were docile. Contrary to legend, the dictator didn't quite succeed in making the trains run on time, but he earned bravos for trying.

From the outset, Mussolini relished the job of governing. He never worked as hard as his publicists suggested, but neither was he a dilettante. Aside from epic-level philandering, a love of swimming, and a taste for swordplay, he had few outside interests. He sought to govern well, but to do that, he felt the need to rule absolutely. He had full trust in his own judgment, and there was no satiating his hunger for power.

In 1924, Mussolini pushed through an electoral law that put Fascists in control of parliament. When the leader of the Socialists produced evidence of vote rigging, he was kidnapped by thugs and murdered. By the end of 1926, Il Duce had abolished all competing political parties, eliminated freedom of the press, neutered the labor movement, and secured the right to name municipal officials himself. To enforce his edicts, he took control of the national police, expanded it, and multiplied its capacity to conduct internal surveillance. To constrain the monarchy, he claimed the power to approve any successor to the king. To mollify the Vatican, he shut down brothels and fattened the stipends of priests, but in return he gained the right to approve all bishops. Looking ahead, he turned schools into human factories, where black-shirted schoolboys marched with muskets, celebrated the prospect of a heroic death, and shouted the Fascist credo: "Believe! Obey! Fight!"

Mussolini told his mistress, "I want to make a mark on my era . . . like an alien with its claw." To that dubious end, he exhorted Italians to abandon romantic conceptions about human equality and embrace what he referred to as "the century of authority, a century tending to the 'right,' a Fascist century." "Never before," he said, "have the peoples thirsted for authority, direction, order, as they do now. If each age has its doctrine, then . . . the doctrine of our age is Fascism."

Even an aroused citizenry can't remain forever in a state of mobilization if it lacks a sense of forward movement. Mussolini supplied this through his grandiose rhetoric, which evoked the image of a dominant Italy, reborn with more *spazio vitale* (living space), holding sway throughout the Mediterranean. The road to this paradise was war, which Mussolini urged Italians to embrace, renouncing all comforts. "Live dangerously," he beseeched them. To back his words, he embarked on an aggressive foreign policy that placed intense pressure on Albania, then invaded a nearly defenseless Ethiopia, the last independent kingdom in Africa. To raise money for this brutal venture, Italy's women, led by Queen Elena, donated their wedding rings to be melted down into gold or exchanged for cash; Italian women abroad were encouraged to do the same, and thousands did. Mussolini described the Ethiopia expedition as "the greatest colonial war in all history." When machine guns and poison gas forced that country to surrender, he called on his people to "raise up your banners, stretch forth your arms, lift up your hearts and sing to the empire which appears in being after fifteen centuries on the fateful hills of Rome."

Mussolini was not a keen judge of individuals, but he was sure he knew what the mass of people wanted: a show. He compared the mob to women who are helpless (he fantasized) in the presence of strong men. He posed for pictures in the government-controlled media while driving a sports car, standing sans shirt in a wheat field, riding his white stallion, FruFru, and posing in his military uniform, complete with shiny boots and a chest bedecked with medals. He accepted invitations to every wedding, factory opening, and patriotic event his schedule would allow.

When giving a speech, he stood on a small platform (as I do) to appear taller. He sometimes claimed credit (as I do *not*) for the sun breaking through the clouds just prior to an address. In addition to the inevitable Blackshirts, his usual audience included soldiers in khaki field uniforms, peasant women in white-sleeved dresses, and members of the *squadristi*, the Fascist veterans of the early days, wearing red-and-yellow sashes. To the side might be a small group of foreign reporters who would be pointed to and mocked by preliminary speakers, then greeted by the audience with catcalls and boos. Finally, in the words of a contemporary witness, "when Signor Mussolini stepped out, the crowd seemed to lift itself up as bayonets, daggers, caps and handkerchiefs were waved in the air amid deafening shouts."

During the peak years of his reign, the great man's image was displayed on products ranging from hair tonic and baby food to lingerie and pasta. When a would-be assassin shot him in the nose, he slapped on a bandage and went ahead, later the same day, with a speech to a conference of surgeons, telling them that he would now put himself in their hands. He commissioned street banners bearing the declaration IF I ADVANCE, FOLLOW ME; IF I RETREAT, KILL ME; IF I DIE, AVENGE ME! He put foundries to work building a bronze statue, never completed, of a 260-foot-tall figure looking down on the cupola of Saint Peter's, its body that of a half-naked Hercules and its face a dead ringer for Il Duce.

By the late 1930s, the adoration accorded him had reached the level of parody. Visitors to his office were expected to run the twenty yards between the door and Mussolini's desk before halting and raising their arm in the Fascist salute, then, when exiting, reverse the process.

For all his success as a politician, he was not comfortable as a diplomat. This was an age when international affairs in Western Europe were still primarily the province of aristocrats proud of their tailored suits, refined manners, and ability to banter about trivialities for hours at a time. Before becoming prime minister, Mussolini had never worn formal clothes. He had not learned which spoon or fork to use at a social dinner. He didn't think it sanitary to shake hands, didn't smoke, and had no taste for liquor, not even Italy's fine wine. He was a poor listener who disliked hearing other people talk. He was loath to spend nights away from his own bed, and the time he allotted for meals—either alone or with his family—averaged about three minutes.

Mussolini promised to make Italy unfathomably rich, but economics was a second arena where he failed to shine. He thought a great country required a robust currency and so pegged the lira to the dollar, causing an abrupt increase in public debt, a problem made worse by his failure to understand how interest rates worked. He promoted the idea of national self-sufficiency without ever grasping how unrealistic that ambition had become. He sought to bring labor and management together but ended up creating a haphazardly organized and inefficient corporate state. He emphasized wheat production when prices were low while neglecting other crops that would have yielded more revenue. These errors might have been avoided had he appointed good advisers and heeded their counsel. Instead he discouraged his cabinet from proposing any idea that might cause him to doubt his instincts, which were, he insisted, always right. He told a gathering of intellectuals, "Only one person in Italy is infallible," and said to a reporter, "Often, I would like to be wrong, but so far it has never happened."

As the 1930s wore on, the new Roman empire, the Fascist empire, was beginning to fray. As a circus master, Mussolini was still without peer, but Italy lacked the resources—and he the strategic prowess—to transform the political map of Europe. Not so Adolf Hitler.

THREE

"WE WANT TO BE BARBARIANS"

Heidelberg, Germany: That night at the Inn, I noticed that a lint-haired young man at the next table was fixing me with an icy gleam.... He suddenly rose with a stumble, came over, and said: "So? Ein Engländer?" with a sardonic smile. "*Wunderbar!*" Then his face changed to a mask of hate. Why had we stolen Germany's colonies? Why shouldn't Germany have a fleet and a proper army? Did I think Germany was going to take orders from a country run by the Jews? A catalogue of accusation followed, not very loud, but clearly and intensely articulated. His face, which was almost touching mine, raked me with long blasts of schnapps-breath. "Adolf Hitler will change all that," he ended. "*Perhaps you've heard the name?*"

—MEMOIR OF A BRITISH TRAVELER, DECEMBER 1933

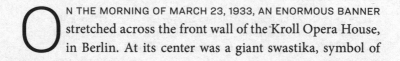

O N THE MORNING OF MARCH 23, 1933, AN ENORMOUS BANNER stretched across the front wall of the Kroll Opera House, in Berlin. At its center was a giant swastika, symbol of the Nazis.* The Opera House was the temporary home of the Reichstag, the German parliament, whose permanent headquarters had been ravaged by arson four weeks earlier. Approaching the lectern was the country's new chancellor, an Austrian by birth, who on January 30 had assumed power not via popular acclaim but because he commanded the most violent gangs and had Communists for enemies. The building in which he was about to speak was guarded on the outside by Heinrich Himmler's secret police and on the inside by the brown-shirted Sturmabteilung (SA), the Nazi paramilitary force, already larger than the German army.

Adolf Hitler spoke quietly, in a soothing tone. The forty-three-year-old appealed to the legislators for their trust, hoping that they would not think too hard before voting themselves into oblivion. His goal was to secure approval of a law authorizing him to ignore the constitution, bypass the Reichstag, and govern by decree. He assured his listeners that they had nothing to worry about; his party had no intention of undermining German institutions. Should they pass the law, the parliament would remain intact, freedom of speech would be unhindered, the rights of the Church would not be altered, and Christian values would, as ever, still be cherished. The powers requested under the "Law for Removing the Distress of the People and Reich" would be used only to shield the country from its adversaries. There was no need for concern: legislators could count on the Nazis to act in good faith.

The chancellor sat down so that the leaders of other parties could have their say. One by one, the Catholics, conservatives, and centrists fell in line and slipped Hitler's bit between their teeth. Only the spokesman for the Social Democrats resisted, saying that

---

* In 1920, the Nazis had adopted the swastika, or *Hakenkreuz* ("hooked cross"), as a symbol of their movement. The swastika had its origins in ancient Indo-European culture and was considered a talisman of good luck.

to be defenseless did not mean to be without honor. Hitler, no longer the conciliator, stormed back to the rostrum. "I do not want your votes," he screamed at the Socialists. "The star of Germany is in the ascendant, yours is about to disappear, your death knell has sounded."

The legislators cast their votes, approving the Enabling Law by a wide margin. Within weeks, the compliant political parties were abolished and the Socialists put under arrest. The Third Reich had begun.

ADOLF HITLER WAS BORN ON APRIL 20, 1889, IN RURAL BRAUNAU, near the frontier between Austria and Bavaria. The son of a minor civil servant and an indulgent mother, he developed into a mediocre student, described by a teacher as "cantankerous, willful, arrogant, and . . . lazy." Leaving school at sixteen, he embarked on what seemed an unpromising career, filling sketchbooks with architectural drawings, falling in love with Wagnerian opera, and applying without success to prestigious art schools. He spent his early twenties bedding down in a men's hostel in Vienna, doing odd jobs, selling small paintings for modest sums, and reading prolifically. To an observer, the young man might have appeared unattractive, malnourished, ill-housed, underemployed, and without close friends; but in his own eyes Hitler was one of the elect, a superior being. His acquaintances found him full of unrealistic ideas, passionate about politics, and almost always livid about the folly of others. He scorned the laboring class for swallowing the bromides of Socialists and priests. He vilified the Reichstag for doing nothing in the face of dire threats to the nation, and he embraced theories—then widespread—about the evildoing and monstrous conspiracies of Jews.

Hitler, at twenty-five, welcomed the start of World War I. He enlisted in the Bavarian Army, saw combat at the outset, then, for four years, served as a courier between the regimental head-quarters and the front lines. Unlike many soldiers, he did not complain about the war, which he considered an opportunity for the German people to show their mettle. In October 1916 he suffered a leg injury, but he returned to duty in the spring and was promoted to lance corporal. In the summer of 1918, he was exposed to a gas attack that temporarily blinded him.

His sight returned in November, but with it came the shock of Germany's defeat. The government in Berlin had, until that final autumn, spoken only of victory and the rich rewards an end to the conflict would bring. Instead the silencing of the guns had been accompanied by the dishonor of surrender and so, also, the victors' demand for blood money, the loss of territory, and the dissolution of the imperial regime. To Hitler and many other soldiers, this startling and humiliating outcome was not something they could accept. The war had reduced the ranks of German men between the ages of nineteen and twenty-two by a numbing 35 percent. The fighting and economic deprivation pulverized the nation. In the minds of enraged survivors, the cause of their disgrace had nothing to do with events on the battlefield: Germany had been betrayed, they told themselves, by a treasonous cabal of greedy bureaucrats, Bolsheviks, bankers, and Jews.

The abdication of Kaiser Wilhelm II led to the installation of multiparty democracy at an inauspicious time. The new Weimar Republic confronted a spiteful Europe, an indifferent America, and a wounded citizenry. As the government, it could not avoid responsibility for the harsh terms of the Versailles Treaty, which dictated that Germany accept blame for the war, disarm, cede territory, and pay reparations. The republic's leaders were held accountable, as well, for the hyperinflation that soon followed, wiping out the life savings of many in the middle class. As in Italy, the conflict's end prompted agitation on the part of labor unions, with frequent strikes and protests, while millions of soldiers returned from the front, scarred in body and mind, scrounging for jobs that weren't there. Feelings of alienation were amplified by the sense Germans had developed of themselves during the nineteenth century as the custodians of a nation apart, with a divine mission and a unique cultural heritage. They were winners, were they not?—but now they felt lost.

In the fall of 1919, Hitler joined the Bavaria-based German Workers' Party, a group of rabble-rousing nationalists so small that it had immediate room for him within its leadership. Though in truth the fifty-fifth member, he was designated "party comrade 555," to give the appearance of larger numbers. Put in charge of propaganda, Hitler began holding public meetings and sought to attract new members through a platform demanding the abrogation of the Versailles Treaty, the unification of all Germans, the exclusion of Jews from citizenship, and share-the-wealth measures directed at the rich. To seduce the left, the movement changed its name to "National Socialist German Workers Party"—or Nazis.

Early on, Hitler forged an alliance with army captain Ernst Röhm, who began to steer veterans toward the new party. Röhm organized his recruits into a militia, the Sturmabteilung, with the mission of beating up Communists; he also stole money from the army to finance a newspaper. The party's biggest asset, however, was the man its members referred to as "the drummer," its public voice.

Now in his early thirties, Hitler was an undisciplined but mesmerizing orator. The Iron Cross he had earned while in the military steeled his nerve, and his time on the streets gave him an intuitive sense of what delighted audiences—and it wasn't abstract theories or objective arguments. He used simple words and did not hesitate to tell what he later described as "colossal untruths." He sought to incite hatred toward those he considered traitors— the "November criminals" whose treachery had cost Germany the war—and he returned each day to what Nietzsche had called the ideology "of those who feel cheated": anti-Semitism.

Speaking in town squares, beer halls, and circus tents, Hitler employed over and over again the same action verbs—*smash, destroy, annihilate, kill.* In a typical address, he would shout himself into a lather of arm-flailing, screaming fury at the nation's enemies, only to grow abruptly calm as he painted a word picture of what a new era of German ascendance might look like. Gradually, party membership expanded and so did the show-business aspects. The Nazis adopted a stiff-armed salute and—in another bow to Mussolini—started wearing brown shirts. They organized rallies, at which Röhm's swelling cadre of thugs conveyed an aura of menace. Hitler designed a flag in the colors of the old German Republic. "We National Socialists," he wrote, "regarded our flag as being the embodiment of our party programme. The red expressed the social thought underlying the movement. White the national thought. And the swastika signified the mission allotted to us—the struggle for the victory of Aryan mankind." These efforts paid off; the Nazi Party was establishing a presence, but—amid the chaos of the early 1920s—few were paying close attention.

In November 1923, Hitler's impatience got the better of his judgment and he tried to replicate Mussolini's already legendary March on Rome. It was a harebrained scheme. The Nazis hoped to spark a nationwide coup by seizing control of Bavaria, but to prevail, they needed the army's support, which they didn't get. The ringleaders were arrested and the coup went nowhere. Of the conspirators, Hitler alone was brazen enough to admit that he had intended to overthrow the government. In his first appearance on the national stage, he made the case for an uprising that would cleanse all Germany, then told the court that he had no choice but to perform his duty as "a man born to be a dictator." Given a five-year sentence, he was released on probation after thirteen months, having made productive use of his time. The manuscript tucked under Hitler's arm as he exited the prison bore the title *Four and a Half Years of Struggle Against Lies, Stupidity, and Cowardice*, later shortened by his publisher to volume one of *My Struggle*—or *Mein Kampf.*

The failed putsch left Hitler doubly resolute but newly cautious; he decided to pursue power through what he called a "policy of legality." This approach didn't rule out the use of violence, but it did demand something more: a nationwide political organization. The Nazis set to work broadening their base. By 1929 they had daily and weekly newspapers and special clubs for young people, women, teachers, lawyers, and doctors. To whip up enthusiasm, Hitler continued to decry the government's payment of war reparations, an act that was, to his mind, a craven admission of national guilt. He denounced the British and French for plotting to keep Germany poor and weak. He lambasted mainstream politicians for ignoring the needs of the common people. Above all, he heaped scorn on the Communists, a strategy that won him friends in the financial community and favorable coverage in some of the nation's largest media outlets.

Still, as the twenties stumbled to their tumultuous end, the Nazis remained a minor party and at the mercy of events. For them, good news was bad news. The economy had begun to perk up. Inflation was tamed. Hitler's countrymen were feeling better about the future and therefore less interested in the supposed cure-all he had to sell.

Then, suddenly, the Great Depression blocked the road to recovery and Germany went into a tailspin. With excess capital earmarked for war reparations, the nation's investments had been financed entirely by borrowing. Now debts had to be repaid and credit was no longer available. Global markets shrank, squeezing the demand for exports. Production declined, unemployment quadrupled, and businesses shut their doors while pawnshops opened theirs. Leaders of the traditional political parties did little but squabble, creating a deadlock in the Reichstag, followed by a series of elections that settled nothing. An angry man for an angry age, the future Führer had found his audience at last. With Deutschland once more on its knees, he offered himself as a bullhorn for its misery. He lashed out again at the November criminals and argued that the time had come for a new generation of fearless Germans led by a party that would fulfill the fatherland's destiny, lift the people up, and crush their foes.

In September 1930, unhappy voters marched to the polls with protest on their minds. The Nazi tally went up, and the party's position in the Reichstag improved as Hitler scored impressive gains among women, small businesspeople, peasants, and the young. Overnight, what had been the ninth-largest party became the second, trailing only the Social Democrats. Communists, too, did well as the political extremes assaulted the bastions of democracy from both sides, shrinking the center to an island whose sole inhabitants were pious aristocrats and bewildered liberals.

Tall, dignified Paul von Hindenburg, the German president, was a revered former war hero, but his face was hardly a fresh one. The old general had first fought for his nation in 1866, in a long-forgotten war against Austria. In his prime, he had represented the epitome of the Prussian officer class, devoted to Kaiser and flag, with no higher calling than duty and no greater fear than change. As a political figure in the modern age, he seemed a time traveler, without relevant skills and unable to decipher the meaning of contemporary events. The aged president was not well served by the officials around him, who clung to their ambitions like life jackets, trying to outmaneuver one another for prime seats on a sinking boat.

Two years on, in the spring of 1932, the old man was persuaded to stand for reelection. He defeated Hitler, but with the Depression still holding the country back, the Nazi vote rose again in the July balloting for parliament, enabling the party to capture one hundred more Reichstag seats than any of its opponents. A shaken Hindenburg invited Hitler to join a coalition government, but the upstart demanded full executive power, a proposal that the president bravely refused. This led to yet another round of elections. In November, the Nazi momentum slowed, but the party still won enough seats to provide leverage. Because bringing the Communists into a coalition was out of the question, Hindenburg was seemingly left with a choice between accepting Hitler as leader or continuing to hold elections with little hope of a decisive outcome. His advisers were split about what to do, but his son, Oskar, a Nazi sympathizer and also corrupt, argued on behalf of the intemperate Austrian. On January 30, 1933, Hindenburg folded his hand. Like Mussolini a decade earlier, Hitler was given the keys to power by an elderly man who felt he had no better option—and, like Il Duce, he arrived in the nation's highest office without ever having won a majority vote, yet by constitutional means. The new German chancellor called the historic transfer "a legal revolution."

THE COUNTRY'S POLITICAL ESTABLISHMENT—BIG BUSINESS, THE military, and the Church—had initially dismissed the Nazis as a band of loudmouthed hooligans who would never attract wide support. Over time, they saw value in the party as a bulwark against Communism, but nothing more. As for Hitler, they were not nearly so scared of him as they should have been. They underestimated the man because of his lack of schooling and were taken in by his attempts at charm. He smiled when he needed to and took care to answer their questions with reassuring lies. He was, to members of the old guard, clearly an amateur who was in over his head and unlikely to remain popular for long. Though they misread Hitler, the young chancellor was an acute judge of them. "The reactionary forces believe they have me on the lead," he confided to a colleague in February 1933. "I know they hope I will achieve my own ruin by mismanagement. . . . Our great opportunity lies in acting before they do. We have no scruples, no bourgeois hesitations. . . . They regard me as an uneducated barbarian. Yes, we are barbarians. We want to be barbarians. It is an honorable title."

Empowered by the Enabling Law, Hitler launched a political blitzkrieg, destroying what remained of German democracy. He began by abolishing local assemblies and replacing provincial governors with Nazis. He sent SA thugs to brutalize political opponents and, when necessary, cart them off to newly opened concentration camps. He disposed of the unions by declaring May 1, 1933, a paid national holiday, then occupying union offices throughout the country on May 2. He purged the civil service of disloyal elements and issued a decree banning Jews from the professions. He placed theater, music, and radio productions under the control of Joseph Goebbels and barred unsympathetic journalists from doing their jobs. To ensure order, he consolidated political, intelligence, and police functions in a new organization, the Gestapo.

The Nazi revolution moved ahead with quicksilver speed, but for some party members it was not ploughing deeply enough. Hundreds of thousands had signed on to the party with the expectation of immediate rewards. In the cities, they wanted jobs; in the countryside, land. The oversize SA, the Sturmabteilung, hungered to replace the regular army. Hitler, however, was not the servant of his followers. His goal was to rebuild the foundations of German national power and, to do that, he would need the skills and experience of people outside the party. He had no intention of dismantling big agricultural enterprises, disrupting core industries, or picking a fight with the military. Instead he used the personal diplomacy he was capable of, and the fear he had engendered, to enforce discipline within the party. Generally, that effort went well—but there was one notable exception.

The Nazis had recruited the SA to provide the clenched fist they needed to knock aside obstacles along the path to power. Now that the finish line had been crossed, the force was without a mission, and party leaders made plans to trim it. Rather than acquiesce, the militia's chief of staff, Ernst Röhm, rebelled, arguing that there were many more tempting targets to attack, including corporations, landed estates, and anyone with property the SA could plunder. From Röhm's perspective, a revolutionary movement needed a revolutionary army, and a revolutionary army devoured everything in its way. Hitler tried to reason with his old friend, but Röhm was intransigent, even adding firepower to units assigned to the capital—a threatening gesture.

On June 4, 1934, Hitler and Röhm met again. The chancellor, at his most ingratiating, proposed a cooling-off period in which the SA would go on leave for a month, with any final decisions about its fate put off until its return to duty. Röhm—who really should have known better—saluted and dropped his guard. On June 30, the Gestapo arrested him and rounded up several hundred alleged co-conspirators. Given a revolver with a single bullet and allowed ten minutes to commit suicide, Röhm replied defiantly, "If I am to be killed let Adolf do it himself." When the ten minutes were up, two of Hitler's aides shot Röhm, who reportedly died gasping, *"Mein Führer, mein Führer."*

Operation Hummingbird, known also as "the Night of the Long Knives," eliminated the SA as a threat to the regular army. This secured Hitler's ties to the military establishment and cleared the way for him to succeed Hindenburg when the aged president died shortly afterward. Hitler emerged from the crisis as head of government, head of state, and commander in chief of the armed forces. From then on, the army was required to swear allegiance not to the country or the constitution, but to the Führer personally.

HITLER'S CLAIM TO DISTINCTION RESTED NOT ON THE QUALITY OF his ideas, but instead on his extraordinary drive to turn warped concepts into reality. Where others hesitated or were constrained by moral scruples, he preferred to act and saw emotional hardness as essential. From early in his career, he was a genius at reading a crowd and modulating his message accordingly. In conversations with advisers, he was frank about this. He said that most people earnestly desired to have faith in something and were not intellectually equipped to quibble over what that object of belief might be. He thought it shrewd, therefore, to reduce issues to terms that were easy to grasp and to lure his audiences into thinking that behind the many sources of their problems there loomed a single adversary. "There are...only two possibilities," he explained, "either the victory of the Aryan side or its annihilation and the victory of the Jews."

Hitler felt that his countrymen were looking for a man who spoke to their anger, understood their fears, and sought their participation in a stirring and righteous cause. He was delighted, not dismayed, by the outrage his speeches generated abroad. He believed that his followers wanted to see him challenged, because they yearned to hear him express contempt for those who thought they could silence him. The image of a brave man standing up against powerful foes is immensely appealing. In this way, Hitler could make even his persecution of the defenseless seem like self-defense.

The chancellor's average height, dark hair, and unathletic body—so at odds with the Aryan ideal—may have added to his support. He referred to himself as a true representative of the people, a workingman, a veteran, without a bank account, investment income, or a mansion. "Workers," he declared, "you must look upon me as your guarantor. I was born a son of the people; I have spent all my life struggling for you."

Citizens of the Reich were fed a steady diet of propaganda at the workplace, in public rallies, and over the rapidly evolving medium of radio. The Führer was the first dictator with the ability to reach eighty million people in a single instant with a unifying summons. Radio was the Internet of the 1930s, but, being a one-way means of communication, it was easier to control. Never had such an efficient tool for manipulating the human mind been available. For a time, Hitler's major speeches were global events. In schools, meanwhile, *Mein Kampf* was a sacred text. "We studied it as a Bible. Hatred was our creed," recalled one student.

Pundits talk today about the importance of authenticity in politics. Hitler lied shamelessly about himself and about his enemies. He convinced millions of men and women that he cared for them deeply when, in fact, he would have willingly sacrificed them all. His murderous ambition, avowed racism, and utter immorality were given the thinnest mask, and yet millions of Germans were drawn to Hitler precisely because he seemed authentic. They screamed, "*Sieg Heil*" with happiness in their hearts, because they thought they were creating a better world.

They were not the only ones deceived. Writing in 1935, Winston Churchill observed:

> *Those who have met Herr Hitler face to face in public business or on social terms have found a highly competent, cool, well-informed functionary with an agreeable manner, a disarming smile, and few have been unaffected by a subtle personal magnetism. Nor is this impression merely the dazzle of power. He exerted it on his companions at every stage in his struggle, even when his fortunes were in the lowest depths. One may dislike Hitler's system and yet admire his patriotic achievement. If our country were defeated I should hope we should find a champion as indomitable to restore our courage and lead us back to our place among the Nations.*

Hitler was smart enough not to try to reinvent the economy. In his first two years, the gloom of the Depression started to lift and unemployment was cut in half. The boom created three million new jobs, with the armaments industry leading the way.

The timing was critical, because Germany's military might had shriveled. The country had virtually no air force or navy, and its army lacked modern equipment. What it did have was a leader who fully grasped the need to prepare for war because he was bent on initiating just such a conflict. While the British and the French were hesitant to spend money in anticipation of a clash they hoped to avoid, Germany plunged into a massive campaign of semi-clandestine rearmament. For years Hitler insisted that his intentions were peaceful and that he was just trying to compensate for the unfair treatment Germany had received. When he took a step forward, such as in remilitarizing the Rhineland in 1936, he insisted that he planned to go no further, that this limited action satisfied Germany's demand for justice. But there was always a next step.

Hitler was not going to stop. He urged his followers to awaken so that they might "grow the German Reich of which great poets have dreamed." He had read enough philosophy to appreciate the concept of world historical figures, agents of destiny, supermen, who could transform an entire age through the majestic power of their will. He knew to the root of his being that he was such a figure, and, in all Europe, he saw but one other.

FOUR

"CLOSE YOUR HEARTS TO PITY"

N 1940, CHARLIE CHAPLIN RELEASED *THE GREAT DICTATOR*, HIS first talking movie. In the film, the incomparable actor performed the dual roles of a Jewish barber and the self-aggrandizing Adenoid Hynkel, tyrant of a fictional country in the center of Europe. Born just four days apart, Chaplin and Hitler were two of the world's most famous men, similar also in height, build, and mustache.* During the movie, Benzino Napaloni, a neighboring dictator, comes to visit Hynkel and the two exchange views on their plans for war. The clownish duo sit in a barbershop, side by side, each feverishly adjusting the height of his chair so that he might look down on the other.

---

* Chaplin, whose mustache was fake, financed *The Great Dictator* personally because U.S. studios did not want to appear political. British authorities intended to ban the movie for fear of offending Hitler, but the war had started by the time the film was complete.

Hitler and Mussolini met more than a dozen times. Each had a lofty vision of his personal destiny and each harbored an unquenchable rage toward a world that, when he was young, had failed to recognize his talents. Both resented their more educated and socially correct contemporaries and both were Fascists, though only Hitler was a Nazi. During his political ascent, Hitler considered the older man to be a trailblazer worthy of emulation. Il Duce paid little heed to Hitler at first, then, when he came to know him, thought him a potentially useful maniac.

Mussolini rejected Hitler's racial theories, which he privately called "stupid, barbarous, and unworthy of a European nation." As an Italian, he had no cause to rhapsodize about the myth of a master Nordic race. He had also, early in his career, been recognized by Jewish newspaper publishers as one of the world's leading Christian defenders of their people.

Memories of the twentieth century would be far different had Italy chosen to align itself with France and Great Britain in the Second World War, as it had in the First. Sadly, Mussolini had resentments left over from the earlier alliance and felt that British and French officials looked down on him as one might on an uncouth third cousin. The decisive break came in 1935 when the League of Nations slapped economic sanctions on Italy for invading Ethiopia. Mussolini deemed it hypocritical for Europe's leading imperial powers to punish his homeland for wanting an empire of its own.

Mussolini caught Hitler's fancy because they both favored the same machismo-laden rhetoric of daring, nationalism, antiCommunism, and war. In *Mein Kampf*, the German lauded "the great man south of the Alps, who, full of ardent love for his people, made no pacts with the enemies of Italy." Many of the tactics Hitler employed to seize and consolidate power, Mussolini had adopted previously: the reliance on violent gangs, the intimidation of parliament, the strengthening and subsequent abuse of authority, the subjugation of the civil service, the affinity for spectacle, and the insistence that the leader, whether Der Führer or Il Duce, could do no wrong.

Hitler and Mussolini had moments of genuine collegiality, and the former's appreciation for the Italian dictator's early triumphs never waned. But Chaplin's comic satire had a real-life mirror. The two leaders and the countries they represented were an imperfect fit. A diplomatic troll might have scripted the chancellor's first Italian visit, to Venice in June 1934. Problems began at the airport, where Hitler exited his plane wearing a drab khaki raincoat, only to be welcomed by Mussolini in full military dress. At their meeting, Mussolini tried to get by without an interpreter and so failed to understand much of what Hitler said. The next morning, Mussolini showed up for a parade thirty minutes late, then made a speech in Piazza San Marco that barely acknowledged Hitler's presence. At lunch, a mischievous chef added salt to the Führer's coffee. The German leader chose an afternoon boat tour to discuss the racial inferiority of Mediterranean peoples. Halfway through that evening's reception, Mussolini walked out, and later, in a calculated leak to reporters, he compared his guest to Genghis Khan. Hitler thought of Victor, the Italian monarch, as "King Nutcracker."

Over time, the personal dynamics improved, but not by much. Hitler became frustrated with Italy as an ally, and Mussolini was exasperated that, when conducting business, his German counterpart rattled off statistics like machine-gun fire and never seemed to shut up. Il Duce's son-in-law noted at the time, "Hitler talks, talks, talks. Mussolini suffers—he, who is in the habit of talking himself, and who instead has to remain silent." After one encounter, the two had to fly to Berlin in the Führer's plane. As soon as they were aloft, Mussolini took his revenge by insisting—to Hitler's white-knuckled terror—on piloting the aircraft.

The ugliness in Italian Fascism was displayed most graphically before the party took power, when its armed squads killed an estimated two thousand leftist rivals, and in Ethiopia, where

Rome's designated occupiers ran viciously and without a leash. In office, however, Mussolini did not feel called to conduct domestic purges of the type orchestrated by Hitler, and for all his tough words, he could still be shocked. In 1934, when Hitler ordered the murder of a hundred of his own supporters, Mussolini was astonished by his cruelty to onetime friends. A short time later, a Nazi assassination squad in Vienna shot the Austrian chancellor in the throat and sat around for three hours while he bled to death on a sofa. At the time, the chancellor's wife and two young children were guests of Il Duce's, staying at a villa close to his along the Adriatic coast. Mussolini went to the villa and, in halting German, personally conveyed to the widow the sad news of her husband's homicide.

MUSSOLINI'S EGO LIFTED HIM TO THE PINNACLE OF POWER, THEN betrayed him. The man had such faith in his instincts, and believed so fully in what he heard himself say, that he failed to either seek or to take sound advice. For much of his tenure, he occupied Italy's principal cabinet positions himself, as many as six simultaneously. Unlike Hitler, who left the bulk of hard work to others, Mussolini took pride in the art of government. He just wasn't that good at it.

His most telling failure was in preparing Italy for what was to come. Nothing made him more eager than the expectation that his country would prove itself in conflict. "War is to a man what motherhood is to a woman," he liked to say. Raising his fists for emphasis, he implored his countrymen to do what worthy Romans did: hate their enemies, steel themselves for battle, and offer their lives for the nation.

Playing Caesar, he regarded the conquest of Ethiopia as an auspicious start; and in March 1938, he ordered his air force to strike Barcelona on behalf of General Francisco Franco and the right-wing military in Spain's Civil War. For two terror-filled days, liquid-air bombs pelted the city's undefended streets, exploding trolleys and buses, flattening apartment buildings, breaking windows, and leaving rescue workers to scoop into baskets the human fragments they found on blood-spattered streets. Mussolini exulted that the time had come for Italians to "horrify the world by their aggressiveness . . . instead of charming it with their guitars." He also hoped to impress the Germans who he said "love total, pitiless war." If his goal was to generate horror, he succeeded. The pope demanded that the bombing stop. When the death toll climbed above thirteen hundred, so did Franco. So, even, did Hitler.

Beating up on soft targets was one thing, but after a decade and a half of Fascist rule, Italy was in no shape to fight a modern war against a capable foe. It didn't have an adequate supply of men, planes, ships, guns, or even uniforms. Unlike Germany and Czechoslovakia, Italy had never invested in a serious domestic armaments industry. Mussolini had promised his people economic self-sufficiency, but his country remained dependent on imported coal and fertilizer and lacked the seaborne military clout to safeguard its ships and ports. The Ministry of War Production estimated that Italy might be ready for combat—in 1949. Mussolini knew all this but preferred his own truth. He was so quick to boast about the number of available army divisions that he cut in half the size of each, then forgot he had done so. Despite a 20 percent increase in population, the country was to mobilize fewer troops in World War II than it had in World War I.

In 1939, when Germany and Italy signed a mutual defense treaty, Mussolini urged Hitler to delay starting a conflict for several years. The Führer had no such intention. On August 22, he urged his senior officers to "close your hearts to pity. Act brutally. Eighty million people must obtain what is their right. Their existence must be made secure. . . . I shall give a propagandist reason for starting the war, no matter whether it is plausible or not. The victor will not be asked afterward whether he told the truth."

Early on September 1, fifty-six German divisions, supported by fifteen hundred aircraft, swarmed into western Poland, leaving the eastern half to be devoured by the Soviet Union. The Wehrmacht followed up in the winter and spring of 1940 by invading Norway, Denmark, Belgium, Luxembourg, and the Netherlands. Hitler invited Mussolini to join in taking the next step, the invasion of France. Il Duce hesitated. Only after the Nazis had made a sieve out of the Maginot Line and were about to enter Paris did Mussolini declare war. Typically, he made the decision without consulting his military staff—a costly mistake. His country had a large merchant fleet at sea, one-third of which was forced by the British to surrender with Italy barely firing a shot.

Mussolini hoped for a short war and a seat on the winning side of the table when peace returned and the plunder was divided. He told advisers that, to validate his claim for money and land, at least a thousand Italian troops must die in combat, but that meant his country would have to fight. He could have taken the initiative against the British in North Africa, but his military was reluctant to strike. Then the Führer double-crossed him by securing German access to Romania's oil fields, which Italy also coveted. "Hitler always presents me with a fait accompli," he complained to relatives. "This time I am going to pay him back in his own coin. He will find out from the newspapers that I have occupied Greece. In this way, the equilibrium will be re-established."

This was Mussolini's bright idea: to invade Greece. He did so—in October 1940—contrary to the warnings of his own generals and with no heads-up to his German ally. In his fantasies, he imagined a triumphant march into Athens that would stamp the Balkans with Italy's brand and match Hitler's grand entrances into Vienna, Prague, and Paris. When advisers pointed to the potential dangers, he told them not to worry, that he was privy to a secret: the top Greek officials had been bribed and would not fight. He was misinformed. The defenders trounced the poorly equipped Italian troops as Mussolini's tanks got stuck in the mud, his planes couldn't fly because of fog, and his ships couldn't operate effectively due to high winds and heavy seas. Instead of advancing to Athens, the Italians were driven back, thirty miles into Albania. Within weeks, a sheepish Duce had to turn to Hitler for help. The German rescue operation forced Hitler to delay his invasion of the Soviet Union until June 1941, narrowing to four months the window Nazi troops had to reach Moscow before Russia deployed its most lethal weapon—winter.

AS THE WAR HE HAD LAUNCHED SPREAD ACROSS EUROPE, HITLER thought it would be a good plan to bring Franco and Spain into the contest on his side; Mussolini agreed. They viewed the Spanish general as a fellow autocrat who could help them to secure the Mediterranean and who could furnish battle-hardened troops for future expeditions.

In 1931, Spain's King Alfonso XIII was forced out and a democratic republic proclaimed. This was during the Depression and, as in Italy and Germany, the Spanish electorate was sharply divided between left and right. One weak government after another tried to assert authority amid crippling strikes and a rash of politically motivated assassinations. In 1936, a Socialist coalition headed by Francisco Largo Caballero, a colorless yet dogmatic prime minister, was given its chance to get Spain moving again. Army leaders, backed by some of the country's wealthiest families, decided they had seen enough of democracy and more than enough of Socialism, then launched a rebellion that Franco was chosen to lead.

The Spanish general had neither the look nor the commanding voice of a dashing military leader. He was short, pudgy, and balding, had a droopy countenance, was prone to crying, and—when

issuing orders—tended to squeak. Colleagues referred to him behind his back as "Miss Canary Islands," a comment on both his
demeanor and the remote site where he was stationed when the
first shots were fired; but Franco was the sort of leader who could
find his way through a minefield without putting a foot wrong.
Unlike many, he expected the Civil War to be long, dirty, and
closely fought. In preparation, he solicited and received aid from
Hitler and Mussolini.

To the irritation of both dictators, Franco resisted pressure for
bold actions that, in his judgment, would have entailed taking ex-
cessive risks. Instead he waged war like a safecracker, turning the
dial one click at a time. He used aerial bombardments to soften up
any opposition before attacking on the ground. He paid careful
attention to logistics and didn't squander his ammunition, equipment, or men. He moved his headquarters close to the fighting
and insisted that a field commander lead in retaking any territory
he lost. All this he managed while ever mindful of his position
on the global stage, for the Spanish Civil War (1936–1939) was of
interest not solely to Spain.

For liberals in the West, the showdown between the Spanish
Republic and Franco's nationalist rebels seemed the first real
chance to stop Fascism's terrifying advance. Volunteers from
fifty-four countries, including three thousand from the United
States, formed international brigades to assist in the cause. The
Largo Caballero government, still desperate for help, turned to
Stalin, who offered men and equipment in return for a clandestine
shipment of the country's entire supply of gold. Celebrity pho-
tographers, poets, and writers—Ernest Hemingway included—
hurried to chronicle and at times glamorize the competition
between the forces of light, as they saw it, and darkness.

The conflict, though, was anything but romantic. It lasted three
years and killed more than half a million people. There were long
lulls, but the clashes were savage. Each side executed prisoners,

and each cast a wide net in arresting enemy sympathizers. For Franco, the systematic rooting out of potential foes was just good strategy. One of his subordinates told allied mayors, "It is necessary to spread an atmosphere of terror. We must create an impression of mastery. Anyone who is overtly or secretly a supporter of the Popular Front must be shot."

Spain, divided by ideology and class, was split by religion as well. Some priests opposed the nationalists, but the Roman Catholic hierarchy was clearly identified with Franco. Its officials were among the more vocal advocates of harsh measures, and a few took delight in personally gunning down "reds." Meanwhile, the left was generally hostile to the Church and hungry to seize its land. Republican forces murdered an estimated ten thousand bishops, priests, nuns, and monks. These atrocities helped color foreign reporting and prompted most major newspapers in the United States to support Franco. When Eleanor Roosevelt urged her husband to send arms to the Spanish Republican government, he told her that if he were to do so, no Catholic would ever vote for him again.

Militarily, neither side was very potent, but Franco benefited from the failure of the Republican factions to coalesce. The Spanish left was a political battleground that encompassed Communists loyal to the party, laborers partial to the exiled Bolshevik theorist Leon Trotsky (a bitter rival of Stalin), internationalists who meant well but lacked military skills, anarchists who detested everyone including each other, and a Socialist government trying to present an attractive face to the world. While Franco was taking his time, the opposition factions were beating one another up, squabbling over supplies, and tossing some of their most committed partisans into jail. George Orwell, who went to Spain to fight Fascism, ended up getting shot by a Communist sniper and exiting the country one jump ahead of the Socialist police.

There are aspects of the Spanish Civil War that remain relevant today. The bloodshed generated controversy within neighboring countries, especially France, about whether to accept or turn back the tens of thousands of refugees who sought relief from the fighting. The Russian troops and tanks that appeared in Spain did so without markings or insignia, just as their successors would do in the 1961 Berlin crisis and, more than fifty years later, in Ukraine.* The German bombing of Guernica, immortalized by Picasso, sparked calls for an international war crimes investigation that never took place. Instead the perpetrators first denied that any bombs had fallen, then blamed the carnage on the victims.

Franco was Spain's youngest general and possibly its most cruel. He personally ordered the executions of thousands of alleged enemy combatants and sympathizers, without the least sign of remorse. He was deliberative, but ambitious. Even before the war had been won, he was designated the future chief of state, with full dictatorial powers. Everywhere he went, Nationalist posters proclaimed, UN ESTADO, UN PAÍS, UN JEFE—"One state, one country, one leader," an echo of the Nazi slogan *"Ein Volk, ein Reich, ein Führer."*

The last of the Republican forces surrendered to Franco on April 1, 1939. The general vowed at the time that he would never pick up his sword again except to defend his country from invasion. When Hitler urged him to bring Spain into the wartime Axis alliance, he refused as a matter of principle, then asked how much Germany was willing to pay. He set his own terms: generous amounts of economic and military aid, plus Morocco, a possession of Vichy France. The Germans viewed the price tag as exor-

---

* During the showdown in Berlin, Russian tank markings were obscured, and soldiers wore black uniforms without insignia. CBS radio correspondent Daniel Schorr dubbed them "un-tanks" and speculated, "We might one day be told that they were just Russian-speaking volunteers who bought some surplus tanks and came down on their own."

bitant and knew that handing Morocco to Spain would so outrage the Vichy regime that it would no longer collaborate.

To break the deadlock, Hitler traveled from Berlin to the town of Hendaye, along the French-Spanish border, where, on October 23, 1940, he met with Franco. The chancellor was confident that his willingness to journey eleven hundred miles to visit the Spaniard would produce a breakthrough. After all, wasn't he the master of Europe? Instead, in a nine-hour meeting, Franco evaded every request. When Hitler pressed him for a commitment, he replied with questions. Asked to moderate his demands, he repeated them. When the Führer predicted a quick victory over England, implying that Spain could wait no longer if it wanted to share in the triumph, Franco doubted the scenario before adding that, even if the Germans were to capture London, the British would keep fighting from Canada.

Barely containing his fury, Hitler had no choice but to make the long trip back home empty-handed. The following February, he tried a final time, writing to Franco, "We three men, the Duce, you, and I, are bound together by the most rigorous compulsion of history. . . . In such difficult times . . . a bold heart can save nations." Flattery didn't work with Franco, who politely declined the chance to link his fate to the Nazis. Writing again, this time to Mussolini, Hitler predicted that Franco—who would die in his bed at the age of eighty-two—was "making the greatest mistake of his life."

FIVE

VICTORY OF THE CAESARS

W HEN WORLD WAR I ENDED, THE AUSTRO-HUNGARIAN Empire was dismantled. Two-thirds of Hungary was amputated and the severed pieces were parceled out to neighboring states. For a brief time, Bolsheviks—trying to seize the moment—took power in Budapest, but they were soon routed by what remained of Hungary's battle-weary armed forces. Throughout the interwar period, the country's majority was trapped by poverty while many from the old upper class craved a return to the influence and wealth they had enjoyed previously. Rich and poor alike felt compelled to recover the precious lands their nation had lost.

Amid the unhappiness, several Fascist organizations arose, most prominently the Arrow Cross, a group that preached what it called "Hungarism." This was an eclectic doctrine promising jobs, revenge, freedom from foreigners, eternal salvation, and the restoration of the stolen territory. Evidently, the menu was appealing because, by 1939, the Arrow Cross was the largest

right-wing party. Its members, however, were so vituperative—
and other Hungarian officials so cooperative—that when World
War II broke out, Hitler had no need to work with the Fascists.

The Hungarian government joined the Axis in the hope of
sharing in a rapid triumph, but when the prospects for success
dimmed, that same government sought out the Western allies to
negotiate a separate peace. Rather than tolerate such a betrayal,
the Nazis gave full authority to the Arrow Cross, whose leaders
promptly sent gangs of armed teenagers into the streets to ter-
rorize the population. In the war's final months, a wretched and
wrenching drama played out in which tens of thousands of Hungarian Jews were worked to death at home or deported by train
or on foot to concentration camps from which few ever returned.
Arrow Cross members did not hesitate to murder Jews in the
Budapest ghetto, including those with paperwork that showed
them to be under international protection.

The 1920s, '30s, and early '40s were a time of rising nationalism
coupled with technology-driven angst and revulsion at governments that appeared to be both corrupt and relics of an earlier
age. The widespread questioning and tottering of faith caused prospective Fascist leaders to test their training wheels and spurred
movements and fads of every description, from mysticism and
belief in fairies to flagpole-sitting and a flirtation across the political spectrum with eugenics and its accompanying racial theories.

Mussolini's early success energized those whose primary fear
was Bolshevism or what they imagined to be Bolshevism: loud
demands for higher wages, for example, or campaigns for land
reform. In virtually every country, there were veterans who—
regardless of which side they had fought on during the war—were
contemptuous of civilian politicians. Anti-Semitism, whether
casual or visceral, flourished in politics, the professions, academia,
and the arts. The bewildering rush of globalization prompted
many to find solace in the familiar rhythms of nation, culture,
and faith; and people everywhere seemed to be on the lookout

for leaders who claimed to have simple and satisfying answers to modernity's tangled questions. Oswald Spengler, a German schoolteacher turned philosopher, argued that history moved in cycles. In 1918, he wrote:

> *The last century was the winter of the West, the victory of materialism and skepticism, of socialism, parliamentarianism and money. But in this century, blood and instinct will regain their rights. . . . The era of individualism, liberalism and democracy, of humanitarianism and freedom, is nearing its end. The masses will accept with resignation the victory of the Caesars, the strong men, and will obey them.*

One man who saw himself in such a leading role was Sir Oswald Mosley, an adventurous Brit with a toothbrush mustache to match Hitler's, a libido to equal Il Duce's, and what was described by an acquaintance as "an overwhelming arrogance and an unshakable conviction that he was born to rule." Well-bred and a consummate fencer (despite a clubfoot), Mosley spent World War I in recovery from a pair of broken ankles, the first incurred in a drunken brawl, the second when he crashed his airplane after flying in loops to impress his mother. Starting in 1918, he served in Parliament as a conservative, then as an independent, and next under the banner of the Labour Party, from which he resigned when its leaders rejected his plea for an enormous infrastructure program. Undaunted, Mosley founded the New Party, which ran candidates for Parliament in the 1931 election, with zero success. A still-game Mosley traveled to Italy for a close look at Mussolini's effort to create a new Rome. To a frustrated politician harboring big dreams, the Italian model—with its freshly constructed though not yet fully paid-for bridges, aqueducts, grand halls, and broad avenues—seemed just the ticket.

Returning to London, Mosley founded the British Union of Fascists (BUF) on a platform featuring his signature public works program, anti-Communism, protectionism, and the liberation of Britain from foreigners, "be they Hebrew or any other form of alien." In the tradition of Il Duce, he recruited a tough-looking security force, tutored his minions in the Roman salute, and distributed black shirts based on the design of his fencing jackets. By 1934, Mosley's rallies were drawing large crowds of workers, shopkeepers, businessmen, elements of the nobility, disgruntled Tory politicians, and a smattering of reporters, soldiers, and off-duty bobbies. Party membership reached forty thousand. Eager to branch out, the BUF organized drinking clubs and football squads, but its effort to conduct a beauty pageant failed because of a shortage of interested applicants. At this juncture, Mosley's personal evolution from British patriot to German lackey was complete: in 1920, George V had attended his first wedding; in 1936, Joseph Goebbels hosted his second, with Adolf Hitler among the half dozen guests.

British Fascism did not die quickly, but it did fade away. This was due in part to the government's official policy of appeasement, which provided a more socially respectable home for Nazi empathizers. But what really dampened enthusiasm for Mosley's Blackshirts was the spectacle of Hitler's Brownshirts marching into the Rhineland, Austria, the Sudetenland, Prague, and—the move that finally triggered war—Poland. Suddenly the stakes were much higher, and being a Fascist was not so acceptable. William Joyce, BUF's propaganda chief, fled to Berlin, where he began a second career as the infamous Lord Haw-Haw, a traitorous radio broadcaster. Mosley was arrested in the first year of fighting, but, this being England, Churchill allowed the highborn prisoner and his wife the courtesy of a small house with a vegetable garden and the right to hire fellow inmates as servants.

NONE OF THE EUROPEANS WHO, LIKE MOSLEY, SOUGHT TO FOLlow in the footsteps of Mussolini and Hitler reached the top of their country's power pyramid. In Spain, Franco invited the Fascist Falange party into his coalition, then swallowed it up. Portugal's dictator, Antonio de Oliveira Salazar, embraced the authoritarian attributes of Fascism but rejected any rebellion against the Church or its doctrines. In France, the blue-shirted Solidarité Française was one of several right-wing groups that served as sparring partners for the left; the movement was openly pro-Nazi, campaigned on the slogan "France for the French," and was banned by the Socialist government in 1936. Members of Iceland's Nationalist Party wore gray shirts and red swastika armbands, swore to protect Icelanders' ethnic identity, believed in Aryan supremacy, and never received more than one percent of the vote. In Romania, the army alternately suppressed and collaborated with the Legion of the Archangel Michael, a charismatic group with an impoverished rural following drawn to its mix of revivalist religion, revolutionary politics, and violence against Jews.

In these and other cases, Fascism was less defeated than diluted. Zealous foot soldiers helped drive nationalist passions in many countries, but the insurrectionary elements of the movements were contained before they could threaten the powerful. In Italy and Germany, former corporals called the shots; everywhere else, generals and their upper-crust civilian counterparts retained their grip on power.

Czechoslovakia, poised tensely in the Third Reich's shadow, was a special case. There, Konrad Henlein, a shrewd, paunchy, nearsighted former gymnastics instructor, attached himself to the Nazi locomotive and let it pull him along. At Hitler's instructions and with Berlin's money, Henlein became the principal mouthpiece for Fascist elements within Czechoslovakia's politically diverse German community. To foreign officials and the press, he spun tale after tale of his people's mistreatment at the hands of brutal Prague. His fabrications, rebroadcast by the Nazis, had their effect. Many Europeans came to sympathize with

Hitler's declarations of outrage and found reasonable his desire to intervene on behalf of his country's ethnic brethren.

As that day of reckoning drew near, Henlein shed earlier disavowals and embraced Nazism, salute and all. His disciples differed from those of Hitler only in the color of their shirts (white) and the design of their banners (scarlet with a white shield, no swastika). In September 1938, the clash between Nazi lies and the rule of law came to a head; the lies won. Under the 1938 Munich Pact, France and Great Britain agreed that Germany was justified in gobbling up 30 percent of Czechoslovak territory, a third of its population, and more than half of its strategic minerals. Less than six months later, Hitler returned for the rest.

CONTROVERSY OVER FASCISM'S RISE, DIRECTION, AND FATE TRANscended the boundaries of Europe. Though the word "Aryan" tends to conjure up the image of a blue-eyed Nordic blond, some pro-Nazi racial theorists traced its origins to "the people that descended, several millennia ago, from the Central Asian plateau into the valleys of the Indus and Ganges and who remained pure by observing strict caste laws. . . . These people call themselves the Aryans . . . the noblemen."

Many in India endorsed this designation. Angry at their British overlords and worried about Muslim encroachment, Hindu nationalist leaders admired Mussolini's attempt to turn easygoing Italians into a warlike people; they yearned for a similar transformation among their own followers. In March 1939, ten days after the Wehrmacht's invasion of Czechoslovakia, spokesmen for the Hindu Party hailed Germany's "revival of the Aryan culture, . . . her patronage of Vedic learning, and the ardent championship of the tradition of Indo-Germanic civilisation." During the Second World War, thousands of militant Hindus found their way to Germany, where the Nazis organized them into a legion to fight British forces on the subcontinent.

The forces that nourished Fascism elsewhere—economic hardship, ambition, and prejudice—were present, too, in the United States. A self-educated writer, William Pelley, founded the Silver Legion of America in January 1933, only a few hours after Hitler's ascension to the chancellorship of Germany. Headquartered in Asheville, North Carolina, the Legion attracted a membership of some fifteen thousand. Followers wore blue pants and silver shirts with a scarlet "L" over the heart, standing for Love, Loyalty, and Liberty. The Silver Shirts were militantly anti-Semitic and sought to duplicate the Nazi model of organizing armed bands. Undercover investigators from the U.S. Marine Corps testified that Pelley's operatives promised them money in exchange for access to weapons from military arsenals in California, but the inquiry did not lead to arrests. In 1936, Pelley ran for president on the slogan "Down with the Reds and Out with the Jews," but was on the ballot only in Washington State and received fewer than two thousand votes.

The Silver Shirts soon disappeared, but the prejudice they espoused found a voice in such organizations as the Ku Klux Klan and in the nationwide broadcasts of Father Charles Coughlin, a polarizing and isolationist radio personality based in Detroit. Not every bigot was the same, however, for although many of those with Fascist tendencies were anti-immigrant, others had not been in the United States for very long.

Nearly a quarter of the United States population had some German ancestry and most of them hoped that a second war between their native and adopted homelands wouldn't be necessary. Within this group were some, a small fraction, who declared their support for Hitler. Fritz Kuhn was such a man. A chemical engineer who came to the United States in 1928, Kuhn organized the German American Bund (GAB) eight years later. Members of the group wore brown shirts and black boots, and displayed the swastika at rallies alongside a portrait of George Washington, whom they hailed as America's "first Fascist" because of his alleged distaste for democracy. "Just as Christ wanted little children to come to him, Hitler wants German children to revere him"—this was the message conveyed at the Bund schools that sprouted around the country, most commonly in the Midwest.

The Bund fully expected a National Socialist victory in Europe and saw a chance to copy that anticipated triumph on U.S. shores. To bring that goal closer, the GAB demanded full obedience from members and urged the United States to remain neutral in any dispute involving Germany and the Allied powers. Despite their foreign roots, Bund enthusiasts portrayed themselves as the truest and purest Americans, defending the country against such perils as Communism, miscegenation, and jazz. The movement reached a rowdy climax at Madison Square Garden in February 1939, when Kuhn spoke to an amped-up crowd of twenty thousand. To shouts of "*Sieg Heil*," he gleefully mocked President Frank D. "Rosenfeld" and his "Jew Deal."

The GAB encountered stout opposition from mainstream German-American organizations, trade unions, Jewish activists, and at least a few gangsters. "The stage was decorated with a swastika and a picture of Adolf Hitler," recalled notorious mob boss Meyer Lansky of one Fascist rally. "The speakers started ranting. There were only fifteen of us, but we went into action. We threw some of them out the windows. Most of the Nazis panicked and ran out. We chased them and beat them up. We wanted to show them that Jews would not always sit back and accept insults." Given the connection with the underworld, it seems appropriate that the career of Fritz Kuhn ended not in an act of violence but—as with Al Capone—in a prison sentence for tax evasion and, in Kuhn's case, an added conviction for embezzling GAB money to support a mistress.

In hindsight, it is tempting to dismiss every Fascist of this era as a thoroughly bad guy or a lunatic, but that is too easy, and by inducing complacency, also dangerous. Fascism is not an exception to humanity, but part of it. Even people who enlisted in such movements out of ambition, greed, or hatred likely either were unaware of, or denied to themselves, their true motives.

Oral histories from the period testify to the hope and excitement that Fascism generated. Men and women who had despaired of political change suddenly felt in touch with the answers they had been seeking. Eagerly they traveled long distances to attend Fascist rallies, where they discovered kindred souls keen to restore greatness to the nation, traditional values to the community, and optimism about the future. Here, in this crusade, they heard explanations that made sense to them about the powerful currents that were at work in the world. Here were the chances they had sought to participate in youth groups, athletic organizations, charity drives, and job-training activities. Here were the connections they needed to start a new business or take out a loan. Many families that had stopped after bearing two children, thinking that number all they could afford, now found the confidence to bear four or five or six. In the congenial company of fellow Fascists, they could share an identity that seemed right to them and engage in a cause that each could serve with gladness and singleness of heart. These were prizes, they believed, worth marching for and even giving up democratic freedoms for—provided their leaders could do as promised and make their fantasies real.

For a long while, it appeared that those leaders could do exactly what they pledged. Throughout the 1920s, Mussolini had the look of a winner, and so, after 1933, did Hitler. They—more than any other European statesmen—were trusted to deliver where conventional politicians fell short. They were the trailblazers, the visionaries firmly in touch with the disturbing yet exhilarating zeitgeist, the spirit of the time.

In *Cabaret*, there is an electrifying moment at a beer garden

when a young Nazi rises to his feet and, joined by most but not all
of those present, belts out an anthem of promise and horror:

> *The branch of the linden is leafy and green,*
> *The Rhine gives its gold to the sea.*
> *But soon, says a whisper: "Arise, arise,*
> *Tomorrow belongs to me."*
> *Oh Fatherland, Fatherland, show us the sign*
> *Your children have waited to see.*
> *The morning will come when the world is mine.*
> *Tomorrow belongs to me.*
> *Tomorrow belongs to me.*

Fascism caught on because many people in Europe and elsewhere saw it as a mighty wave that was transforming history, that
was owned by them alone, and that couldn't be stopped.

SIX

THE FALL

Poděbrady, January 1942. People here are sad and everyone is taking the war with difficulty. This includes Aryans and non-Aryans, to use this rather peculiar naming into which God's creation are now divided. We wear stars as you know, some proudly, some hide them even though you are not allowed to. . . . We live in strange times and are viewed by some as members of a less valuable race. Of course, blacks are also underrated and yet the world is quiet about that, even Jews. When God enlightens our brains and we understand that we are all equal before God, it will be better.

THE SENTENCES ABOVE ARE FROM THE JOURNAL OF RŮŽENA Spieglová, a widow living alone, mourning her daughter's recent death, and observing from within the shackles that—during the severe winter of 1942—tightened around Jews in Nazi-occupied Czechoslovakia.

Her words illustrate the capacity of an ordinary person living with extraordinary stress to feel empathy toward men and women she has never met and to seek comfort in the conviction that all humans are of equal worth. This generosity of spirit—this caring about others and about the proposition that we are all created equal—is the single most effective antidote to the self-centered moral numbness that allows Fascism to thrive. It is a capacity that can be found in most people, but it is not always nurtured and is sometimes, for a period, brutally crushed.

Poděbrady, April 1942: We were taken for departure and categorized for work. There were four health gradations. I was in the second category which means that my health is pretty good. Now they are saying that we will soon be moved out of Poděbrady and that is why all Jews are leaving by train to Cologne for registration. . . . It is possible that the troubles, which await us, I will survive. Perhaps, we will see each other, dear ones, who are abroad. May God give you health. When I come back (I hope I will, a person never knows), I will write down what it was like in Cologne. [Journal ends]

On June 9, 1942, Růžena Spieglová was one of a group of Czechoslovak Jews sent by rail transport to the Nazi concentration camp in Terezín. On June 12, they were transported farther east to a destination we do not know for sure, probably a forested area in occupied Poland. There were no survivors from that transport. My maternal grandmother was fifty-four years old when she was murdered.

IN THE SUMMER OF 1940, AFTER LESS THAN A YEAR OF DECLARED war, the Third Reich held sway over Austria, all segments of a divided Czechoslovakia, half of Poland, Norway, Denmark, Belgium, the Netherlands, and much of France. Between April and June, it had seized 400,000 square miles of Europe, taken control of air bases from the North Sea to Marseille, secured access to a bounty of oil and other strategic minerals, and, on the continent at least, wiped out the only significant armies that opposed it. Nothing on earth appeared equal to the Nazi juggernaut, but, contrary to all expectations including his own, Hitler would not again know such a high point.

The descent began when, in July, Winston Churchill brusquely rejected the Führer's offer of a peace settlement. To teach the British a lesson, Hitler ordered the Luftwaffe to destroy the Royal Air Force and make possible a land invasion across the Channel. For five months, Stuka bombers and Messerschmitt fighters did battle with British antiaircraft guns, Hurricanes, and Spitfires. German air raids set sirens wailing in coastal and industrial regions and in the heart of London itself, igniting thousands of fires, destroying factories, docks, rail stations, apartment buildings, pubs—even damaging Buckingham Palace.

These events would be among my own earliest memories. Having said our farewells to family and friends, my parents and I departed Prague soon after the March 1939 invasion, then traveled by train through Slovakia, Hungary, Yugoslavia, and Greece. From there we took passage on a boat that brought us to England, first to a dingy boardinghouse in London that I was too young to remember, then to a modest flat I will never forget. The apartment, with a tiny kitchen and bath, was on the third floor of a redbrick building in Notting Hill. Our neighbors included fellow refugees, some from Czechoslovakia, others from Poland, Germany, and Spain.

During air raids, our routine was to hurry down the cramped gray concrete stairwell to the basement, which was divided into several small rooms and one larger. There were about two dozen of us at any given time, occasionally more when buildings nearby had to be evacuated. We sipped tea or coffee prepared by the volunteer wardens and shared snacks of bread and biscuits. We slept—when we could—on camp beds or mattresses in the biggest room. Although the building was new and structurally sound, the cellar had hot water and gas pipes suspended from the ceiling; they warmed the rooms, but had a bomb fallen close by, we'd have been scalded or asphyxiated. Being so young, I did not think of such possibilities and instead enjoyed every minute of the stiff-upper-lip camaraderie.

Notting Hill lacked strategic value and was therefore not a prime target, but bombs still struck more than a dozen locations nearby, killing scores. One of our neighbors was pulled by the fire brigade from the rubble of the Freemasons Arms, a local pub. She had thought she was done for but proved tough as rawhide and lived to celebrate her 103rd birthday. Another time, a bomb came hurtling down but did not detonate, so all the buildings in the area were evacuated and an emergency team arrived. After investigating, the crew told us not to worry: the explosive had been made by factory workers in occupied Czechoslovakia and carefully rigged not to explode.

My father's job was to broadcast news back to our homeland on behalf of the London-based Czechoslovak government-in-exile. This was to counter the stream of lies put forth each day by the German occupiers. One morning near the beginning of the Blitz, my father—Josef Körbel—had a radio script he needed to finish and decided to ignore the sirens and remain in our apartment working. A friend who was with him later remembered:

> The whiz of a flying bomb was so loud that we both threw ourselves down and Dr. Körbel quickly jumped under the table. The airborne assault was deafening, and our house swayed so much that it reminded me of a ship on the high seas. I would never have believed a huge iron-and-concrete building could vibrate that dramatically and still not fall to pieces. When we felt ourselves out of danger, we could not resist a laugh of relief.

From September 7, 1940, until the end of October, over fifty-seven consecutive days, an average of two hundred bombers dropped their deadly payloads on London. There was no reliable refuge. The shelters, whether in home gardens or public parks, provided protection only against collateral blast and debris. Families who retreated to basements were often crushed or suffocated by collapsed buildings. In the first six weeks, sixteen thousand houses were obliterated and another sixty thousand seriously damaged; more than 300,000 people were displaced.

Londoners, however, are an adaptable species. Knowing that they might be stranded for days between trips home, office workers arrived at their desks with toiletries, pillows, blankets, and extra clothes. As evening approached, the parade of mattresses began moving into cellars, shelters, and the Underground. Weather data were classified, so people made their own forecasts—fair skies meant a lovely day for Hitler; clear nights at certain times of the month provided a bomber's moon. The social divisions that defined British culture momentarily melted away as people from all walks of life wished one another well. Defiant shopkeepers displayed signs: SHATTERED, NOT SHUTTERED or KNOCKED, NOT LOCKED. Banks and the postal service promised BUSINESS AS USUAL; enterprising streetwalkers did the same.

Despite the hard blows and the many in political circles who saw no alternative but to give in, the British refused to yield. Hitler had expected to dispose of England before turning his attention to the Soviet Union, but in this aggressive scheme he was denied. He was frustrated, as well, in his effort to persuade Franco to bring Spain into the war and aggravated by Mussolini's impetuous decision to invade Greece. Meanwhile, in North Africa, British and Indian forces were defending successfully against German and Italian attacks, and in March 1941, courageous Serb patriots overthrew a pro-Nazi government and forced Hitler to intervene there. The Germans were immensely powerful, but as the chancellor was beginning to discover, so—when fully aroused—is the will to resist.

TEN DAYS BEFORE THE WAR BEGAN, GERMANY AND THE SOVIET Union had announced that each would remain neutral in any war involving the other. The agreement was shocking in that the governments were ideological adversaries, yet understandable because they were equally cynical. As arranged, the two invaded Poland from opposite directions and split the country between them. For Stalin, the pact was well-timed. He had spent the late 1930s conducting show trials of allegedly disloyal officials, executing hundreds of thousands. This exercise in paranoia left Russia unprepared for an armed confrontation with the Germans.

Hitler, too, appreciated the timing. He didn't want to be forced to fight on two fronts—as the Germans had been in the Great War. It made sense, therefore, to delay, but Hitler saw enough of himself in Stalin not to trust. He thought old Joe would try to outfox him and attack as soon as the Red Army was able; better, he surmised, for Germany to land the first punch. War with the USSR had always been a question of when, not if. The vast lands to the east were the prize the Führer coveted most. Part of the reason was material—his military had a bottomless need for grain, meat, oil, and other resources—but he also had a manic desire to expand *Lebensraum* (living space) in the only direction not blocked by an ocean, channel, or sea. His planners fantasized that, after the war, the whole fertile expanse between the Urals and the Polish frontier would be adorned by gleaming cities populated exclusively by the racially pure—their food supplied by Slav peasants toiling outside the gates, cultivating the soil, raising livestock, eating scraps, and educated only to the level required to understand and obey orders.

Hitler's decision to invade the Soviet Union in June 1941 was made with the understanding, and indeed the hope, that it would disrupt the food supply of the local population. Four weeks prior to the attack, Göring predicted that "many tens of millions of people in the industrial areas will become redundant and will either die or have to emigrate to Siberia. Any attempt to save the population there from death by starvation . . . would reduce Germany's staying power in the war." This was the same Göring who boasted, "I have no conscience." That was Nazi morality in a nutshell.

On the first day of summer, German planes, tanks, and infantry roared to the east, catching the Soviet Union by surprise and advancing more than two hundred miles in the first week. Military experts in Berlin and other Western capitals were sure that the storm troopers would prevail quickly. Stalin thought his own staff might kill him because of his stupidity, but that didn't happen. The Soviets had built an integrated economic and political system that allowed them to mobilize all their resources. After absorbing large initial losses, the Red Army rallied and was able to establish strong defensive positions. Distance and climate gave Russia a crucial strategic edge. Every mile the Germans moved forward lengthened their supply lines, and every passing week brought shorter days, colder winds, more rain, and, starting in October, snow. With the advantage of surprise dissipated, the warriors of the Third Reich—for the first time—found themselves in a real fight.

As Germany's momentum slowed, Hitler's rage mounted. He had thought the people of Ukraine and the Baltic States would greet his troops as liberators, and some did, because anti-Russian feeling in these areas was high. The Nazi governors and SS commandos, however, were heavy-handed. Instead of treating the local populations as allies, they drove them into opposition by confiscating food, stealing property, enslaving millions of workers, and beating people up.

Hitler was a student of military history and understood the value of preparation and surprise. What he failed to grasp was the need to adjust his strategy to accommodate unwelcome facts. In his thirst for another conquest, he underestimated Russian resilience and the Red Army's capacity to find replacements for the men who were killed or taken prisoner. With unwavering trust in his own judgment, he frequently overruled his generals, ordering them to accomplish what no one could. This left his troops, many without boots or winter coats, trudging wearily through the frozen countryside thousands of miles from home.

By early December, the frostbitten Germans had reached the forests west of Moscow, but the Soviets soon launched a counteroffensive that drove them back and put the capital out of reach. In 1942, Hitler tried again and once more attempted too much. On the second day of February 1943, in Stalingrad, the German Sixth Army surrendered some ninety thousand men. The fighting would drag on for months, but the Führer's eastern expedition was doomed.

MUSSOLINI AND HITLER WERE THE EMBODIMENTS OF FASCISM, but neither could engineer a fully totalitarian state. There was always a gap between theory and reality, between orders from on high and implementation at lower levels. The governments were never quite as efficient as they wished to appear. In Germany, the Gestapo committed countless hideous crimes but also had to work hard to make average citizens believe the regime had agents on every corner and ears on duty in every building. Behind its intimidating facade, the organization was understaffed, swamped with paperwork, and politically unreliable—half its members were not even Nazis. Many Gestapo informants were opportunists who found satisfaction in making trouble for unpleasant neighbors and people to whom they owed money. Then there was the lady from Saarbrücken who informed on her husband to make room—as she told her young son—for "a much better" new dad.

Almost as soon as he took office, Hitler removed women from the bureaucracy, promising them "emancipation from emancipation." Women were counseled to tend the hearth, mend, sew, make *Apfelkuchen*, and give birth to the next generation of Aryan supermen. That ambition proved no easier to fulfill than conquering the Soviet Union. From 1933 to 1939, the number of women in the workforce rose from four million to five million as Frauen and Fräuleins helped the economy to keep pace with the demands of war.

In Italy, where Communists and Socialists were outlaws by definition, many survived the Fascist years by keeping their heads down, pretending to be apolitical and—like Mussolini's father in an earlier era—concealing the family's red flag in a box buried in the backyard. The prudent tactics enabled leftist movements to resurface with considerable strength even before the war's end. In Germany, open dissent was rare, but there were pockets of anti-Nazi activity in the trade unions, the private sector, the religious community, and the military. Disgust with Hitler came to the fore most dramatically when, on July 20, 1944, Claus Philipp Schenk (Count von Stauffenberg) tried to blow up the Führer with a time bomb concealed in his briefcase. The explosion left the intended victim with scorched hair, a burned leg, damaged eardrums, and the conviction—due to his narrow escape—that Providence still had his back.

THE TIME BOMB AWAITING MUSSOLINI WAS LESS NOISY BUT ULTImately more lethal and came from a source even closer to home. Who would have thought that the founder of Fascism would be brought low by members of his own party?

The pivotal moment came toward the end of 1942, when Allied forces knocked the Axis out of North Africa, creating a platform to liberate Europe from the south, through Italy.

That country's deteriorating position was mirrored by changes in its leader. Mussolini the boastful and swaggering was no more. Where once he had prided himself on making snap decisions and keeping his desk clean, now he allowed paperwork to stack up while he pored over news clips, underlining key sentences in crayon. He became erratic, often changing his mind and sometimes checking both boxes on a memo presenting opposing options. He took stomach medicine to ease his ulcer, but there was no prescription for the central dilemma he faced: his disappointing countrymen wanted out of the war.

Neither the average Italian nor the nation's armed forces nor the beleaguered king wished to be associated with the Third Reich. Hitler's transparent paganism didn't sit well with Roman Catholics, and many grumbled when, in 1938, Mussolini consented to the same anti-Semitic statutes that had been approved years earlier in Germany. Even, and perhaps especially, those who loved Il Duce didn't enjoy seeing him play junior partner to a Teutonic racist. The military was upset by the deployment of tens of thousands of its men to the East, where they had fought— many wearing cardboard shoes—alongside the Germans. Now their homeland was about to become a new front in what seemed an endless war. The Fascist movement, once so eager to trumpet the return of Italian glory, would surely be held responsible for Italy's defeat.

On July 10, 1943, the first of 160,000 Allied troops landed in Sicily. Two weeks later, the Fascist Party's Grand Council convened in Rome. Uncertain what to expect, many attendees concealed knives or grenades in their pockets. However, this wasn't Hitler's Germany or Stalin's Russia. Instead of roaring threats, Mussolini was morose. He greeted party leaders with a two-hour harangue, defensive in tone, full of irrelevant statistics and utterly dispiriting to those still searching for a way out of the dilemma they faced. While he was speaking, delegates furtively passed around a statement proposing that the full constitutional powers of king and parliament be restored. The principal author, Dino Grandi, had originally been among Mussolini's more militant colleagues. Now he stood and confronted his old boss:

You believe you have the devotion of the people, but you lost it the day you tied Italy to Germany. You have suffocated the personality of everyone under the mantle of a historically immoral dictatorship. Let me tell you, Italy was lost on the very day you put the gold braid of a marshal on your cap.

Grandi's resolution, put to the test, was approved 19–8–1, with Mussolini's son-in-law among those demanding change. The infallible dictator no longer had the backing of the party he had forged on the anvil of his own will—and so a twenty-minute vote brought down the curtain on twenty years of Fascism. In a last bid for salvation, Il Duce sought a renewed declaration of solidarity from the king—to no avail. For more than two decades, Victor Emmanuel had bent before Mussolini because he felt he had no choice and because he was a coward. Now, at long last, the high cards had fallen into his hand. "Today," he said to his visitor, "you are the most hated man in Italy." "If that is true," came the reply, "I should submit my resignation." "And I," said the king, "unconditionally accept it."

News of Mussolini's departure touched off celebrations throughout Italy. Framed pictures of the deposed dictator were removed from walls by the thousands and dropped in bins; suddenly there was no rarer creature than an admitted Fascist. The new government agreed to an armistice with the Allies and prayed that its war was over, but the plea went unanswered. Hitler's troops seized the northern part of the country and insisted that Mussolini serve as head of a puppet regime. This he did unhappily, a virtual prisoner of the Germans.

During his final months, Mussolini had little to do except brood about how his audacious dreams had turned sour. He speculated that the outcome might have been different had he found it in his heart to equal Hitler in cruelty. He faulted his own citizens for their lack of appetite for battle and the Nazis for their paucity of interest in anything else. He admitted to his few remaining advisers that he had been too susceptible to flattery and that dictators "lose any sense of balance as they pursue their obsessive ambitions." He took confession and made other sporadic efforts to gain the blessing of the Church. He also stopped comparing himself to Caesar, wondering aloud if Jesus Christ might be a more apt comparison.

In the war's final days, both American troops and Italian Communists converged on Mussolini's weakly defended headquarters. The fallen dictator went on the run, at first hoping to meet up with what he imagined to be a substantial residue of followers preparing for a last stand. Failing in that, he and his companions joined some German soldiers who were fleeing toward the Austrian border. On April 28, 1945, despite wearing a Luftwaffe greatcoat and helmet, he was recognized by the members of a Communist detachment. A firing squad shot him, his longtime lover, Claretta Petacci, and others in their group, loaded the bodies into a truck, and dumped them in Milan.

IN GERMANY, THE INESCAPABLE DRUMBEAT OF GOEBBELS'S PRO-paganda had created what historian Ian Kershaw has labeled the "Hitler myth." This was the feeling that, however shocking the country's setbacks, the Führer would soon make all things right. To the extent a problem lingered, it was because it had not been brought to the top man's attention. Others, and only others, were to blame when the bureaucracy was inept, the military blundered, or the SS committed acts of gratuitous brutality. Hitler was considered the embodiment of the nation, the creator of an economic miracle, the clear-eyed dispenser of justice, the protector against all enemies, and the military and foreign policy genius whose strategy—the heavens would ensure—must be crowned with success.

In 1943, the hero of this myth began to experience a tremor in his left arm and leg that did not respond to treatment. Walking, he had to drag his foot. He had other ailments as well, and came to rely on a physician who prescribed an unhelpful combination of placebos, stimulants, aphrodisiacs, and mild poisons. As Hitler's body wore down and his energy level slumped, the German war machine was pummeled. Following D-Day, the two-front war Hitler had feared became a reality. From east and west, the Allies closed in, freeing countries the Nazis had sought to enslave. High school boys, without training, were given uniforms and ordered to fight to defend every square meter of land, just as the Führer was doing, or so they were told. By then, the famous voice was no longer heard at public rallies or on radio broadcasts. Hitler did not even dare to venture outdoors. In July 1944, Russians liberated the Majdanek death camp, and in January of the following year, Auschwitz. In April, Americans flung open the gates of Buchenwald and the British did the same at Bergen-Belsen. The world could no longer deny what it had not wanted to believe.

The now feckless Führer spent his final months shuffling around his bunker twenty-five feet belowground in the center of Berlin. As he moved, the whole left side of his body twitched and shook. Incessantly, he complained, mused aloud, and shared the tattered remnants of his fantasies with an audience of secretaries, who grew bored listening—which they had no choice but to do— often until dawn. Unlike Mussolini, Hitler did not acknowledge mistakes, regret decisions, or care that he was hated. He spewed vitriol at the many he claimed had betrayed him, was adamant that any German deserters be shot, and clung to the hope that a final miracle would validate the exalted standing that he had, in his own unseeing eyes, always merited. In mid-April, he was buoyed briefly by the news that Franklin Roosevelt had died, "removing," he said in a statement, "the greatest war criminal of all times from the earth." On April 30, 1945, two days after the demise of Mussolini, Hitler and his wife of thirty-six hours, Eva Braun, committed suicide, she by cyanide, he by pistol shot.

IN *THE GREAT DICTATOR'S* CLOSING SCENES, CHARLIE CHAPLIN'S timid Jewish barber is, through a complicated plot twist, mistaken for the film's Hitler-like character, also played by Chaplin. Clad in a German military uniform, he finds himself standing before a microphone, expected to address a mammoth party rally. Instead of the rapid-fire invective the crowd anticipates, Chaplin delivers a homily about the resilience of the human spirit in the face of evil. He asks soldiers not to give themselves to "men who despise you, enslave you . . . treat you like cattle, use you as cannon fodder . . . unnatural men—machine men with machine minds and machine hearts. You are not machines! You are not cattle! You are men! You have the love of humanity in your hearts."

"Even now my voice is reaching millions throughout the world," the humble barber tells the crowd, "millions of despairing men, women, and little children—victims of a system that makes men torture and imprison innocent people. To those who can hear me, I say—do not despair. . . . The hate of men will pass, and dictators die, and the power they took from the people will return to the people. . . . Liberty will never perish."

Chaplin's words are sentimental, maudlin, and naïve. I cannot listen to them without wanting to cheer.

SEVEN

DICTATORSHIP OF DEMOCRACY

J OSEPH STALIN CONDEMNED WITH RELISH THE REACTION-
ary policies of Italian and German Fascists, but to a Communist, "Fascist" was the most versatile of insults. Rather
than reserve the epithet for the real thing, Soviets used the F-word
to discredit capitalists, nationalists, democrats, the religious, and
any faction—whether Trotskyite, Socialist, or liberal—that did
battle with the USSR for the hearts and minds of the left. In Stalin's universe, you were either with him or no better than Hitler;
there wasn't any middle ground. One might think, therefore, that
the two—Fascism and Communism—were opposites, but the
contrast is more complicated.

In 1932, Mussolini described Fascism as a closed universe in
which "the State is all-embracing," and outside which "no human
or spiritual values can exist." In so doing, he acknowledged its
overlap with Communism in its disdain for democracy and all its
trappings. Publicly, Il Duce denounced Bolsheviks but in private

he confessed his admiration for the effectiveness of Lenin's brutal tactics. Both Fascism and Communism had utopian aspirations and both took hold amid the intellectual and social ferment of the late nineteenth century. Each purported to deliver a level of emotional sustenance that liberal political systems lacked.

However, there were also stark differences. The Nazis sorted humans based on nationality and race; to Communists, the key determinant was class. In Germany, Jews and Roma were persecuted; in the Soviet Union, the principal targets were landowners, the bourgeoisie, and only later the Jews. The Nazis perverted religion while exploiting the impulse for worship; the Communists shunned religion while treating certain secular texts as sacred. The Nazis seized control of state institutions; the Communists dismantled and then rebuilt them, replacing a slothful czarist bureaucracy with a lumbering and inefficient Soviet one. Each system had its ironies. The Nazis chased the dream of a racially pure society through occupation and conquest, thus ensuring intimate contact with people of many non-Germanic nationalities and races. The Communists insisted that national identity was irrelevant but obsessively persecuted men and women because of who they were: Latvians, Poles, Ukrainians, Armenians, Finns, Chechens, Koreans, and Turks.

As for the two leading men, Hitler, once in power, showed his indolent side, generally starting his day around noon and leaving the details of government to others. Stalin rose with the roosters, worked long hours, and demanded to be kept current on every development, whether economic, political, or military. Hitler was a teetotaler and vegetarian; Stalin drank plenty and ate omnivorously—his chefs, including Vladimir Putin's grandfather, prepared the cuisine of the leader's native Georgia: kebabs, stews, salads, dumplings, plenty of walnuts, and bread you could sink your hands into. Hitler preferred oral briefings; Stalin read detailed policy papers—and edited them.

For all their dissimilarities, the two men spoke a common language: violence. Both despised the Jeffersonian ideals of popular governance, reasoned debate, freedom of expression, an independent judiciary, and fair electoral competition. Both struck remorselessly at enemies within and outside their parties. In the 1920s, when the Nazis were still struggling to establish themselves, the Soviets implemented their revolution by forcibly reorganizing industry, sending millions of "class enemies" to Siberia, and triggering a horrendous famine through the collectivization of agriculture. In 1937, Stalin ordered the executions of 680,000 people judged politically unreliable, including military officers, party officials, and members of the politburo—an incredible number. The Communists, almost as much as the Nazis, knew how to turn the state into a fearsome killing machine.

Also like the Nazis, the Communists sought to shape the minds of citizens by overwhelming their senses with propagandistic spam. Each day, the men and women of the USSR were called on to sacrifice for the revolution, unite for a better tomorrow, and labor harder for the good of the whole. The hectoring was constant from billboards and radios, newspapers and party bosses; its purpose was to mold conformists who would do what the government demanded because they could no longer conceive of an alternative. Their mission, and they had no safe choice but to accept it, was to follow orders—to become human robots who equated obedience with virtue.

Communists and Nazis both thought it their calling to forge a "new man," a creature of modernity who would rise above the individual quest for money, property, and pleasure that pitted workers against one another and, in their view, made of democracy a moral cesspool. In 1932, at a meeting hosted by the social realist writer Maxim Gorky, Stalin urged his country's literary elite to be "engineers of human souls." For their part, Soviet filmmakers churned out a thousand variations of the same story: a protagonist is forced by greedy capitalists to choose between self-interest and the well-being of the community. Invariably, the wrong choice leads to tragedy, and the correct one to comradely bliss.

The scenario's attraction is readily apparent. The Bolsheviks—which translates as "the Majority"—won millions of converts, in part because of the stark inequities that persist in capitalist societies. The notion of giving everyone a seat in the same boat is appealing and seems fair. However, there is a reason the Communists had to apply such a heavy hand to put their theories into practice. Had their ideas been a better fit for real life, their campaign to indoctrinate wouldn't have been so arduous and their gulags would have been unnecessary. Whatever might be the case in principle, the best farmers don't like collective agriculture, because there's nothing in it for them except more labor and less profit. In factories, the most productive workers won't remain so unless rewarded for their efforts—and an occasional "employee of the month" ribbon isn't enough. In any society, men and women with imagination will rebel at being told what to do, what to believe, and not to think.

A dictatorship by any other name is still a dictatorship, whether its symbol is the czarist two-headed eagle or the hammer and sickle. During World War II, the Red Army pressed into service millions of soldiers who loathed their commander in chief but still fought to defend Mother Russia against German Fascists. Soviet fact spinners later claimed that their troops had stormed into battle proclaiming their allegiance to Stalin, but that was nonsense. Communism doesn't work.

IN JULY 1945, AT THE AGE OF EIGHT, I BOARDED A BRITISH BOMBER, found a makeshift seat in its belly, and flew home to my native Czechoslovakia. My father, having returned some six weeks earlier, met us at the airport. The postwar era had begun. In the next three years, our country would balance precariously between Soviet-style Fascism and the kind of robust democratic republic we had cherished in the 1920s and '30s.

With the German occupation at an end, the divide between the two major components of the anti-Axis alliance—the Soviet Union and the West—was laid bare. During the war, most Czechoslovak exiles found refuge in London, but thousands of others were in Moscow, zealously preparing for what would come next. The brave souls who had resisted the Nazis from inside the country included loyalists from both camps. The unanswered question was whether the Czechoslovaks who had combined forces in time of war would cooperate in time of peace—and whether they would be allowed to do so.

Our country's president, Edvard Beneš, wished to preserve firm ties to both East and West—a sensible approach and, with the Cold War yet to emerge fully from its womb, seemingly possible. While I was en route from London to Prague, Stalin was chatting amiably in Potsdam with Truman and the soon-to-be-replaced Churchill. Publicly, we were still all on the same side. Behind closed doors, however, an epic clash had begun.

May 1946 saw the first elections in postwar Czechoslovakia. Prior to the conflict, Communists had received but a small fraction of the vote. They had expected to do better this time, but no one anticipated that they would rack up 38 percent, finishing well ahead of any other party. Beneš remained president while the hardline Communist leader, Klement Gottwald, a former cabinetmaker fond of wearing caps instead of hats, stepped in as prime minister. The cabinet was equally divided between moderates and the extreme left. The balloting gave Communists the hope that they could do what Mussolini and Hitler had done earlier—achieve power by democratic means, then kill democracy.

The second round of elections was scheduled for May 1948. The Communists sought an absolute majority; the democrats were determined to prevent that and gain momentum themselves. Calculations on all sides had to be adjusted in June 1947 when U.S. Secretary of State George Marshall put forward a generous loan program for the reconstruction of Europe. Every country in the region that had been damaged in the war, including the USSR, was invited to participate. For Czechoslovakia, the Marshall Plan offered a way to refloat its economy until farm conditions improved and factories resumed normal operations. On July 4, the cabinet voted unanimously to sign up.

Seven days later, that bright green light turned red in every sense. Officials from Prague went to Moscow, where Stalin told them that the American proposal was a trick, a trap designed to isolate Russia and undermine him. To press the argument, he declared that he was the only protection Czechoslovakia had against the resurgence of German power. Should the government choose to defy him, that protection would be withdrawn. Further, he would consider it a breach of Czechoslovak treaty obligations.

This is how the Cold War truly commenced. Not only my country, but the entire constellation of Soviet satellites—Poland, Hungary, Romania, Bulgaria, Albania, and Yugoslavia—had to reject the Marshall Plan because the Red Army was close and the Western allies had put down their guns. The plan could have held the continent together. Instead, Russian insecurity—a trait that would resurface in the twenty-first century—caused barbed wire to be strung across Europe's heart.

Back in Czechoslovakia, the democratic and Communist camps jockeyed feverishly in preparation for the scheduled balloting, with the latter having the advantage of superior organization, control of most major ministries, the backing of the Soviet Union, and the ability to summon large numbers of people to the streets on short notice. They also had the sharper elbows. Democrats pleaded with their countrymen to recognize the Communists' hypocrisy—that the same partisans who bragged about opposing

Fascism were now aping its techniques. The Communists were simply replacing pictures of Hitler with portraits of Stalin and, like Mussolini's Blackshirts, attacking the press, smearing political rivals, demanding total loyalty from party members, and threatening anyone who stood in their way.

My family watched all this from nearby Belgrade, where my father was Czechoslovak ambassador. Under strongman Josip Broz (better known by his pen name: Tito), Yugoslavia had emerged from the war with a fully committed Communist government. From his contacts with local officials, my father knew that vultures were circling our homeland. A Yugoslav army officer told him, "I do not agree with the policy of your government . . . you have too many parties." In his country, he said, the Communists "lead in parliament, in the army, in public administration, on the collective farms, in industry—everywhere. They act on behalf of the nation . . . it is a dictatorship of democracy." This peculiar conception, too, was right out of the Fascist game plan: a single party, speaking with one voice, controlling every state institution, claiming to represent all people, and labeling the entire sham a triumph of the popular will.

Deeply worried, my father went to Prague in January 1948 to consult with President Beneš. Having witnessed the cutthroat proclivities of Communist leaders in Yugoslavia, he hoped to find a leader fully aware of the danger that democratic forces faced and in possession of a clear strategy to fight back. However, when he was ushered into Beneš's office, my father was greeted by a man obviously ill, with silver hair thinning, deep bags beneath his eyes, and a slowing gait.

Beneš had been a world figure of near-legendary energy for three decades, but had recently suffered a stroke and was plainly worn down trying to hold his country together. My father, intent on making the most of his opportunity, warned the president about the inroads the Communists were making in the army, police, trade unions, media, and foreign ministry. He insisted that time was short. The older man's soothing response—that he was not alarmed—couldn't have been more frightening. Beneš dismissed the possibility of a coup and said he was certain the democrats would prevail in the coming elections. He urged my father to stop worrying, return to his job in Belgrade, and carry on.

A quarter of a century earlier, Mussolini had taken the reins of power from an indecisive king. In 1933, Hitler had done the same from an ailing and aged president. Beneš was neither as passive as Victor Emmanuel nor as old as Hindenburg, but he shared with them an inability to marshal democratic forces at a critical time. The showdown came in February 1948, when Communists were caught trying to subvert the police and distribute rifles to supporters in Prague. The revelations coincided with a large trade union rally scheduled for the capital on February 22, in what looked like a Moscow-orchestrated version of Mussolini's March on Rome.

Instead of keeping their nerve, the democratic cabinet ministers resigned, in the vain hope of forcing immediate elections. The resulting chaos created an opening that Gottwald, the Communist leader, did not hesitate to seize. He demanded that Beneš replace the ministers who had resigned with a list of men he considered "more reliable." His agents in the media echoed this call, and tens of thousands of labor activists cheered it. Then, on February 25, freedom was mugged beneath the spires of Prague. Democratic leaders on the way to work were barred from entering their offices; some had their homes searched or were handcuffed and thrown into jail. The last independent newspapers and radio stations were taken over and trashed. The Communist unions called for a nationwide strike; workers who refrained from joining were dismissed from their jobs. Gottwald went to Beneš and threatened him: *Either appoint a new cabinet or more blood will flow.* Reluctantly, the president gave in.

One major democratic official who did not resign was Foreign

Minister Jan Masaryk, a close friend of my father and of our family. The man I knew as "Uncle Jan" much preferred playing the piano to playing the diplomat; he had eyes that tried to mourn but twinkled anyway and a habit he could not shake of telling the truth. On the morning of March 10, his broken body was found in the ministry's courtyard, below an open bathroom window. The new government, headed by Gottwald, insisted that the death was suicide; evidence pointed to murder.

The story of the Communist takeover of Czechoslovakia holds lessons that still need absorbing. Good guys don't always win, especially when they are divided and less determined than their adversaries. The desire for liberty may be ingrained in every human breast, but so is the potential for complacency, confusion, and cowardice. And losing has a price. After 1948, Czechoslovakia had no room for democrats. In that Kafkaesque environment, the Czechs who had devoted every hour of World War II to fighting Hitler from London were accused of having spent their days instead plotting to enslave the working class. So, for the second time in my life, I was uprooted from the land of my birth. My father was asked to chair a UN commission investigating the dispute over Kashmir between India and Pakistan. When that assignment was complete, he applied for political asylum in the United States for himself and our family, a petition granted in June 1949.

CONTEMPLATING THE DEVASTATION WREAKED BY WORLD WAR I, the leaders of the international community showed what they had learned: not enough. The European victors wanted nothing more than to grab territory and exact revenge. The losers were impoverished and spoiling to get even. The United States arrived at the peace conference in Paris with lofty principles and a short attention span, ultimately rejecting its own proposed League of Nations and withdrawing smugly to its side of the ocean. The overall lack of effective joint action—following an ordeal that had left twenty million people dead and twenty-one million wounded—enabled Fascism to rise and led the world into the abyss of a second and even more catastrophic war.

After V-E Day, President Truman and his transatlantic colleagues were determined to work together where their predecessors had not. They hoped that their wartime alliance with the Soviet Union could be extended, but the Communist coup in Czechoslovakia, coupled with Masaryk's murder, destroyed that illusion. Stalin had no intention of keeping his wartime promises; his plan was to dominate Central and Eastern Europe.

The West countered by forging a military alliance (NATO) and helping Greece and Turkey to fend off Communist subversion. Instead of retreating again into a cocoon across the sea, the United States championed an array of multilateral organizations, including the UN, the International Monetary Fund, and the World Bank. In 1949, Truman unveiled Point Four, a technical aid initiative designed to help people in distant corners of the globe raise their standard of living. Each of these steps was the product of enlightened international engagement, and each was implemented in the United States with strong bipartisan support. These accomplishments and the painstaking diplomacy that brought them into being should not be taken for granted or forgotten.

The Soviet Union in this period continued to exhibit many of the classic symptoms of Fascism. When the liberal columnist I. F. Stone visited Moscow in May 1956, he encountered a Communist party functionary who seemed eager to say what was on his mind, but when Stone prompted him, the Muscovite quickly developed second thoughts, finally muttering in German, "*Ili Schweigen ili Gefängnis*"—"Either silence or prison."

That grim choice was a real one, because Communist governments showed a tendency to devour their own. Many postwar Communist leaders in Czechoslovakia and elsewhere in the region were later imprisoned or hanged, some on the direct orders of Stalin, some almost certainly because they were Jews. A distinctive vocabulary was developed to justify the arrests. Those condemned by show trials were called class traitors, enemies of the people, running dogs, bourgeois pigs, imperialist spies—and, naturally, when the Berlin Wall went up, the excuse given was to protect against Fascists.

In the West, we invented our own list of disparaging labels: red, pinko, fellow traveler, commie-symp. Concerned by the danger of Soviet espionage and determined not to replicate the appeasement policy that had smoothed Hitler's path, U.S. politicians tried to outdo one another in appearing the most vigilant. Congressional committees demanded to know "Who Lost China?" and sought to root out traitors in the media, arts, labor movement, and all branches of government. The times called for a leader of wisdom and strength who could protect the country against subversion without getting tangled in the snares of paranoia and unreasoning fear. That was the need, but it was not who barged through the door.

SENATOR JOSEPH MCCARTHY—ANGRY, JOWLY, AND PERPETUALLY indignant—had the instincts of a Mussolini, but without the intellectual foundation. Like Il Duce, he was a showman who loved politics and craved power. Unlike him, he began his public life largely ignorant of policy. His temperament was that of a Fascist bully, but he was uncertain at first where to direct his fury. During McCarthy's early years in the Senate, he tried to think up an angle that would make sensational news out of fur tariffs, public housing, sugar quotas, or Pentagon procurement. It was hard going. Early in 1950, with his reelection campaign on the horizon, he stepped up his quest for a headline-grabbing idea.

The answer, according to contemporary accounts, came during

a friendly dinner in a Washington restaurant with three fellow Roman Catholics: a lawyer, a professor, and a prominent Jesuit priest. The lawyer recommended that McCarthy make a big push on behalf of the St. Lawrence Seaway—a massive construction project. Too dull, the group decided. The professor proposed a plan to give each old person in America a hundred dollars a month. Too expensive, they agreed. Finally, the priest spoke up: What about Communism and the threat to national security? How's that for an issue? Just right.*

Thus was conceived a phenomenon that would split America from right to left and raise ominous questions—of a type we still face—about whether a democratic citizenry can be talked into betraying its own values.

Joe McCarthy had a barrel chest, blue eyes framed by shaggy brows, an abundance of restless energy, and experience as a chicken farmer. His down-to-earth speaking style pleased many voters, as did his reputation for shouting things that more conventional politicians were too timid to whisper. The senator's skin, however, was paper-thin, and he seemed not to care very much whether his startling disclosures had any basis in fact.

Just one month after his fateful dinner in Washington, McCarthy told a women's club in Wheeling, West Virginia, "I have in my hand a list of 205 names that were made known to the secretary of state as being members of the Communist Party and who nevertheless are still working and shaping policy in the State Department."

There followed a three-year spectacle during which McCarthy captured enormous media attention by prophesying the imminent ruin of America and by making false charges that he then

---

* McCarthy's helpful Jesuit friend, Father Edmund Walsh, SJ, was dean of the Georgetown School of Foreign Service, later renamed in his honor. I teach at the Walsh School and have done so for more than twenty years. The faculty does not talk much about Father Walsh's dinner date with McCarthy.

denied raising—only to invent new ones. He claimed to have identified subversives in the State Department, the army, think tanks, universities, labor unions, the press, and Hollywood. He cast doubt on the patriotism of all who criticized him, including fellow senators. McCarthy was profoundly careless about his sources of information and far too glib when connecting dots that had no logical link. In his view, you were guilty if you were or ever had been a Communist, had attended a gathering where a supposed Communist sympathizer was present, had read a book authored by someone soft on Communism, or subscribed to a magazine with liberal ideas. McCarthy, who was nicknamed Tailgunner Joe, though he had never been a tail gunner, was also fond of superlatives. By the middle of 1951, he was warning the Senate of "a conspiracy so immense and an infamy so black as to dwarf any previous such venture in the history of man."

McCarthy would neither have become a sensation, nor ruined the careers of so many innocent people, had he not received support from some of the nation's leading newspapers and financing from right-wingers with deep pockets. He would have been exposed much sooner had his wild accusations not been met with silence by many mainstream political leaders from both parties who were uncomfortable with his bullying tactics but lacked the courage to call his bluff. By the time he self-destructed, a small number of people working in government had indeed been identified as security risks, but none because of the Wisconsin senator's scattershot investigations.

McCarthy fooled as many as he did because a lot of people shared his anxieties, liked his vituperative style, and enjoyed watching the powerful squirm. Whether his allegations were greeted with resignation or indignation didn't matter so much as the fact that they were reported on and repeated. The more inflammatory the charge, the more coverage it received. Even skeptics subscribed to the idea that, though McCarthy might be

exaggerating, there had to be some fire beneath the smoke he was
spreading. This is the demagogue's trick, the Fascist's ploy, exem-
plified most outrageously by the spurious and anti-Jewish Proto-
cols of the Elders of Zion. Repeat a lie often enough and it begins
to sound as if it must—or at least might—be so. "Falsehood flies,"
observed Jonathan Swift, "and the truth comes limping after it."
McCarthy's career shows how much hysteria a skilled and shame-
less prevaricator can stir up, especially when he claims to be fighting in a just cause. After all, if Communism was the ultimate evil,
a lot could be hazarded—including objectivity and conventional
morality—in opposing it.

DURING MUCH OF THE COLD WAR, THE SOVIET EMPIRE WAS AN
overextended colossus, battling internal contradictions and driven
more by paranoia than by any ambition for global conquest.
That empire, however, was formidably armed, cynical, and cruel
enough to merit a vigilant response from free societies. Thank-
fully, there were leaders on every continent prepared to argue
for democratic representation, a strong defense, and respect for
liberal norms. In Europe, these principles were wedded to a process of regional integration that eased border restrictions, eliminated tariff barriers, and developed a common currency. In the
United States, administrations from both parties made major
contributions through such measures as Eisenhower's "Atoms for
Peace" program, Kennedy's Alliance for Progress, Nixon's opening to China, Carter's commitment to human rights, and Reagan's
support for democracy. These and other initiatives showed the
fundamental difference between a state-run system that ignores
individual rights and one that derives its power from the people.

The saga of the Cold War, however, was not quite as black-and-
white as this duality suggests. In 1920s Italy and 1930s Germany,
fear of Communism propelled Fascism's rise. After World War II,

the same fear gave life to McCarthy's reckless allegations and to a willingness on the part of many democratic leaders to overlook repression when the governments involved were anti-Communist. By the early 1970s, the Nixon administration counted among its "free world" partners the dictatorships of South Korea, the Philippines, Indonesia, Pakistan, Iran, Saudi Arabia, Egypt, Zaire, Spain, Portugal, Greece, Argentina, Chile, Paraguay, Brazil, and all of Central America except Costa Rica—an embarrassing list.

I'm reminded of a dream that the aunt of a friend of mine had; the woman's name is Cleo and she grew up in Kansas during the Great Depression. In the dream, she is lifted to Heaven when just a child. There, she is greeted by an angel who says, "Take my hand and I will show you to your new home." The angel and Cleo stroll through Heaven's shining streets, more radiant than anything the small and nervous girl had seen. However, instead of stopping before one of the lovely houses, they keep walking, then walking some more. The lights begin to dim, the houses are smaller now and the streets not so smooth. Finally, they arrive at a tiny hut near the edge of a dense forest with just enough light to see. Cleo asks, "Is this my new home?" The angel replies, "I'm afraid so; you were just barely good enough to get in."

During the Cold War, many governments thought it sufficient to define themselves by what they were against. When the Berlin Wall fell and the Iron Curtain parted, mere anti-Communism was no longer the credential it had been. To win respect, governments would have to aim higher than "barely good enough." That, one might hope, would prove welcome news.

EIGHT

"THERE ARE A LOT OF BODIES UP THERE"

TEN WEEKS AFTER THE DEATH OF FRANKLIN ROOSEVELT and less than two months subsequent to the German surrender, President Harry Truman flew to San Francisco to address representatives of the newly founded United Nations. The message he conveyed was one of profound optimism and hope, but included a word of caution. "Fascism did not die with Mussolini," he warned. "Hitler is finished, but the seeds spread by his disordered mind have firm root in too many fanatical brains. It is easier to remove tyrants and destroy concentration camps than to kill the ideas that gave them birth."

Foremost among the ideas Truman referred to was the belief that one's own nation has attributes and rights above all others. The aggression shown by Tojo's militaristic Japan, Mussolini's New Rome, and Hitler's supposed thousand-year Reich could all be traced, at least in part, to the unbridled nationalism of those countries' leaders and followers. The world—East and West—had paid an unconscionable price to withstand the folly unleashed by their "fanatical brains." However, this did not mean that as history moved from hot war to cold, the Soviet Union and its adversaries would view nationalism in the same light.

In Communist theology, preoccupation with national identity is a mortal sin, an obsession devised by the rich to distract the proletariat and prevent it from asserting its own interests. In this view, the nurturing of ethnic pride is little more than a tactic for dividing workers, persuading them to don opposing uniforms and slaughter one another for the benefit of arms manufacturers and banks. Thus, Communist regimes, especially in diverse societies like the USSR and Yugoslavia, banned the public display of nationalist sentiments. In the non-Communist world, however, nationalism is often thought to be a basic human instinct that becomes dangerous only when taken too far. Ordinarily, it is manifested in benign ways. For example, as a child, I marked Czechoslovakia's National Day by wearing a traditional dress and handing out flowers in front of the embassy where my father had his office; that was my job.

As an adult, I have never concealed my pride in being an American, even to acquaintances who consider that kind of chauvinism unsophisticated. The identification we feel toward the places where we live or were born can give us an anchor in a chaotic world and strengthen our connections to family, community, and the generations that preceded and will follow us. At their best, such feelings are a celebration of culture and all that comes with it in the form of literature, language, music, food, folktales, and even the wildlife we associate with our homelands—the eagle in America, for instance, or in the Czech Republic what's left of our lions, wolves, and bears.

There is, however, a tipping point where loyalty to one's own tribe curdles into resentment and hatred, then aggression toward others. That's when Fascism enters the picture, trailed by an assortment of woes, up to and including the Holocaust and global war. Because of that history, postwar statesmen established organizations to make it harder for deluded nationalists to trample on the rights of neighbors. These bodies include the United Nations—hence Truman's speech—and regional institutions in Europe, Africa, Asia, and the Americas.

When the Cold War ended, the Soviet bloc lost its ability to stifle the expression of nationalist attitudes. At the same time, many countries were given the chance to join groups from which they had been excluded. The combination brought some peoples closer together and tore others apart. In Central Europe and the Baltics, citizens of the newly liberated states looked eagerly to the West as they prepared to enter NATO and the European Union. In other parts of the world, the pent-up forces of sectarian anger took advantage of the thawing earth to crawl like poisonous snakes from their holes.

In 1993, I began serving as America's permanent representative to a very busy UN, where diplomats confronted conflicts that had arisen almost overnight in Georgia, Armenia, Azerbaijan, Somalia, Angola, Liberia, Mozambique, Sudan, Haiti, Cambodia, Afghanistan, and Tajikistan. Until that time, the world body had focused on wars between states. Now we were often called on to respond to mayhem within states, the most horrific of which was the genocide perpetrated by Hutu militants in Rwanda. Yet another region of prolonged and vicious fighting was the Balkans.

Early in my tenure, I flew across the Atlantic and half of Europe to a garbage dump in the corner of a plowed field a few miles outside the Croatian city of Vukovar. As I looked around at the debris, not much was visible—just a few rusted refrigerators and scraps of farm equipment, surrounded by coils of razor wire. But in the ground below lay the bodies of more than two hundred Croat hospital patients—innocent men, women, and children who, some months earlier, had been rousted from their beds, taken outside, and murdered by their Serbian neighbors. I wanted to know the reason. Later that day, I met with local Serb leaders. They made no effort to deny that the mass killing had taken place; they just marveled at my concern. Didn't I understand the influence of the past? Why, after so many years of jealousy and hate, should I expect anything to change?

SLOBODAN MILOŠEVIĆ WAS A YUGOSLAV BUSINESSMAN WHO MA-neuvered his way upward through the ranks of Communist officials following the death, in 1980, of the country's longtime leader Tito. While establishing himself, Milošević adhered to the party line, favoring a Yugoslavia of "brotherhood and unity," as the slogan had it, in which all groups were treated equally. His attitude hardened when, just prior to the end of the decade, he was elected president of Serbia. Though he continued to pay lip service to the ideal of a multinational Yugoslavia, he also cooked up bits of red meat to whet the appetites of Serb partisans:

> We must secure unity in Serbia if we wish, as the largest and most populous republic, to dictate the course of future events. . . . If we must fight, then my God, we will fight and I hope they will not be so crazy as to fight against us. Because if we don't know how to work well or to do business, at least we know how to fight well.

Like other nationalist orators, Milošević drew heavily on the literary, religious, and artistic traditions that had bound his people together through centuries of foreign domination. He exploited the anger born of past defeats at the hands of the Ottoman Turks and Nazis and called for vigilance against such imagined present-day foes as the CIA, Germany, and the Vatican. He took inspiration from a memorandum signed by two hundred members of the Serbian Academy of Arts and Sciences, describing Serbs as a repressed people and calling for the inclusion of them all within a single state.

When, in 1991 and 1992, Yugoslavia broke uneasily into five pieces, the dissolution was most wrenching in Bosnia-Herzegovina, which had a Muslim majority but also housed significant Serb and Croat communities. As part of the breakup, Milošević allowed Bosnian Serbs from the Yugoslav Army to return home with all their weapons, giving them the upper hand in what quickly became a grisly civil war.

Every party to the Bosnian bloodbath could be faulted for human rights violations, but the Serbs had the greater firepower and committed by far the most egregious crimes. As early as the summer of 1992, there were ninety-four Serb-run concentration camps in which, all told, tens of thousands of prisoners were beaten, starved, or raped. Even though Milošević, from his vantage point in Belgrade, didn't personally direct these operations, he knew what was taking place—as did the whole world. He continued nevertheless to furnish financial and military support to the killers and rapists.

The Bosnian Muslims had no air force or munitions plants to attack, but the absence of strategic targets did nothing to slow the Serb assault; shells rained down on open-air markets, shops, cyclists, and children sledding or playing in the snow. Apartment buildings were gutted, with gaping holes where windows should have been. Serb marksmen turned the main boulevard in Sarajevo into what became known as "Sniper Alley." In the countryside, the disruptive effects of the fighting made bad conditions even worse. Desperate for medicine and food, villagers depended on airdrops that often missed their targets and on convoys that rarely came. Many people grew hungry, some starved, babies died. Doctors were forced to operate without anesthetics, extracting bullets from bodies by candlelight. Half of Bosnia's population was displaced; one out of twenty perished.

Years earlier, I had traveled through the region and was impressed by Yugoslavia's reverence for its heritage and by the existence, often in a single town, of Roman Catholic and Orthodox churches and one or more mosques. Now the holy places were damaged and the Sarajevo National Library, with its collection of rare Ottoman-era books, had been shelled and burned.

The horror reached its apex in 1995, when, in the space of ten July days, troops commanded by General Ratko Mladić executed 7,800 Muslim men and boys in and around the town of Srebrenica and deposited their bodies in mass graves. After four years of dithering, the killings finally triggered a serious diplomatic effort by Western and UN officials to end the war. However, even while that process was under way, Bosnian Serbs attacked a Sarajevo food market, murdering thirty-seven civilians. Given their earlier crimes, the provocation was sufficient that two days later, more than five dozen NATO aircraft, flying from bases in Italy and the Adriatic, pounded Serb positions around Sarajevo. French and British artillery joined in. It was, to that time, the largest NATO combat operation in history.

The air strikes had a military impact, but the more telling effect was psychological. With NATO on watch, the Bosnian Serbs could no longer play the bully; their reign of terror was over. During the first week of September, the parties agreed to silence their guns and live side by side within a single state. The arrangement served as a basis for the Dayton Accords, initialed on November 21, 1995, ending the Bosnian War.

The Balkans crisis was inseparable from the history that preceded it. Muslim victims accused Bosnian Serbs of ethnic cleansing and genocide, the worst war crimes in Europe since the Fascist atrocities of World War II. Milošević pointed at the abuses committed by Croat nationalists, some of whom had taken Hitler's side in that conflict. Observers around the world were reminded of photos from half a century earlier of malnourished prisoners—

their skin pulled tight against their skeletons—languishing in concentration camps. Until NATO finally acted, the years of inept diplomacy made me think of Europe's inglorious and unavailing attempt to appease Hitler prior to the invasion of Czechoslovakia. On one point only was there consensus. With the fighting finally over, and more than 100,000 killed, we should never again allow the Balkans to be riven by sectarian violence.

EARLY ON SATURDAY, JANUARY 16, 1999, I WOKE TO THE SOUND OF all-news radio. Lying there in the pale light of a midwinter dawn, I heard a bulletin about events nearly five thousand miles away. "There are a lot of bodies up there," said a voice. "Men have been shot in various ways, mostly very close up." Already, "never again" was happening.

The massacre in the town of Račak left forty-five civilians dead; the youngest, age twelve; the oldest, ninety-nine. Račak is in Kosovo, a province of Serbia that was home to just over two million people and situated on the jagged line that once divided Europe's Muslims from its Christians. The tragedy was an outrage that might have passed with little international notice had it not been for the ghosts of history.

In Kosovo in 1389, Serb forces had suffered a closely fought defeat at the hands of the mobile cavalry of the Ottoman Empire. The Serb leader, captured by the Turks, was brought before the sultan and beheaded. Through the centuries, many Serbs, while honoring the bravery of their forces, hungered to avenge the loss. For them, Kosovo was a place central to their identity.

As the years passed, the population of the province was heavily affected by its proximity to neighboring Albania and by the cultural impacts of Turkish rule. By the 1990s, most Kosovars were Albanian in ethnicity and Muslim by faith. The Christian Serbs were a small minority. Under Tito, the Kosovo Albanians had obtained the right to run their own schools and other institutions. This upset the local Serbs, who complained of religious discrimination and of being crowded out of their ancestral home by Muslims, with their high birth rate. Milošević, when he came to power in 1989, revoked the privileges granted to the Albanians, pleasing the Serbs. That, in turn, caused militant Albanians to organize the Kosovo Liberation Army (KLA), a band of resistance fighters who demanded full independence.

The KLA's aggressive tactics provided an excuse for Milošević's hardline policies and helped him diplomatically. Had he been wise, he could have turned world opinion against the guerrillas by accommodating the aspirations of moderate Kosovars for autonomy. However, he didn't see the ethnic dispute as a political and diplomatic problem to be solved; he saw only an enemy to be destroyed. This was the attitude that led to the massacre at Račak and, before long, to the unhappy final chapter of the dictator's reign.

I WAS THEN IN MY THIRD YEAR AS U.S. SECRETARY OF STATE. PRESident Clinton and I felt a duty to use the national security tools we had available to prevent the loss of more innocent lives. After huddling with colleagues in Europe, we pressed the Serbian leader to find a peaceful way out of the crisis. For leverage, I warned that, as in Bosnia, NATO was prepared to conduct air strikes to protect civilians. Under the plan we developed, Kosovo would be entitled to autonomy, but the KLA would be required to disarm, and its demand for independence put on hold. We were asking both sides to compromise. After much hesitation, the Kosovo Albanians said yes. To seal the deal, I had to persuade the man in Belgrade.

Slobodan Milošević did not fit the stereotype of a Fascist villain. He wasn't flamboyant like Mussolini or a screamer like Hitler. His face was ruddy, fleshy, and unlined. He cultivated an affable manner and tended to act the innocent in conversations.

Many thought he was influenced by the inflexible attitude of his wife, Mirjana Marković, a Marxist professor whose mother had been tortured and murdered by the Nazis.

Milošević, who insisted that he was a democrat, harbored a peculiar notion of what that calling entailed. He exercised a despot's control over his country's media, repressed political opposition, and created a paramilitary force to intimidate domestic rivals. Even when fueling the terrible fighting in Bosnia, he claimed to want peace; and even amid the slaughter of civilians in Sarajevo, he insisted that Serbs were the primary victims. A year earlier, when I met with him in Belgrade, he had lectured me about the history of his people. I pointed out that I had lived for a time in Yugoslavia and that my father had written a book about the country, which he dedicated to the people who lived there. My father confided to me that had he not been born a Czech, he would have loved to be a Serb; so I was well enough informed.

I told Milošević that the United States was eager to have a good relationship with him, but that didn't mean we were willing to sit back and do nothing while he pushed others around. This was the message I repeated as the crisis in Kosovo heated up. I emphasized that a negotiated settlement was within reach; the KLA had promised to put down its arms, provided an international force was deployed to prevent further massacres. "This is a deal you should be willing to take," I argued. "Solving Kosovo will end Serbia's international isolation and allow you to concentrate on expanding your economy and moving closer to Europe."

Milošević assured me of his desire for reconciliation and of his allegiance to cultural diversity. He valued pluralism so much, he said, that he couldn't possibly sign on to an agreement that would leave Albanian Muslims with the upper hand in Kosovo. I noted that Muslims made up 90 percent of the population and that the plan we had in mind would protect the Serb minority. Milošević, however, was in love with an alternative set of facts. He insisted that half or more of the people in Kosovo were not Albanian but instead were Serbs, Turks, Montenegrins, or Roma and asked if I expected him to stand by and watch the Albanians force them from their homes. Kosovo, he said, had been defending the Christian West against Islam for five hundred years.

I argued that the whole purpose of sending international peacekeepers to the province was to ensure that citizens of every nationality and faith could live there in peace. Milošević was stubborn by nature, and his experience as a Yugoslav Communist convinced him that he had the right, as head of state, to impose his will. When it became clear, after our conversation, that we were not going to back away from our principles, he sought to preempt the issue.

Without warning, he ordered his security forces into Kosovo to burn houses, arrest political leaders and journalists, and sow panic. His goal was to drive Albanians out of the country so that they would no longer be the majority in Kosovo. Within weeks, hundreds of thousands had been compelled to leave by train, by truck, by car, or on foot and to find temporary shelter in the hastily constructed tent cities that sprouted in surrounding fields and hills. As we had threatened, NATO initiated air strikes to force the Serbs to back down. After two and a half months of fighting, the alliance prevailed, Milošević gave in, the refugees returned, and, with international help, the Kosovars set up their own government.

The crisis in Kosovo involved a small place and a big issue. There had been a time, not much earlier, when the global community would have disclaimed any official interest in what a government did to men and women within its own jurisdiction. National sovereignty was the acknowledged cornerstone of the international system. Hitler, however, had shown how a dictator can make the arguably legal morally intolerable. After the death camps, there had to be a line drawn by people of conscience—a line beyond which a ruler (and those under his command) couldn't go.

The Nuremberg trials established the principle that neither "obeying the law" nor "following orders" is a sufficient legal defense for those accused of violating basic standards of civilization. In 1948, the Universal Declaration of Human Rights spelled out a framework for holding governments accountable, followed in three years by the Convention on the Prevention and Punishment of Genocide. In the 1970s and '80s, international sanctions were lodged against racist Rhodesia and South Africa, ultimately transforming both countries. In the same period, the United States and Western Europe began making respect for human rights a condition of foreign military assistance. During the Bosnian conflict, an international tribunal was established to prosecute the perpetrators of crimes against humanity. I was a firm advocate of the tribunal because only through a judicial process is it possible to establish individual culpability for crimes that might otherwise be attributed to an entire group—and nothing does more to trigger additional cycles of violence than perceptions of collective guilt. Among those indicted by the tribunal was Milošević, who was charged with genocide in Bosnia and the forced deportation of hundreds of thousands of people from Kosovo.*

THE END OF THE SUPERPOWER RIVALRY WAS A MOMENT OF INCALculable promise: the third make-or-break opportunity of the twentieth century. The first had arisen in the aftermath of the

---

* Milošević's trial began in 2002, but in 2006 it was terminated without a verdict upon his death from a heart attack. In 2016, in a separate case, the tribunal noted both Milošević's role in funding the Bosnian Serbs and a lack of evidence implicating him in planning Bosnian Serb atrocities. In 2017, Ratko Mladić, who had been the Serb commander at Srebrenica, was convicted of genocide and war crimes.

Great War, the conflict that President Woodrow Wilson hoped would leave the world safe for democracy; instead, Germany's quest for vengeance on one side of the Atlantic and America's retreat into isolationism on the other ignited Fascism and gave space for its flames. The second opening accompanied the Allied victory in World War II. This time, the international community built institutions that, for all their flaws, fostered prosperity and helped avoid yet another global conflict. The fall of the Berlin Wall marked the third turning point—a fresh chance to make the world more stable, civilized, and just.

During President Bill Clinton's two terms, the United States was at the forefront of this effort—and not solely in the Balkans. We helped safeguard nuclear materials following the breakup of the Soviet Union. We gained approval of an international convention to ban chemical weapons. By opening the doors of NATO, we created an incentive for countries in Central Europe to strengthen their democracies and prevent the kind of sectarian strife that had made the region vulnerable to Fascism. We encouraged China and India to liberalize their economies and streamlined rules for international commerce through a new World Trade Organization. We pioneered the Summit of the Americas process to enhance cooperation throughout the Western Hemisphere and worked with African leaders to end wars caused by ethnic and religious differences. We spoke out frequently on behalf of human rights, the empowerment of women, better conditions for workers, and stronger protections for the environment.

Finally, in June 2000, we brought together representatives from more than one hundred nations at the first Community of Democracies conference, an event hosted by Poland. The conference's theme was that countries should help one another live up to the responsibilities that come with the democratic label. This was not a celebratory event. We assembled in Warsaw because we recognized that consolidating democratic gains would be long and difficult. We were heartened, nonetheless, by the impressive turnout and by the apparent sincerity of the commitments made. I left Poland thinking that, in the battle for world opinion, democracy—more than ever before in history—occupied the high ground. I did not know then what the new century would bring.

NINE

A DIFFICULT ART

I N 1895, THERE APPEARED A CARTOON IN THE BRITISH HUMOR magazine *Punch*. The line drawing showed a bishop and his family sharing breakfast with a young curate, or priest. Studying the egg his guest is eating, the bishop worries aloud that it might be rotten. The curate responds politely, "Oh no, my Lord, I assure you—parts of it are excellent!"

Today, across the globe, we might say something similar about the condition of democracy. The difference is that little can be done to salvage the curate's half-eaten egg. With help from its friends, however, democracy can almost always be repaired, then made better.

OVER A SPAN OF MORE THAN THREE DECADES, I WORKED FIRST AS vice-chair then as chair of the National Democratic Institute (NDI), which, with its sister organizations in the United States and abroad, aids indigenous efforts to develop democratic institutions and skills. In this role, the organization has observed historic milestones such as the People Power movement that in 1986 foiled Philippine dictator Ferdinand Marcos's effort to steal a "snap" presidential election; and two years on, the plebiscite that ended the repressive rule of Chilean general Augusto Pinochet. NDI was also present during the historic 1994 election in South Africa that brought down the curtain on apartheid, and—in the Cold War's wake—the rebirth of democracy in Central Europe and the more recent transitions in Indonesia, Nepal, Nigeria, and Tunisia.

NDI's stance is strictly a supportive one. It neither advocates for any specific party or policy agenda, nor views democracy as a rigid system that will look the same in Asia, for example, as in Africa or the Americas. Within the framework of certain core principles, democracy is a means by which very different peoples express their freedom. NDI's mission is to help local officials and activists profit from the experiences of others, and to do so across borders and regions. The lessons learned might facilitate an electoral process free from the taint of unfairness and corruption; or offer practical ideas on how to modernize a legislature, professionalize political parties, create space for civil society, or ensure that women, young people, and minorities are fairly represented when decisions are made.

NDI is careful to stress that democracy requires far more than choosing a leader via the ballot box. That is essential but never enough. No error is more common than to assume that the winner of an election has license to do whatever he or she may want. In a true democracy, leaders respect the will of the majority but also the rights of the minority—one without the other is not enough. This means that constitutional protections for the individual must be defended, even when those protections become inconvenient to the party on top. Years before taking office, Hitler told his fellow Nazis, "The Constitution only maps out the arena of the battle, not the goal . . . once we possess constitutional power, we will mold the state into the shape we hold to be suitable."

NDI and similar groups offer a counterpoint to this kind of arrogance. Their efforts are vital because when free governments fail, authoritarian leaders are emboldened—and because elected officials in many regions are engaged in a constant struggle to meet the expectations of their citizens. The Central American states of El Salvador, Honduras, and Guatemala, for example, emerged from a searing period of left–right civil wars only to find themselves—due to gang violence—with three of the world's highest homicide rates. Afghanistan and Iraq continue to be threatened by terrorists while attempting, often with immense courage on the part of ordinary citizens, to put democratic principles into practice. In Africa, many governments lack the financial resources to meet the needs of their people. In Myanmar, the long-awaited emergence of democracy has been marred by an ugly campaign of ethnic cleansing directed at the Rohingya Muslim minority.

Cicero declared that "it is a difficult art to rule a republic." Between his era and ours, governing hasn't become any easier. Consider that, of the people celebrating their sixteenth birthday this year, almost nine in ten will do so in a country with a below-average standard of living. In the world's four dozen poorest nations, the adult population will more than triple by midcentury. Globally, more than a third of the workforce lacks a full-time job. In Europe, youth unemployment is above 25 percent, and the level is even higher for immigrants. In the United States, one out of every six young people is both out of school and out of a job. Wages, in real terms, have been stagnant since the 1970s.

These figures would be disturbing at any time, but they are particularly worrisome now, when so many countries have populations coming of age that are anxious to start careers but have no realistic chance to do so. Think of the PhD candidate who ends up driving a taxi; the college graduate who digs ditches; and the high school dropout who can't get hired at all. People want to vote, but they need to eat. In many countries, the climate is reminiscent of that which, a hundred years ago, gave birth to Italian and German Fascism.

INNOVATION IS THE PRIMARY GENERATOR OF EMPLOYMENT, BUT also the number one destroyer. Technology has enabled companies to increase their productivity—a boon for consumers but not for those whose jobs become obsolete. That's why we have fewer coal miners, field workers, riveters, welders, cobblers, bank tellers, dressmakers, blacksmiths, typists, print journalists, traveling salesmen, and telephone operators—a deficit not quite balanced by an increase in code writers, consultants, health care technicians, addiction counselors, and reality TV stars. The most difficult competitor for any worker is a machine that can do the same job essentially for free. This unequal contest between our inventions and our workforce has depressed salaries and robbed millions of the dignity that comes from regular employment— and along with it the precious sense of being useful and optimism about what lies ahead.

Against this backdrop, the celebration that erupted among many—including me—when the Cold War reached its end has dissipated. In 2017, *The Economist*'s Democracy Index showed a decline in democratic health in seventy countries, using such criteria as respect for due process, religious liberty, and the space given to civil society. Among the nations scoring less well was the United States, which for the first time was rated a "flawed democracy," not a "full" one. The analysts didn't blame Donald Trump for this fall from grace but rather attributed his election to Americans' loss of confidence in their institutions. "Popular trust in government, elected representatives, and political parties has fallen to extremely low levels," the report concluded, adding,

"This has been a long-term trend." The number of Americans who say that they have faith in their government "just about always" or "most of the time" dropped from above 70 percent in the early 1960s to below 20 percent in 2016.

Yes, there continue to be gains. In Africa, forty heads of state have relinquished power voluntarily in the past quarter century, compared with a mere handful in the three decades prior to that. However, progress there and in a select number of other countries has failed to obscure a more general leveling-off. Today, about half the nations on earth can be considered democracies—flawed or otherwise—while the remaining 50 percent tend toward authoritarianism.

Surveys indicate that most people continue to believe that representative democracy—like the curate's egg—is excellent in parts. However, the same polls show a rising curiosity about potential alternatives. On average, one person in four thinks well of a system in which a strong ruler can govern without interference from a parliament or the courts. One in five is attracted to the concept of military rule. Predictably, support for nondemocratic options is most evident among those, whether on the political right or left, who lack a higher education and are unhappy with their economic circumstances—precisely the groups hit hardest by the evolving nature of the workplace. The 2008 financial crisis reinforced this trend by causing many citizens to doubt the competence of their leaders and to question the fairness of systems that seem to protect the wealthy at the expense of everyone else.

A FURTHER REASON FOR DISCONTENT WITH DEMOCRACY IS THAT public officials are having a harder time communicating their intentions and actions. The old days of one person broadcasting a story to many have been supplanted by networks that connect all to all; each day, there are more people with megaphones on the street. This expansion of awareness has benefits, but can also stir resentment among people who see what others have and they do not. Respect for the rights of others is a lofty principle; but envy is a primal urge.

Meanwhile, advances in technology have provided both the blessing of a more informed public and the curse of a misinformed one—men and women who are sure they know the truth because of what they have seen or been told on social media. The advantage of a free press is diminished when anyone can claim to be an objective journalist, then disseminate narratives conjured out of thin air to make others believe rubbish. The tactic is effective because people sitting at home or tapping away in a coffee shop often have no reliable way to determine whether the source of what they are reading is legitimate, a foreign government, a freelance impostor, or a malicious bot.

What we have witnessed thus far is just the beginning. Each year, more states employ squads of opinion-shapers to flood online sites—North Korea, China, Russia, Venezuela, the Philippines, and Turkey are already among the leading practitioners of this dark art. Extremist political movements, including terrorist groups, engage in the same practice. Many of these troublemakers can generate products that show people—including democratic politicians—doing things they didn't do and saying things they never said. For maximum impact, the phony information is then distributed to recipients based on personal profiles derived from social media posts. Imagine a foreign agent creeping into your bedroom every night to whisper lies in your ear, then multiply the number of agents and lies by a billion or more.

Disinformation campaigns are hardly novel. During the American War for Independence, the rebel minister to Paris, Benjamin Franklin, used his printing press to circulate stories he had made up about British atrocities. However, just because a technique isn't new doesn't mean it's not dangerous. The cost of spreading falsehoods via social media is minimal and so, for those who are adept at it, is the effort required. As a defense, the deployment of fact-checkers is helpful but can seem like dispatching a tortoise in pursuit of a hare that, unlike Aesop's, has no intention of slowing down.

This puts a burden on the operators of social media platforms to re-examine their role. The view that they have no responsibility to screen content is convenient and, when articulated as a defense of freedom, seductive to many. However, that approach carries with it the risk that governments will choose to move in another direction entirely—toward China's use of firewalls, for example— thereby serving neither democracy nor freedom. At a minimum, Internet users require tools that will enable them to identify bot-generated and other forms of faux news services. Regulations are also needed to ensure that the source of online political messaging is as transparent as the sponsorship of campaign commercials that appear on radio and television.

Most of us lived through the years when spam threatened to destroy e-mail. Today, democracy is being weakened by lies that come in waves and pound our senses the way a beach is assaulted by the surf. Leaders who play by the rules are having trouble staying ahead of a relentless news cycle and must devote too much effort trying to disprove stories that seem to come out of nowhere and have been invented solely to do them in.

All this has consequences. Small "d" democrats riding to power on the promise of change often begin to lose popularity the day they take office. Globalization, which is not an ideological choice but a fact of life, has become for many an evil to be fought at all costs. Capitalism is considered a four-letter word by an increasing number of people who—if not for its fruits—would be without food, shelter, clothing, and smartphones. In a rising number of countries, citizens profess a lack of faith in every public institution and the official data they produce. One pro-Brexit

British politician said smugly that voters "have had enough of experts."

We need to take a deep breath. A whole generation has been born and come of age since the Communist bloc disintegrated. What does this mean? It means that we no longer judge established democracies by comparing them with the Soviet alternative; and that we don't evaluate emerging democracies by looking at their totalitarian predecessors. We have tossed the measuring-sticks we used in the past into the waste bin. Our attention spans are shorter today, our expectations higher, and we are less likely to overlook flaws that have become ever easier to detect.

This transition has led "we the people"—including editorial writers, columnists, talking heads, and bloggers—to demand more of our governments. That would be fine if only we matched the request by asking more of ourselves. Instead, we are spoiled. Even those too lazy to vote feel it their birthright to blast our elected representatives from every direction. We complain bitterly when we do not get all we want as if it were possible to have more services with lower taxes, broader health care coverage with no federal involvement, a cleaner environment without regulations, security from terrorists with no infringement on privacy, and cheaper consumer goods made locally by workers with higher wages. In short, we crave all the benefits of change without the costs. When we are disappointed, our response is to retreat into cynicism, then start thinking about whether there might be a quicker, easier, and less democratic way to satisfy our wants.

We've all heard the excuses. Freedom can be noisy and frustrating; money undermines fairness; and the wrong people get elected more often than we wish. Personally, I have been involved in five winning presidential campaigns—and eight losing ones. Winning is better, but we can learn as much or more from finishing second. As for promoting democracy overseas, the 2003 invasion of Iraq and the hyperbolic claims attached to it caused many to associate such efforts less with altruism than imperialism. The seemingly endless strife in the Middle East and Afghanistan, moreover, has fed the notion that trying to expand democratic practices to areas where they do not already exist is folly. Such concerns have merit and should cause us to gauge carefully what we attempt. But by ignoring freedom's accomplishments, they tell only a small part of the story—and giving up on democracy because it isn't easy is the coward's way out.

In my view, no country has the right to dictate to others how they should be governed; but we all have good reason to speak up on behalf of democratic values. Our support will not make a difference in all cases, but when we do make a difference, it should be in the direction of greater respect for the individual and improved governance for society.

Democracies, as we know, are prone to every error from incompetence and corruption to misguided fetishes and gridlock. Therefore, it is astonishing, in a sense, that we would be willing to submit the direction of our societies to the collective wisdom of an imperfect and frequently disengaged public. How could we be so naïve? To that fair question, we must reply: how could anyone be so gullible as permanently to entrust power—an inherently corrupting force—to a single leader or party? When a dictator abuses his authority, there is no legal way to stop him. When a free society falters, we still have the ability—through open debate and the selection of new leaders—to remedy those shortcomings. We still have time to pick a better egg. That is democracy's comparative advantage, and it should be recognized and preserved.

In 1918, Tomáš Garrigue Masaryk was sworn in as president of an independent Czechoslovakia. With his erect bearing, old-world manners, modern outlook, and fearless commitment to democratic principles—including feminism and pluralism—Masaryk commanded a global reputation, despite the modest dimensions of the nation he led. Due to his age, his health declined even as the

threat from the Third Reich grew—in the 1930s, no fully democratic nation was more endangered. His response, when asked to
explain what was at stake:

> *Democracy is not only a form of state, it is not just some-*
> *thing that is embodied in a constitution; democracy is a view*
> *of life, it requires a belief in human beings, in humanity. . . .*
> *I have already said that democracy is a discussion. But the*
> *real discussion is possible only if people trust each other and*
> *if they try fairly to find the truth.*

For all its shortcomings, there is no other form of government
to which such words apply. It is up to us to remedy democracy's
faults when and wherever we can, but never to forget the underlying strengths. Up to us, as well, to realize that democracy has
enemies who do not advertise that fact.

MUSSOLINI OBSERVED THAT IN SEEKING TO ACCUMULATE POWER,
it is wise to do so in the manner of one plucking a chicken—feather
by feather. His tactics live on in our no-longer-new century. When
we awaken each morning, we see around the globe what appear
to be Fascism's early stirrings: the discrediting of mainstream
politicians, the emergence of leaders who seek to divide rather
than to unite, the pursuit of political victory at all costs, and the
invocation of national greatness by people who seem to possess
only a warped concept of what greatness means. Most often, the
signposts that should alert us are disguised: the altered constitution that passes for reform, the attacks on a free press justified
by security, the dehumanization of others masked as a defense of
virtue, or the hollowing out of a democratic system so that all is
erased but the label.

We know from experience that Fascism and the tendencies

that lead to it are subject to imitation. Surveying the world today, we see apprentice autocrats copying repressive tactics that had their tryouts in Venezuela or Russia fifteen years ago. Undemocratic practices are on the rise in, among other places, Turkey, Hungary, Poland, and the Philippines, each a treaty ally of the United States. Radical nationalist movements—some violent, some not—are achieving notoriety as they draw media attention, make parliamentary inroads, and push the boundaries of public discussion toward bigotry and hate. America, the rock against which Fascism crashed in the last century, may have begun to slide; and in North Korea, a zealot armed with nuclear weapons boasts of his might.

It would be easier to raise the alarm against this trend if Fascism, too, were not excellent in parts—at least for a time, at least for the privileged. Italians in the 1920s and Nazis in the 1930s were, by and large, upbeat people. One German woman, not a Fascist, recalled:

> *The little lives of my friends went on, under National Socialism as they had before, altered only for the better, and always for the better, in bread and butter, in housing, health, and hope, wherever the New Order touched them. . . . I remember standing on a Stuttgart street corner in 1938, during a Nazi festival, and the enthusiasm . . . after so many years of disillusion, almost swept me, too, off my feet. Let me tell you what it was like in Germany: I was sitting in a cinema with a Jewish friend and her daughter of thirteen, while a Nazi parade went across the screen, and the girl caught her mother's arm and whispered, "Oh Mother, Mother, if I weren't a Jew, I think I'd be a Nazi!"*

As regularly as we use the term, few current heads of government fully embody the spirit of Fascism. Mussolini remains in his grave and Hitler never had one. But that is no grounds for relaxed vigilance. Every step in the direction of Fascism—every plucked feather—causes damage to individuals and to society; each makes the next step shorter. To hold the line, we must recognize that despots rarely reveal their intentions and that leaders who begin well frequently become more authoritarian the longer they hold power. We must acknowledge, as well, that anti-democratic measures will often be welcomed by some of the people, some of the time—especially when those measures are deemed to favor their own.

TEN

PRESIDENT FOR LIFE

N SEPTEMBER 1999, BILL CLINTON AND I SAT DOWN AT THE UN with the ebullient, youngish leader of Venezuela, Hugo Chávez. Chávez had been elected president the previous December. In June, he had rung the closing bell at capitalism's highest altar, the New York Stock Exchange, then visited the *Washington Post*, where he took care to distance himself from "irresponsible populism." He assured everyone that he wasn't an ideologue; instead he flaunted the plumage of a visionary and promised to restore luster to his country by rescuing it from a nightmare of stagnation and debt.

Chávez had a face made for smiling. Words gushed out of him like water, and the emotions behind them centered on the poor. Venezuela sat above a significant fraction of the world's petroleum reserves, yet the gap between its wealthier citizens and the impoverished majority had been widening. Chávez vowed to change that. He told us of his plan for an array of oil-financed funds to help families with low incomes gain access to food, shelter, health care, job training, and schools. He wanted to diversify the nation's economy, attract foreign investment, and transform the government into a true servant of the people. Clinton, one of the few who could match Chávez word for word, was clearly intrigued by him; so was I. Here, we dared hope, was a young leader with passion who wanted also to be a problem solver, someone who had learned from earlier mistakes and sought to earn the world's respect.

Sadly, the honeymoon was short. Three months later, Genesis-scale rain inundated the coastal region just north of Caracas, causing mudslides that buried whole towns, killing tens of thousands. Horrified, I immediately contacted the White House, where President Clinton agreed to help. Within days, the United States had helicopters and soldiers in Vargas state to assist in emergency rescue and relocation, but a disaster of this size required more. Working with Venezuela's defense ministry, the Pentagon prepared to ship bulldozers, tractors, and hundreds of U.S. Marines and Navy engineers to construct a new coastal roadway—literally a lifeline to the devastated region. Our supply vessel was fully loaded and en route to the Caribbean when we received a disappointing message from President Chávez: "We'll take your equipment, but not your people." Unwilling to proceed without knowing how our assistance would be used, we turned the ship around.

IN DECADES PAST, LATIN AMERICAN MILITARIES DEVELOPED A well-earned reputation for catering to the needs of the wealthy, but there were a few cases where an army officer stood apart, and championed the cause of social change. Argentina's Juan Perón, husband of the legendary Evita, served as military attaché to Rome in the 1930s. He saw in Mussolini a leader who ruled with a strong hand but also enjoyed the loyalty of many peasants and workers. Later, as his country's cabinet minister for labor and social welfare, Perón forged such an intimate bond with trade unions that less forward-looking officials grew nervous and had him arrested. They soon learned that incarcerating the spouse of Eva Perón was not a wise move. She organized a demonstration that brought thousands of supporters to the streets and set her husband free, then catapulted him to the presidency via an election the following year.

Perónism evolved into a left-leaning cousin of Italian Fascism, with a corporatist economy, restraints on the press, a heavy-handed police force, and real gains in average income. Like Mussolini, Perón and especially Evita could electrify crowds, but unlike him, they did not preach aggression or poke the hornets' nest of hate. They loved power and abused it, but remain among the more iconic names in Argentine history. Their reputations will be forever tarnished, however, by Perón's decision to provide a haven for Josef Mengele, Adolf Eichmann, and other high-level Nazis, apparently in return for technological advice and cash.

In 1968, Panamanian general Omar Torrijos used the power gained via a coup to expand social services and end the monopoly on economic clout enjoyed by the very rich. However, Torrijos is best remembered for the Panama Canal Treaty, which gave his government control of the engineering marvel known as the path between the seas. I was on the staff of Jimmy Carter's White House at the time and can attest that the politics of the negotiation were tricky in both Panama and the United States. Carter had to contend with Ronald Reagan and other hawkish politicians who claimed that the treaty was a giveaway to a Communist dictator. Torrijos had to ease the concerns of Panamanian nationalists who begrudged the United States any future security role. He compared the challenge for diplomats to that of asking a bootmaker to design the perfect women's shoe: small and chic on the outside, but roomy and comfortable within.

Also in 1968, Peruvian general Juan Velasco Alvarado overthrew a dysfunctional democratic government and instituted land-reform and nationalization programs that, though popular for a time, caused industrial and food production to plunge. Before that abrupt downturn, Alvarado played host to an impressionable group of Venezuelan military cadets, one of whom—Hugo Chávez—would follow the same roller-coaster path but with a more engaging style and a far deeper impact on history.

THE CHILD OF TEACHERS, YOUNG CHÁVEZ WAS A VORACIOUS reader of poetry, politics, and prose. He was raised in the countryside and had a flair for painting, loved to sing, made friends easily, and excelled at baseball. At seventeen, he joined the army, because he thought its sports academy would offer him the best chance to compete at a high level. Though he had dreamed of home runs, not close-order drills, he soon found that he enjoyed parading around with a rifle, thrived amid the camaraderie of barracks life, and was fascinated by the study of military history. At the same time, through his older brother, Adán, he established friendships with socially progressive thinkers and acquired a taste for public affairs. Inspired by the boldness of earlier Latin American revolutionaries, he began to imagine what it might be like to lead a rebellion himself.

Venezuela was given its name, "Little Venice," by a Spanish explorer who admired the way indigenous lake dwellers built their houses on stilts, creating a look that reminded him of the Italian city's famed canals. In 1821, Simón Bolívar liberated the country from Spain, after which it evolved into one of Latin America's more stable republics, known internationally for its oil, beauty queens, and regular elections that allowed the two leading parties to take turns in the presidency without anyone getting too excited. Through the end of the 1970s, the country was also wealthier than most in the region, with a better-educated citizenry and not as sharp a divide between rich and poor.

The next two decades, however, were disastrous. A debilitating mix of low oil prices, mounting debt, a growing population, and indecisive leadership caused a spike in inflation, a decline in real wages, a rise in unemployment, and a shrinking middle class. Carlos Andrés Pérez, new to the presidency in 1989, was persuaded by the IMF to abandon campaign pledges and implement the era's bitter-tasting medicine of choice: a structural adjustment package.

As with the austerity measures that would antagonize Greece and divide Europe twenty years later, the plan's purpose was to establish a platform for renewed growth by imposing budget discipline and clearing away debt. Economically, the approach had logic, but the immediate effects were painful: consumer prices went up; social services were cut back, and protesters vented their rage. The army was summoned to restore order, and more than 330 people were killed. The disturbances were eventually brought under control, but to this day the deaths have not been forgotten.

IN 1923 IN BAVARIA, HITLER ATTEMPTED A PUTSCH THAT FLOPPED due to lack of military support. In 1992 in Venezuela, Hugo Chávez, then an ambitious lieutenant colonel, tried something similar, sending tanks and troops to assault the presidential palace. He, too, failed to dislodge the government, because few fellow officers were willing to put their lives on the line. After arresting Chávez, the authorities allowed him to appear on television and urge his comrades to surrender. For many Venezuelans, this was their introduction to a face that would become almost as familiar to them as their own. Chávez, smartly attired in his khaki-colored uniform and crimson beret, admitted that his movement had failed, *"por ahora"*—for now. A joke quickly made the rounds that Chávez deserved thirty years in prison—one for plotting the coup and twenty-nine for not succeeding. Like Hitler, he had essentially

committed treason and yet was released within two years. Like
Hitler, Mussolini, and Perón, he graduated from prison to politics.

As secretary of state, I paid official visits to Venezuela in 1997
and again the following year. My impression was that tired old
men were botching the job of governing because they had lost
touch with the people they were supposed to lead. I wasn't the
only one who felt that way. Nineteen ninety-eight was the ideal
time for a newcomer to run for president. Voters were demanding
change, and Chávez, the charismatic outsider, promised precisely
that. He did not, however, call himself a Socialist—and would not
do so until years later. Instead, he ran as a patriot who cared about
the laborers, housemaids, campesinos, and cooks whose voices
had gone unheard for too long. His was a winning approach; the
rookie politician received 56 percent of the vote.

Immediately, on taking office, he began to pluck the chicken—
using power to remove obstacles to yet more power. In April 1999,
he held a referendum calling for a special assembly to draft a new
constitution. That document lengthened from five to twelve years
the maximum tenure of a president, abolished the senate, and
gave Chávez control over promotions within the armed forces.
The new president brought a bountiful supply of enthusiasm to
the job, but an unhealthy dose of bitterness as well. His fury may
have stemmed from the poverty of his childhood, though many
Venezuelans endured graver hardships—or perhaps it was simply an intellectual and moral response to all that he had read and
observed.

Chávez's wrath need not have been an obstacle to his success.
Lincoln, Susan B. Anthony, Gandhi, King, Havel, Mandela, and
many other memorable leaders have found in righteous indignation the psychological edge they needed to endure years of doubt
and trial. However, such an emotion is not something everyone
can control, and it has, when unleashed, enough destructive en-

ergy to turn grand potential to failure. Chávez, in his first years in office, had sufficient popular support to bring most Venezuelans together. Instead, he indulged his ire by vilifying one half of the country in search of applause from the other.

Interviewing Chávez at around this time, Colombian novelist Gabriel García Márquez wrote, "I was overwhelmed by the feeling that I had just been traveling and chatting pleasantly with two opposing men. One to whom the caprices of fate had given an opportunity to save his country. The other, an illusionist, who could pass into history as just another despot."

Chávez never lost his ability to charm, but equally often he chose to repel. Rather than heal wounds and broaden his base, he referred to the wealthy as putrid oligarchs, spoiled brats, pickpockets, and pigs; called business leaders vampires and worms; and denounced Roman Catholic priests as perverts. Notwithstanding his cordial encounter with Bill Clinton and me, he regularly insulted the United States for no apparent reason other than to have an enemy to rail against, and, perhaps, to please his new mentor in Havana, Fidel Castro. Chávez's communications strategy was to light rhetorical fireworks and toss them in all directions. Every day and many nights, he was on a podium, in a television studio, or on a radio broadcast, boasting about his accomplishments and deriding—in the crudest terms—real and suspected foes.

Venezuela was not a rich society, but it did have many people of property who were well educated and who positioned themselves politically to the center or right. The military included officers who had worked closely with the United States all through their careers. Many in these groups were targeted by *Chavista* insults and did not like it. They didn't want Venezuela to become another Cuba, and they looked down on Chávez, seeing him as a vulgar man—"that ape"—who had won election by promising the mob what he could never deliver.

On April 11, 2002, the political opposition tried to regain what it had lost by forcing the president from office. Hundreds of thousands of mostly middle-class Venezuelans marched, banging pots, chanting, and moving toward the presidential palace, Miraflores. The army, not wishing to be blamed for a massacre, refused to mobilize. The national guard shot tear gas canisters into the crowd, then fired live ammunition, causing an estimated twenty deaths and many more injuries. Images of the spilled blood dominated the news and intensified calls on the president to quit. Stuck in his office and with no way to shoot his way out, Chávez gave in. He agreed to surrender in return for a promise that he and his family would be allowed to go to Cuba. With safe passage arranged, he boarded a helicopter and was flown to a navy base, then to an island. Despite the assurances he had received, there was a real chance that he would be put on trial or shot. Meanwhile, the coup leaders celebrated. Giddy at their triumph, they chose an interim government headed by a businessman who immediately suspended the constitution and started promising jobs to friends. In Washington, the Bush administration issued a wishy-washy statement that neither endorsed the uprising nor denounced it, but in rebuking the government for the violence, appeared to justify Chávez's ouster.

For a rebellion to fully achieve its purpose, however, the insurgents must enjoy a decisive advantage in coercive muscle or public support. The Venezuelan opposition had some of each but not enough of either. It was also too busy splitting apart to recognize how fragile its position was. Before long, the pro-Chávez elements in the armed forces were organizing their own operation and likeminded peasants and party members were journeying from the countryside to make their presence known in Caracas. Hour by hour, the crowds grew, and those planning for a new government began worrying about the revenge of the old. With the tide visibly turning, the rebels raised a white flag. Chávez withdrew his resignation, found a pilot he could trust, climbed back into the military's helicopter, and returned to Miraflores with a fresh set of complaints to lodge against his enemies in Venezuela and up north.

For years afterward, he told the story of the moments when he felt cornered in his office, with treasonous generals threatening to bombard the palace. It is a tale he related sentimentally, not quite accurately, and to brilliant political effect:

> *How can I forget the feelings of those hours? . . . Suddenly the door opens, and my mother was there. . . . It was a moment of death, not a physical death, but the death of the soul, a death of spirit. I was thinking, is this the end? I remember then that my mother enters the presidential office with the same force of the Arauca River when it enters the Orinoco. And that woman gave a speech, that peasant, because my mother is a peasant, a teacher of the fields, forged in poverty, in battle, and I remember my mother looking at me and telling me: "You will never leave, because your people love you."*

The presidency of Hugo Chávez was both an authentic expression of democracy and a danger to it. One of his first initiatives was to make the judiciary more independent, a move widely applauded; but when the courts later ruled against him, Chávez suspended the judges and packed the bench with more compliant appointees. As year succeeded year, he stripped the bureaucracy of people who opposed his policies, then of those who were not sufficiently servile. He established a grassroots political organization that rewarded loyalists and denied fair treatment to others. He set up a private security force—essentially a gang of thugs—to intimidate opponents and prevent protests from gathering steam. He called dissent a threat to freedom and revoked the operating licenses of television and radio stations that failed to toe the party line.

Like Mussolini, he conceived of politics as a spectacle, a rollicking exhibition of good guy vs. bad guy entertainment. When he decided to take control of the national oil company, he didn't just issue a decree. He personally fired each of the top executives, one by one, on TV. When he wanted to confiscate private businesses, he went to their headquarters and made the announcement in front of a dozen cameras. After the trauma of the nearly success-ful 2002 coup, he complained to Castro about the inadequacy of his security operation and asked for help. The Cuban leader was happy to oblige. Pretty soon, all of Caracas was bugged and the contents of select recordings were played on Chávez's favorite tele-vision and radio programs, humiliating political opponents and wayward cabinet ministers alike.

El presidente adored the spotlight and was at his most skillful onstage. I have known many people in public life who, when the microphone is turned on, are in dire need of a prepared script. Chávez, by contrast, could speak for as long as nine hours at a time, on camera, without notes and without pausing. He per-formed his speeches in the manner of a juggler, tossing up one ball after another, not waiting for the first to complete its arc.

To illustrate a point, he might share a raft of statistics, decry the immorality of his predecessors, vent his sorrow at injustice, recite a poem about resilience and hope, ask a girl in the front row how her family was doing, marvel at Venezuela's natural beauty, recall an experience from his childhood, sing a romantic ballad, curse the enemies of Venezuela, ridicule capitalist greed, reflect on the sweetness of his grandmother and of all grand-mothers, compare himself to Bolívar, suggest that the Great Lib-erator had died from murder not tuberculosis, tell an anecdote about an impoverished farmer who had been given land by the state and another about a woman who had asked for and received lifesaving medicines, then accuse the United States of inventing Al Qaeda and ISIS. And that was just to warm up. On and on he would talk, sing, sometimes dance, wave his arms like pistons, justify every action he had ever taken, think aloud about what he might do next, invite praise from his listeners, and finally, with the audience exhausted, close with the battle cry "Fatherland, Socialism, or death!"

Chávez tried to back his many words with an equal quantity of actions. He was a combative man, not a cynical or devious one. He did all he could to tilt the political process in his favor, but that is not the only reason he won election after election—four in all. He had the luck of a divided opposition, and also of high oil prices, which allowed him to make good on many of his promises. During his tenure, his countrymen received better health care than before and ate more, paid less for gasoline and cooking oil, earned higher wages, and could afford nicer apartments. Just as important, Chávez allowed Venezuelans in humble circumstances to feel that they were an integral part of the country. He spoke directly to them, appointed them to community action councils, gave them decision-making power in farming cooperatives and factories, begged for their votes, answered their requests, asked them about their children, and listened to their stories.

When, in March 2013, he died of cancer, one admirer wrote:

Fourteen years ago, my barrio neighbors didn't dream of going to college, much less becoming doctors in their communities. Fourteen years ago my neighbors could barely fit in their tin or mud homes, much less envision living in a spacious three bedroom house with indoor bathrooms that cost almost nothing. Fourteen years ago, only those on the wealthy east side of my city felt they were citizens. Now we know we all are.

In the flush times, Chávez was handing out money not only to the poor in his own country, but also to buy influence and reward friends in Cuba, Argentina, Nicaragua, Ecuador, Bolivia, and even the South Bronx, where he gave millions of dollars to social action programs and spent one morning dancing salsa with the children of New York, a straw hat atop his head.

This tale would be a happier one had good governance required nothing more than giving stuff away. What made Chávez beloved by many was his unwillingness to admit limits. He wanted to play Santa to his supporters; but a president, unlike Father Christmas, must answer to the rigidities of mathematics.

Chávez wasted enormous sums of money on projects that tripped over themselves because he failed to appreciate the need for expertise in running an oil company, a business, a farm, or a justice system. A leader can become popular by compelling supermarkets and appliance salesmen to charge less for their products but the cheering stops when the stores go out of business and food disappears from the shelves. Ordering cabinet ministers and police chiefs to work for reduced salaries may seem fair, but when the decision leads—predictably—to incompetence and bribery, that should produce second thoughts. Relying on oil revenues to sustain a country's entire economy will satisfy many so long as prices remain high, but when revenues plummet and there is no financial cushion to soften the blow, the result can be disaster. As *Evita* fans might attest, there's a big difference between money "rolling on in" and money "rolling on out."

No one can deny that Chávez brought far-reaching change to Venezuela, but neither can one conclude that he did all he had pledged. By the time of his premature death, many of the country's wealthy professionals had taken their talents elsewhere, the seats they once occupied in fancy restaurants filled instead by currency manipulators, smugglers, narcotics peddlers, and officially empowered thieves. A former planning minister estimated that, under Chávez, a third of Venezuela's oil money was stolen or lost. The president's anti-Washington phobia prompted him to kick the U.S. Drug Enforcement Agency out of the country, causing a 500 percent rise in cocaine imports within three years. Chávez was pro-labor, but when strikes compromised his other priorities, he had the leaders thrown into jail. He urged his followers to adopt a new and higher moral consciousness, but he left behind a nation with one of the grimmest crime rates on earth and a capital city, Caracas, that was a more dangerous place to wake up each morning than Baghdad.

Whatever else one might say of Chávez, he was not in the same dismal league as Mussolini, Hitler, and Stalin. Like them, he exploited national grievances, used enemies to justify the expansion of personal power, wrapped himself in the glory of past heroes, and trampled heavily on the rights of those with whom he did not agree. But it was his style to humiliate opponents, not slaughter them. He bullied incessantly and unapologetically, but he never equated brutality with virility. The fact that common criminals thrived under his rule is evidence that there were lines he refrained from crossing. In a true police state, street crime goes down—and kidnappings for ransom were hardly the problem in the Third Reich that they came to be in Venezuela.

CHÁVEZ INTENDED TO BE PRESIDENT FOR LIFE, AND HE WAS, BUT disease cut the dream short. The Venezuela he left behind is poorer than in 1999, when he took office. His successor, Nicolás Maduro, is a rigidly ideological former bus driver and union boss who possesses every flaw and none of the virtues of the leader he replaced.

Maduro is burly and has a trim mustache. What he doesn't have is enough wit, charm, or oil riches to fill the boots of Chávez, whom he revered. The new president took the helm of an economy in rough waters and steered it toward Armageddon. To repay debts, he tapped the country's financial reserves. Without reserves, Venezuela is hard-pressed to afford imports. Without imports, basic commodities are unavailable. To generate funds, the government printed more money. The value of the national currency—the Bolívar fuerte—has declined to near zero, while the inflation rate is the world's highest. The result is misery. Paychecks and pensions can no longer cover the cost of necessities; the price of a single tube of toothpaste is equal to half the average weekly income. Malnutrition is widespread. No matter how many pharmacies they visit, families are unable to obtain essential medicines. The minimum wage has been raised repeatedly but has failed to keep pace, stalling at about one-eighth the level in neighboring Colombia. Domestic production of coffee, rice, and corn has declined 60 percent. The country's cattle herd is smaller by a third, and a decade and a half of squeezing the private sector has left the business community unable to supply basic needs.

For months in early 2017, angry citizens took their grievances to the streets, shouting anti-Maduro slogans while trying to protect their bodies with bike helmets, cardboard shin guards, and homemade shields painted with the country's colors of yellow, blue, and red.

The president could have eased the crisis by admitting past mistakes and adopting policies to bring the country together. That would have caused foreign investors to take a fresh look at the situation and sparked regional and global initiatives to help. Instead, he doubled down on repression. To Maduro, one either tries to fulfill the *Chavista* revolution or betrays it—and he is a stubborn and unrepentant revolutionary. In July 2017, he engineered a referendum to replace the elected parliament with an all-powerful assembly of partisan puppets. Their job is to write a constitution to supplant the one Chávez wrote, which he predicted would last for centuries. At Maduro's direction, major opposition parties have been banned, while political rivals and even some former allies have been locked up or forced into exile. When responding to street protests, security forces killed more than 120 civilians and roughed up and jailed thousands more. To ensure loyalty, the military and ex-military have taken over many government and private sector functions including the production of oil and the distribution of food.

Maduro has refused to accept a shred of responsibility for the setbacks his country has endured. He blames every woe on domestic reactionaries and on "coup-mongering, power-grabbing . . . tendencies directed and governed by the United States." This last charge was easy to dismiss until Donald Trump decided at his golf club one day to threaten Venezuela with military intervention. That bit of diplomatic clumsiness was a gift that Maduro badly needed and one he is using to reinforce his position both domestically and among anti-imperialist sympathizers throughout Latin America, where past incursions by the U.S. Army and Marines have a troubled history.

THE VENEZUELAN EXPERIENCE SHOWS THAT WHEN ECONOMIC and social conditions deteriorate and democratic politicians fail in their obligation to lead, the lure of a gifted pied piper can be hard to resist. Hugo Chávez was more than an entertainer; he represented a constituency that felt excluded from its own democracy. Members of that constituency brought him to high office, carried him along while wearing their red T-shirts and baseball caps, and delighted in the victory they had wrought. However, governance in the twenty-first century is singularly demanding, certainly more so than Chávez originally perceived. When stymied, he felt the solution was to depart further from democratic mores and use the power he had gathered to drive an even deeper wedge between his backers and the forces arrayed against him. That was not the wisest approach, but it seemed to him the easiest and the one most in keeping with the sense he had developed of his niche in history.

Chávez yearned for a place alongside Bolívar in the pantheon of his country and region. That lofty wish brought him to the outskirts of Fascism. Halfway across the globe, a much different man with a not-so-different ambition was confronting similar temptations in his own way.

ELEVEN

ERDOĞAN THE MAGNIFICENT

ATE IN 1997, THE MAYOR OF ISTANBUL TRAVELED TO SIIRT, IN southern Turkey, to visit his wife's family home and sample the charm of a city known for its colorful handwoven blankets and a cherished nine-hundred-year-old mosque. While delivering a speech, he quoted from a well-known nationalist poem: "The mosques are our barracks, the domes our helmets, the minarets our bayonets, and the faithful our soldiers."

Recep Tayyip Erdoğan's words would have attracted little attention had they not been uttered in what was, for his country, a nervous moment. An insecure government—looking for a fight—arrested him on the charge of inciting religious hatred. He was convicted, forced to resign his position, and barred from public office for five years. The authorities clearly hoped to end the popular mayor's career, but their strategy backfired. The incident gave Erdoğan an aura of notoriety and, in the eyes of some, made him a hero. A two-thousand-car caravan accompanied his journey to prison, and a coterie of admirers returned four months later to greet him upon his release.

For seventy-five years, Turkish authorities had sought to keep religion out of the public square in a society where tens of millions of people are devout Muslims. That was a hard enough assignment when secular leaders were well regarded, but by the time of Erdoğan's arrest, a sputtering economy and bickering politicians had generated a rising tide of popular frustration. Seeking to create a barrier against future protests, the government banned Islamist political parties, but within a few years, comparable organizations with new names took their place. The most dynamic and best run, the Justice and Development Party (AKP), was founded in August 2001. Its leader was Recep Tayyip Erdoğan.

THE TURKISH PEOPLE LIVE AND WORK IN A RUGGED NEIGHBOR-hood, their ancient land bordered on the east by Iran, Iraq, and the Caucasus; on the south by Syria; on the west by Bulgaria and Greece; and on the north, across the Black Sea, by the Russian Federation and Ukraine. Since the time of Alexander the Great, this is where the merchants and militias of Europe, Asia, and the Middle East have met to exchange goods and play king of the mountain. In 1453, the Ottoman Turks swept into Constantinople, gave a good-bye shove to the tottering Byzantine Empire, and founded a Muslim dynasty that ruled a quarter of the world for four hundred years—a domain so vast that it also held sway over the globe's most populous Jewish-majority city, Salonica, and more Christians than any other government.

The industrial age and the rise of nationalism gradually weakened the Ottomans; their defeat in World War I did them in. From the ashes, the fledgling state of Turkey emerged, shooed away the European powers picking at the empire's carcass, and declared independence. At the helm was Mustafa Kemal, an army officer with progressive ideas, who would be known to history as Atatürk, "Father of the Turks." Kemal was determined to create a fully modern society. To that end, he applied a meat-ax to the foundations of Ottoman culture—abolishing the Islamic caliphate, dissolving religious courts, latinizing the Turkish tongue, and looking to Switzerland for civil laws, to Germany for commercial regulations, to France for administrative practices, and, for a criminal code, to Italy.

Atatürk and his successors celebrated the virtues of science and kept a close eye on the practice of Islam. Under their sway, the government dictated what could be preached in mosques, established a nationwide system of secular schools, specified equal rights for women, and jailed anyone who argued that religion should play a bigger role in national life. In 1946, eight years after Atatürk's death, the country became a parliamentary democracy, but it was one that operated within the secular cage the fabled leader had built. His motto, "For the People, In Spite of the People," captured both the lofty intentions of Kemalism and its condescension toward the public at large. In subsequent decades, elections were contested by parties of the center right and the center left, with the former usually coming out on top. Firmly aligned with the West, Turkey joined NATO in 1952 and later set its sights on membership in the European Union. Despite the passage of time, pictures of Atatürk could be found everywhere, and his shadow loomed over all.

RECEP TAYYIP ERDOĞAN WAS A PRODUCT OF ONE OF ISTANBUL'S grittier neighborhoods, yet it was a place he remembers as graced by fruit trees and fields, where children could fly kites, shoot marbles, and—in that age before every inch of ground was paved—get their clothes gloriously dirty while playing in the mud. His father was a sea captain on the Bosporus, and, to help with bills, the boy sometimes sold snacks on the streets. He spent summers visiting his grandparents in a socially conservative province far to the north and east of the city. When he was eleven, his family enrolled him in a religious school, thereby putting his career prospects at risk in Kemalist Turkey. However, once settled on a path, the youth didn't stray. He was diligent, minded his studies, showed a talent for soccer, and developed an aptitude for politics while still in high school.

This was an interval—the 1970s—when the Cold War generated severe clashes between the Marxist left and the nationalist right, in Turkey as elsewhere. A surge in the price of petroleum imports caused the economy to stall and led to shortages of sugar, margarine, and cooking oil. Fearing a revolt, the military stepped in, pushed aside civilian politicians, and virtually obliterated the political left through a combination of torture, murder, and the arrest of half a million people.

Erdoğan and his pious colleagues, especially those living outside the major urban centers, were detached from this confrontation. Their generation had no living memory of Atatürk and no natural affinity for the European culture they were supposed to regard as the Turkish ideal. Many were also anxious about the impacts of globalization on their way of life. They had not set out to be politically ambitious, but they worried that doing nothing might mean the loss of all they valued. Gradually, they opened their ears to the sermons of imams in Egypt and Iran who were saying what their Turkish brethren could not: that the West was determined to divide the faithful, keep them poor, and lure them into depravity. If Muslims were going to improve their lot, they must define their own needs, find their own voice, and act together to make themselves heard.

By crushing the political left, the military created growing room for this new movement. The alienated poor, barred from organizing around ideology, came together around religion. When a party arose calling for a "Just Order" and for breaching the wall that had long separated Islam from the state, Turks signed on in huge numbers: 200,000 in 1991; by 1995, four million. "Other parties have members," boasted one leader; "we have believers." The organization's startling popularity caused panic in secular circles. In 1998, the authorities banned it, hoping to pound the Islamists into submission as they did the Communists. But while Marxist ideology had been imported, the believers had long since established deep roots in the Anatolian heartland.

THE AKP'S BREAKTHROUGH IN THE 2002 ELECTIONS CAME UNDER ideal conditions for a party and a prospective prime minister (Erdoğan) who represented a sharp departure from the past. Less than three years had elapsed since the government's bungled response to a catastrophic earthquake, a show of incompetence that remained fresh in the nation's memory. An economic crisis had followed, draining public confidence. The treasury was deeply in debt, the currency weak, inflation above 100 percent, and foreign investors saw no reason to open their wallets and stanch the bleeding. To right the economic ship, the administration imposed a blend of liberalizing reforms and budget cuts like those that Hugo Chávez's predecessors had tried in Venezuela—with comparable results. Voters were furious. Adding to the stress, Kurdish militants in the southeast were at war against the army, forcing thousands of civilians to pack their belongings and seek shelter in an already overcrowded Istanbul.

None of this meant that the electorate would turn automatically to the AKP. For decades, Atatürk and his disciples had warned voters that the ascension of a religious party would make Turkey appear backward in the eyes of Europe and force them to live as their ancestors had in the Middle Ages. The AKP would get nowhere unless it could address this anxiety. It helped that

Erdoğan, with his Western suits and mild demeanor, seemed the very opposite of a religious zealot. As a mayor, he had been a rousing hands-on success: the trash got picked up, the streets were cleaned, the electricity stayed on, and—when apartment dwellers opened their taps—the water that came out slaked their thirst instead of making them ill. At Erdoğan's direction, the AKP rejected the Islamist label and campaigned instead as a socially conservative but still future-oriented party, with a strong pro-European tilt. Advertisements showed AKP members as businesspeople and professionals, including workingwomen with uncovered hair. Candidates campaigned at restaurants where alcohol was served. Canvassers were instructed to focus on pocketbook issues, smile often, and avoid acting "holier than thou."

The effort to reassure skeptics paid off. On election day, the three parties that made up the governing coalition failed to reach even the 10 percent threshold required for representation in parliament—a shocking outcome. Under the constitution, their ballots were allocated to the party that finished first. This meant that the AKP, which received a plurality of just over one-third of the vote, was awarded twice that percentage of seats in the parliament, a controlling majority.

Representative democracy had always been an uphill climb for Turkey. Atatürk's borrowing from the West did not extend to meaningful elections, independent courts, religious liberty, or free speech. If it had, he would not have been so admired by Hitler and Mussolini, both of whom found a lot to like in his assertive nationalism, persecution of minorities, taming of the imams, and domineering will. Hitler even referred to the charismatic Turk as his "shining star in the darkness." After Kemal's death, the military remained, along with the constitutional courts, a guardian of his legacy. In 1960, again in 1971, and once more in 1980, the armed forces intervened when a civilian government, in their judgment, was not up to the job. As recently as 1997, military pres-

sure contributed to the resignation of a governing coalition and
Erdoğan's arrest. As U.S. secretary of state at the time, I argued
that "whatever issues are going on in Turkey . . . and whatever
changes people are thinking about, they must be within a democratic context." In other words, obey the constitution, please, and
no more military coups.

In March 2003, when the new prime minister arrived in office,
he knew that powerful elements in the establishment were lying in
wait, eager for him to fail. If given an opening, they would accuse
him of undermining secularism and betraying Atatürk's memory. Erdoğan's space to maneuver was further restricted by the
staunchly secular president, Ahmet Necdet Sezer, who had been
chosen by the previous parliament and who possessed the power
to veto legislation and make key appointments. The president
showed his pettiness by refusing to invite the prime minister's
wife to palace receptions because she wore a headscarf.

As a visitor to Turkey during this period, I can testify to the
emotions stirred by that seemingly trivial yet still unsettled issue.
The audience for a talk I had been invited to give included some
women who covered their hair and many who did not. When the
time came for questions, I was asked which option I believed was
correct. The answer, I was sure, was clear: "What you do about
your hair should be up to each of you; it's a matter of individual
choice." My attempt at evenhandedness pleased no one. Where I
saw value in diversity, the women on both sides perceived a fundamental issue of identity, a debate about nothing less than what
it meant to be Turkish. That judgment could not be sidestepped by
suggesting it didn't matter.

During the same visit, I had a chance to reacquaint myself with
Istanbul, which is, aside from my native Prague, the world's most
beautiful city. I have been there many times—even bringing along
two of my grandchildren—and am fascinated by the entire country. However, there has always been a disturbing contrast between

the palatial mansions overlooking the Bosporus and the densely packed apartment buildings where most citizens live. To the average family, Erdoğan in his first term was doing very well, but in the minds of the mansion-dwellers he was on probation.

Prudently, the freshman leader steered his way around issues that might cause religious sparks to fly and concentrated instead on fostering prosperity. The economy he inherited was on the verge of recovery and he made the most of it. Within a year, inflation had dropped from 47 percent to 22 percent, and it soon stabilized in the single digits.

This triggered an explosion in foreign investment, which Erdoğan eagerly solicited, drawing on the experience he had gained while mayor. He poured money into bridges, roads, and airports, attracting yet more capital. He built hospitals and instituted reforms in health and welfare programs that cut infant mortality in half and increased average life expectancy by more than five years. Under his guidance, Turks became more connected as the national airline started flying to scores of additional cities. The government instituted a mortgage system that allowed hundreds of thousands of families to buy a first home. In the suburbs, sprawling shantytowns evolved into blocks of handsome apartment buildings alongside busy cafés and well-stocked stores.

A decade after Erdoğan took office, Turkey was known as the workshop of Europe, the overall economy had tripled in size, the average citizen was earning twice as much as before, and the middle class was twice as big. The AKP even slashed six zeros from the currency, so the parched wouldn't have to pull millions of liras out of their pockets just to enjoy a cup of tea or a glass of raki.

Turkey also advanced its quest for admission to the EU, a goal that had been a centerpiece of Erdoğan's 2002 campaign. Earlier, in the Clinton years, I had prevailed on my European colleagues to consider this request, which had been pending for a long time. To brighten its prospects, Turkey abolished the death penalty and then, under Erdoğan, increased civilian controls over the military and established new protections for speech, minority rights, and women. These steps were enough to score a breakthrough—formal negotiations began.

Even with all this activity, the prime minister never for a second forgot politics. With the opposition spinning its wheels, Erdoğan assembled an AKP juggernaut energized by the devout, bolstered by recruits from the middle class, and financed by businesspeople who wanted to be on the winning side. Volunteers were active all year round, visiting the sick, holding neighborhood meetings, helping the unemployed to find jobs, and placing the homeless in apartments. In the 2007 election, the AKP polled 46 percent, more than twice the support enjoyed by any other party, and earned 341 seats out of 550 in parliament. The margin made it possible for the prime minister to designate a new and more philosophically compatible president as he began his second term.

Buoyed by high poll numbers, Erdoğan was determined to use the power he had accumulated to strengthen his position further. After all, he still had enemies. In 2008, state prosecutors accused the AKP of violating the separation between religion and state. If they had prevailed before the constitutional court, the party would have been banned, ending Erdoğan's political career—and this was a real possibility. When the judges ruled, they did so in the AKP's favor but by the narrowest of margins: one vote.

The prime minister did not want to experience such a close call again, so he set out to transform the institutions that posed a threat to his future, using Atatürk's heavy-handed methods to chip away at the structures his famed predecessor had forged. He began with a scheme to arrest and try hundreds of retired and active-duty military officers for coup planning, corruption, and other violations, some of which were real transgressions, others plainly fabricated. He tightened the AKP's grip on the press through laws empowering the government to seize and transfer the ownership of hostile news outlets. He proposed legislation to expand the courts and thereby his ability to appoint judges on whose loyalty he could count.

Erdoğan also became less guarded in sharing his view of Turkish identity. During his tenure, more than nine thousand new mosques opened their doors for the first time. Children in religious schools increased from 63,000 to more than 1.5 million. Courses in Sunni Islam are now mandatory for all students. In speeches, the no-longer-reticent Erdoğan refers to Islam as the fundamental source of Turkish unity and talks often about the importance of fostering a "pious generation." He has canceled gay pride parades and condemned LGBTI activism as "against the values of our nation." Ever-political, he draws a contrast between the AKP's "holy path" and the supposed atheism of rivals.

Gradually, Erdoğan the onetime unifier has become a polarizer, hurling abuse at secularists and liberals. He has even taken steps to roll back one of Atatürk's historic advances. The constitution grants equal rights to women, but Erdoğan has proposed a "Turkish-style" interpretation, condemning birth control, urging mothers to bear three or more children, and suggesting that women who work are "half-people." In 2016, a parliamentary commission proposed lowering the minimum age for marriage to fifteen and recommended that accused rapists be permitted to avoid prosecution by consenting to marry their victims.

Despite the AKP's winning record at the polls, not everyone is pleased with the new era. In Prague in 1989, demonstrators gathered in Wenceslas Square. In Cairo in 2011, it was Tahrir Square. In Istanbul in 2013, disturbances erupted in Gezi Park, near Taksim Square, a centrally located transit hub boasting patriotic monuments and fast-food outlets. The ostensible cause of the protests was the government's plan to chop down trees and replace the greenery with yet another shopping mall. Fueled by social media, the occupation attracted supporters in seventy cities.

Days of singing, chanting, and camping ensued but were brought to a halt by tear gas and rubber bullets. Though ending in stalemate, the brief popular explosion had the feel of something new. For the first time, the eclectic elements of the anti-Erdoğan world assembled in one place: liberals, environmentalists, feminists, secular nationalists, academics, and dissident Kurds. What took place in Taksim Square might have signaled the beginning of a unified movement in opposition to the AKP—had its momentum not been disrupted by the political equivalent of an earthquake.

ON JULY 15, 2016, A FACTION WITHIN THE MILITARY TRIED TO KILL Erdoğan and take over the government. Around ten o'clock on a Friday night, rebel leaders dispatched tanks to the airport in Istanbul, began arresting loyalist officers, and sent air force jets flying at low altitudes over Ankara. The jets dropped bombs on the parliament building, marking the first time a Turkish capital had been attacked since the fifteenth century. Armed insurgents took up positions at a handful of strategic points in both major cities. They also sent a commando squad to the southwest coast with instructions to assassinate a vacationing Erdoğan. Fortunately, the hit squad arrived too late; the president had been tipped off and was already on a flight back to Istanbul.

The coup never had a chance. News of it had leaked in advance, forcing the conspirators to move before all the pieces were in place. If the plotters had a compelling rationale for their actions, they failed to convey it publicly. Their inability to dispose of Erdoğan gave him the opportunity to appear before the media and summon support from his enormous network of party outlets and mosques. His backers didn't let him down. In the hours of crisis, most senior military officers remained true to the government. Opposition political parties, independent media, and leaders of civil society also condemned the uprising. Through the night, tens

of thousands of Turks gathered on sidewalks and streets to profess their loyalty to the rule of law. Construction firms deployed
heavy equipment to hem in rebel tanks. Loudspeakers broadcast
Muslim prayers. By dawn, the insurrection had collapsed, but not
before some three hundred people, the majority of them civilians,
were dead.

Unlike past rebellions, this wasn't an effort by the military to
preserve the Kemalist tradition, though some may have acted with
that purpose in mind. Many of the leaders were said to be part of a
religious and social movement that had been active in Turkey for
decades and was founded by Fethullah Gülen, a Muslim cleric and
educator who had emigrated to the United States in 1999. If so, it
was a falling-out between friends.

For years, Gülen and Erdoğan had been on the same side. If
a business leader or newspaper editor was favorable toward one,
chances were excellent that he was also for the other. Both men
sought to make the Turkish state less secular and more devout.
With AKP support, many Gülen loyalists took advantage of their
political ties and academic training to climb into positions of influence in the military, police, ministries, courts, and universities.
The Gülen organization's international links—it had a presence
in 160 countries—also helped Turkey to establish valuable new
connections in Africa and Asia.

Just about everyone who had an interest in Turkey in the 2000s
was familiar with Gülen, his many educational and service programs, and his advocacy on behalf of Turkey. I have not met him,
but I did participate in a luncheon event sponsored by the Gulen
Institute in Houston in 2008. On the surface, the organization is
dedicated to humanitarian service, interfaith dialogue, and the
peaceful resolution of conflict. Academic offerings are of a high
quality and teachers are expected to set an example of piety and
assistance to others. Much of its international activity—including
the operation of about 150 charter schools in the United States—is

managed independently from Gülen and has little to do with Turkish politics. Erdoğan's defenders back home, however, are convinced that the cleric and his acolytes are determined to destroy the AKP.

Soon after the 2011 elections, won as usual by Erdoğan, he and Gülen had a falling-out. Who did what to whom is unclear, but suddenly, closeness to Gülen ceased to be an asset for those wanting to land government contracts or a high-level job. In 2013 and 2014, Gülenists struck back by exposing corruption in Erdoğan's administration, including the release of telephone recordings in which the prime minister orders his son to take cash out of their home and hide it. Erdoğan retaliated by labeling Gülen a terrorist and accelerating efforts to remove his supporters from senior positions.

The attempted coup was meant to destroy Erdoğan but instead—like his 1997 arrest—made him stronger. He called resistance to it "the second war of independence" for the republic and has used it as an excuse to plaster pictures of himself—in a manner akin to Atatürk's—just about everywhere, often alongside the many memorials to those who died while opposing the rebellion. To Erdoğan, the uprising has given him carte blanche to move against whomever he chooses and to do so in the name of fighting treason.

With parliament's support, he declared a state of emergency. Security forces rounded up coup plotters and their relatives, friends, and co-workers. In a short time, the net widened to include terrorist suspects of every description, plus people who said, wrote, or blogged opinions deemed critical of the president or dangerous to the state. As the months passed, more than 140,000 government employees were suspended or fired, 16,000 military and police officers cashiered, 6,300 teachers purged, 2,500 journalists sacked, 1,000 businesses seized, 180 media outlets shut down, fifteen universities closed, and one out of every five judges forced to resign.

There were certainly some among the arrested who are guilty and deserve punishment. However, the scope of the government's response went far beyond legitimate law enforcement. Those jailed or targeted for detention included opposition members of parliament, pro-Kurdish activists, respected U.S. academic experts, a professional basketball player, and leaders of nongovernmental organizations who had no connection to Gülen and, in many cases, publicly opposed the coup.

AS EARLY AS 2006, ERDOĞAN HAD TALKED ABOUT THE NEED FOR Turkey to adopt an American-style political system, with a strong president instead of a party-dependent prime minister. There was never much question about whom he would cast in the chief executive's role. Atatürk, after all, had been president, not prime minister—so why not Erdoğan? In 2014, he ran for president and won, the first time the AKP had earned a popular majority, though even then just barely—51 percent. He could not, however, realize his dream of a powerful presidency in the absence of changes to the constitution. The failed coup gave him that chance.

In the spring of 2017, he sought and won approval of a referendum to abolish the office of prime minister and transfer its authorities to him. Under the new arrangement, the president has broader ability to appoint judges and ministers, control budgets, and dictate security policy. The clock on term limits is rewound so that Erdoğan can stay in office, if reelected, until 2028. While the state of emergency remains in effect, he can issue laws by fiat, detain citizens at will, and deny prisoners access to lawyers. The president's initiative, which barely eked out a majority, showed clearly the divisions that have opened in the country. His plan was opposed in most major cities and in areas along the Aegean that face Europe. It was supported in the countryside, where the AKP is still closely associated with prosperity and conservative social values. The outcome sharply diminishes the practical restraints on Erdoğan.

Europe's reaction to the vote was cool. During the run-up to the balloting, the German and Dutch governments prohibited members of Erdoğan's cabinet from campaigning among their countries' Turkish diaspora. Erdoğan combatively referred to this ban as "Nazism . . . risen from the dead." After the balloting, the EU criticized the process as unfairly skewed toward a "yes" vote, an undeniably accurate charge that was, by the president, blithely dismissed.

This war of words is harmful to both Turkey and Europe, and although there are two sides to the story, Erdoğan's thin skin has clearly contributed to the mutual sense of irritation. "If the West calls someone a dictator," he says, "in my view that is a good thing." Addressing a rally in Ankara on the first anniversary of the aborted coup, he showed what he thought of opinion on the continent: "I don't look at what Hans and George say. I look at what Ahmet, Mehmet, Hasan, Huseyin, Ayse, Fatma, and Hatice say."

YEARS AGO, WHEN ERDOĞAN HAD JUST BECOME PRIME MINISTER, I attended meetings with him in New York. His focus then was almost entirely on foreign investment. Asked about religion, he made the point—a good one—that Europe contains many parties that describe themselves as Christian Democrat or Social Christian so why should anyone be upset about people who identify as Muslim democrats? He struck me then as a person with little charm but enormous intensity, not easily swayed. Nothing I have seen since has caused me to alter that assessment.

The positive news is that, through all the political turbulence, Erdoğan's economic plan has not turned inward; the country remains intent on prospering in the global marketplace. That is important because the republic is approaching its centennial with big plans. Should Erdoğan's Vision 2023 agenda be realized, Turkey will become one of the globe's ten largest economies, attract fifty million tourists a year, and join the EU.

However, if any of those goals are to be reached, the president must modify the course he has been pursuing these past few years. It might feel good to castigate Europe and the United States, but Turkey is not going to achieve either its economic or its security goals without help. Erdoğan's original foreign policy mantra, "Zero problems with neighbors," now mocks him. Turkey has misplayed its hand in Syria and exhibited fundamental strategic differences with the Arab states and Iran. Erdoğan won no friends in Israel when he attacked that country's policy toward the Palestinians as having "surpassed Hitler in barbarism." His approach to Russia has swung back and forth between launching verbal attacks one month and the next signing a controversial arms deal. Globally, the government in Ankara has become notorious for jailing more reporters than any other.

In fairness, Turkey faces real terrorist threats, from both ISIS and the Kurdistan Workers' Party, or PKK. It has also borne the brunt of the continent's refugee crisis and could probably have done absolutely everything asked and still not overcome all the obstacles to EU admission, including hostility from Greek Cyprus, Islamophobia, and cultural differences that have caused the goalposts to move whenever the Turks draw closer. The country is right to demand the West's respect, because, as a NATO ally for more than seven decades and currently the possessor of the alliance's second-largest army, it has earned it.

Domestically, Turkey's divisions are deeply etched, and, for as long as he is president, Erdoğan must decide how best to respond to that. He still has a chance to mend his nation's democracy by moving away from recrimination and toward dialogue, heeding criticism from moderates within his own party, and ceasing to equate legitimate political opposition with treason.

No Turkish leader has succeeded in building—or even really tried to build—a democratic society in which citizens who have far different visions of what it means to be Turkish can nevertheless live together productively, freely, and in peace. That would be a worthy monument to any statesman. Might Erdoğan choose that path? I think he could, but only if he were to accept that the primary obstacle to advancement is neither the Gülenists, nor the terrorists, nor rival political parties—it is the voice inside telling him that he and only he knows what's best for Turkey. That's the siren's song that transforms power into an end in itself—and leads toward tyranny.

TWELVE

MAN FROM THE KGB

VLADIMIR PUTIN PLEDGES NO ALLEGIANCE TO THE DEMO-cratic articles of faith, but he does not explicitly renounce democracy. He disdains Western values while professing to identify with the West. He doesn't care what the State Department puts in next year's human rights report, because he has yet to pay a political price in his own country for the sins reported in prior years. He tells bald lies with a straight face, and when guilty of aggression, blames the victim. He has convinced many, apparently including the American president, that he is a master strategist, a man of strength and will. Confined to Russia, these facts would be sobering, but Putin, like Mussolini nine decades ago, is watched carefully in other regions by leaders who are tempted to follow in his footsteps. Some already are.

Though Putin was born in 1952, his story begins earlier, with that of his parents, who survived—just barely—the Second World War. During the Siege of Leningrad, when famine gripped that city, his mother collapsed from hunger and, before reviving, was laid out for burial among corpses. His father, a member of Stalin's secret police, was assigned to carry out sabotage operations behind German lines in Estonia. The unit blew up a munitions depot but was informed on by unsympathetic locals. Enemy soldiers and their baying hounds chased the senior Putin, who escaped by submerging himself in a marsh and breathing through a reed. Of the twenty-eight men in his unit, just four eluded capture or death. Quickly returned to combat, he suffered a leg wound from a grenade and was hauled by a fellow soldier across a frozen river to the hospital. He limped for the rest of his life. Save for these extraordinary events, Vladimir Putin would not exist.

The man who has led Russia longer than anyone since Stalin describes himself as "a pure and utterly successful product of a Soviet patriotic education." A restless, energetic youth, he channeled his physicality into the martial arts, grappling, throwing, parrying, and pinning his way to the judo championship of Moscow. At twenty-three, he fulfilled his childhood dream, engendered by a fascination with spy stories, and became an operative for the KGB. He was in East Germany masquerading as a translator when, in 1989, the Wall came down, shattering the political and ideological system to which he and his family had dedicated their lives. Thus was born Vladimir Putin's redemptive purpose. Two years later, when the Soviet Union disintegrated, he was working for the mayor of St. Petersburg. Colleagues dutifully hung in their offices a photograph of the new president, Boris Yeltsin; Putin did the same with a portrait of Peter the Great.

The former KGB agent's worldview, like mine, was shaped by the Cold War, though from the opposite end of the telescope. There were, as I noted previously, no innocents in this period. Both sides sought allies in every region, and neither was entirely scrupulous about the means used to support favorites. The crucial difference is that the West came down on the side of freedom when it could, while Communists condemned democracy as a bourgeois trick.

In 1991, after Yeltsin took power, the United States hoped for a fresh start in relations with Moscow, and the initial signs were positive. The Russians had supported the senior President Bush in rolling back Saddam Hussein's invasion of Kuwait; Yeltsin then joined in cosponsoring an ambitious conference on Arab-Israeli cooperation. Buried beneath the surface, however, were contrasts in national experience and outlook that a few demonstrations of teamwork could not wish away.

Not long before the USSR's breakup, I participated in a survey of Russian attitudes regarding democracy and free enterprise. What we found was a population worn down by Communism but with little understanding of what democracy entailed. Reliance on the state for jobs, housing, and other benefits was deeply ingrained. People accustomed to the Soviet system had no clue about competitive markets and found alien, even disturbing, the concept of demanding more productive work as a condition for higher pay. Freedom of the press had a nice ring to it but signified little.

My conclusion was that centuries of living under authoritarian rule had left an indelible mark. How could they not have? Patience was essential, therefore, and had the evolution from a centralized system to a market economy been more gradual—perhaps by a factor of ten—the transition might have succeeded, and democracy taken hold. But history is not chess, and Yeltsin had no time to plan his next move. Instead he had to improvise while being assaulted from all sides by half-baked advice, which he half took. Caught between two eras, the nation's economy, like the Soviet Union, fell apart fast.

During the Great Depression, America's economic output declined by one-third. In the 1990s, Russia's shrank by more than half. Tax revenues dried up, and so, too, foreign investment. Supermarket shelves were stripped bare by hungry shoppers and much of the economy had to do business on a barter basis. The average Russian worked less, got sick more, and died sooner. By decade's end, seven out of ten lived at or below a subsistence level. Meanwhile, privileged insiders scooped up publicly owned companies at a small fraction of their value, turned the assets to cash, and lodged the profits in offshore accounts. Well-wishers in the West urged perseverance and attributed the crisis to the country's lack of a democratic tradition. However, on January 1, 2000, a new leader arrived in the Kremlin who blamed every problem on the West and who sought to revive a different tradition—a Russian one.

Like several other men profiled in this book, Vladimir Putin inherited power because his predecessors were thought to have fallen short. Like them, he was not expected to last long. Few in the international community were familiar with him, and even in Russia he was not well known. Who was he, and why had Yeltsin sought him out? Traveling to Moscow that same January, I was determined to find answers.

PUTIN'S FIRST COMMENT WHEN I ARRIVED FOR OUR MEETING WAS about the distinctive pin I was wearing. I said the hot-air balloons were to show how hopes in Russia were rising. He smiled, then looked stern, turned to the cameras, and complained, "The U.S. is conducting a policy of pressure against us." When the media left, he smiled thinly once more, telling me, "I said that so your domestic critics will not attack you for being soft." As soon as we sat down, he gathered up then tossed away a bundle of staff-prepared talking points—a simple gesture but also a way of showing independence from the Kremlin bureaucracy. My own opening words wouldn't be out of place if spoken today. "Russia has become controversial in my country," I said, "and the U.S. is controversial in yours. This is partly due to real differences and partly to the elections in each country. The only answer we can give to those who criticize us for working together is to prove we can get things done."

As our conversation progressed, I was struck by the contrast between the buttoned-down Putin and the "bottoms up" Yeltsin. The new president didn't bully, plead, or flatter. He spoke earnestly about the need to revive his country's economy by enforcing contracts, exposing corruption, and creating a friendly climate for investment. He expressed doubt that the United States—despite its protestations of goodwill—had Russia's best interests at heart. After all, the only leaders America has looked on favorably are Gorbachev, who dismantled the USSR, and Yeltsin, who left office with a domestic approval rating of 8 percent. Putin was particularly annoyed by the alarms we had broadcast concerning human rights in Chechnya and Central Asia. He said that terrorists were overrunning the entire region and that only uncompromising action could bring those dangerous lands under control. "Do not try to squeeze Russia out of these countries," he warned, "or you will end up with another Iran or Afghanistan."

Flying home, I typed up my impressions:

Putin is small and pale, so cold as to be almost reptilian. He was in East Germany when the Berlin Wall fell and says he understands why it had to happen—a position built on walls and dividers couldn't last; but he expected something to rise in its place, and nothing was proposed. The Soviets simply dropped everything and went away. He argued that a lot of problems could have been avoided had they not made such a hasty exit. Putin is embarrassed by what happened to his country and determined to restore its greatness.

Like Chávez in Venezuela, Putin gained momentum early on from rising oil prices and, similar to Erdoğan, he benefited from the unpopular but necessary reforms put in place by his predecessor. In Putin's first years as president, annual economic growth approached 7 percent—Asian Tiger territory. This allowed the government to restore employee salaries and pensions. The value of the ruble went up, making it easier for locally produced crops and goods to find shelf space in markets. Foreign reserves doubled and redoubled while the middle class grew. After the crucible of the 1990s, Russians were pleased to find themselves with thick enough wallets to buy cars, take out mortgages, patronize restaurants, and even go on holiday in Europe or Crimea. Observing all this, our embassy in Moscow reported, "There is a new bounce in the national step."

Putin isn't the most electrifying speaker: he's no arm-waving pounder of lecterns, and he lacks any unique gift for rhetoric, but his unflappable manner conveys steadiness, and he attends to his duties. For years, he has appeared on marathon television shows to answer questions from reporters and citizens alike. Whenever a request is made for help, the government is sure to follow up with a well-reported account of a family assisted or a problem solved. Putin excels at telling people what they want to hear in part because he is genuinely proud to be a Russian. In his visits to St. Petersburg, he touts his country's many contributions to baroque and neoclassical architecture, jewelry, music, literature, and painting. He has brought religion back to the center of national life, understanding that not even seven decades of Communism could stamp out the reverence many Russians feel for their onion-domed churches, sacred rites, and esteemed icons. The president invokes military history, as well. He reminds his people that it was their ancestors who sucked the lifeblood out of Napoleon's Grande Armée in the Patriotic War of 1812—then later saved the world from Hitler with, in his version, little help from anyone else.

Putin is also a show-off. It is hard to imagine any other Russian leader (Yeltsin? Brezhnev? Lenin?) thrusting himself in front of cameras to demonstrate judo moves, pose shirtless with a wriggling fish, shoot a crossbow, shake hands with a polar bear, rub noses with a dolphin, or fire a tranquilizer gun at a rogue tiger. In 2012, the sixty-year-old Putin maneuvered his no longer lithe frame into a white jumpsuit, hopped into the pilot's chair of a small plane, and showed a flock of apparently slow-witted Siberian cranes the proper direction to migrate. Not even Mussolini did that.

SADLY, PUTIN'S SHOW HAS LACKED ENTERTAINMENT VALUE FOR those—including me—who hoped to see Russia develop a more open political system, with warmer ties to the West. The president has pointed to the debacle of the 1990s to discredit democratic institutions and to accuse Washington of trying to encircle his country or, in the vernacular of the Cold War, contain it. In his imagination, American decision-makers lie awake at night thinking up schemes to weaken Russia. How else to explain NATO enlargement, U.S. support for democracy along the Russian periphery, and the deployment of an antimissile system in Central Europe? What Putin refuses to admit is that other countries have rights and that, after decades of being dominated by Moscow, many of the former Soviet republics and satellites valued their independence and were keen on pursuing integration with Europe. NATO took in new members because they were anxious to join and to prevent the resurfacing of old rivalries such as that between the Czechs and Germans. The antimissile system was installed to defend against Iran. And U.S. policy throughout the difficult 1990s was aimed at helping Russia to regain its footing and become part of the West, not at threatening the country or trying to hold it down.

Presented with these facts, Putin refuses to accept them. Politically, he has been under more pressure from the nationalist right than from the smaller and more moderate middle and left. He insists that his government isn't doing anything the West hasn't already done: invade countries, meddle in elections, exert economic leverage, and plant false stories in the media. Every time he complains about America's "almost uncontained hyper use of force—military force—in international relations," he wins plaudits at home. Besides, if Russia didn't have enemies, Putin wouldn't have the excuses he has relied on to tighten his grip on power.

In 1787, Catherine the Great and a group of foreign ambassadors traveled by barge down the Dnieper River to Crimea, which Russia had recently snatched from the Ottoman Empire. At the direction of Catherine's adviser and lover, Grigory Potemkin, feverish efforts were made to impress the visiting dignitaries by creating attractive portable settlements, complete with smiling peasants and trim houses, for the emissaries to marvel at along the way.

There is more than a touch of the Potemkin village in Vladimir Putin's Russia. The political system features opposition parties, but most are mere shells created to foster the illusion of competition. Elections have become rituals for extending the terms of favored candidates. Television networks are propaganda organs. Civil society, when not tame, is condemned as the cat's-paw of foreigners. As one law student told a reporter in Moscow, "We have no democracy, our Parliament is not real, our politicians are not real and our mass media are not real."

Putin isn't a full-blown Fascist because he hasn't felt the need. Instead, as prime minister and president, he has flipped through Stalin's copy of the totalitarian playbook and underlined passages of interest to call on when convenient. Throughout his time in office, he has stockpiled power at the expense of provincial governors, the legislature, the courts, the private sector, and the press. A suspicious number of those who have found fault with him have later been jailed on dubious charges or murdered in circumstances never explained. Authority within Putin's "vertical state"—including directorship of the national oil and gas companies—is concentrated among KGB alumni and other former security and intelligence officials. A network of state-run corporations and banks, many with shady connections offshore, furnish financial lubricants for pet projects and privileged friends. Rather than diversify as China has done, the state has more than doubled its share of the national economy since 2005.

Putin wants his subjects to believe that he is politically invincible. He strives every day to discourage potential competitors from trying—or daring—to develop a serious nationwide coalition against him. He prefers opponents who sit around their apartments, sipping vodka and complaining to one another about how hopeless it all is; and that's what many of them have done.

To retain his appeal, Putin has never tied himself deeply to any ideology or party. Instead he seeks to portray himself as the face of the entire nation. Though he can be vicious in attacking opponents, he isn't intentionally polarizing in the manner of Chávez or Erdoğan. Unlike rightists in Europe, he is respectful toward Jews and Muslims. He saves the bulk of his verbal ammunition for foreign enemies, the arrogant hypocrites who live in glass houses, lie about Russia, and conspire to encircle and strangle his country. When he does go on the offensive against a domestic opponent, it is not to engage on a question of policy but to accuse the adversary of being a traitor. Allegations of treason are the hardest to survive, because, even when the charges are not proven, the aura of disloyalty remains. Putin has stayed in front of the corruption issue by pinning the label on those who have displeased him and then arranging for prominent news coverage of governors, bureaucrats, and other officials being led away in handcuffs, their homes searched, and piles of cash confiscated. Most Russians believe that corruption is a big problem; many think Putin is the remedy.

The president takes nothing for granted. He personally supervises the KGB's successor security service, the FSB. He is creating a new National Guard, separate from the army, to cope with potential protests. Further, in recent years the government arranged with criminal hacking outfits to obtain confidential data about persons of interest.

Late in 2016, the American intelligence community reported that Moscow had used online tools to influence the American electoral process and to help Putin's preferred candidate, Donald Trump, gain entrée to the Oval Office. Comparable disruptive efforts have been directed toward balloting in (at least) France, Italy, Britain, Spain, the Netherlands, the Baltics, the Czech Republic, Ukraine, and Georgia. Methods include the theft and release of campaign e-mails, the generation of phony documents, the use of disguised identities on Facebook, and the dissemination of fictitious and sometimes libelous "news" stories that are then picked up and splashed around by social media. When Russia is confronted with these allegations, the response has been typical of its approach whenever its actions are challenged: to categorically deny any role, then concoct a false equivalency by accusing the West of doing the same thing. As Putin has pointed out, even if Russia did meddle in elections, the United States has an entire branch of civil society devoted to the same purpose. What he fails to acknowledge is the difference between trying to castrate democracy and endeavoring to strengthen and sustain it.

Russia's pioneering use of social media as a weapon reflects not any unusual cultural aptitude for hacking, but rather Putin's experiences in the KGB, where spreading disinformation was both a way of life and an art. The impact, though, is larger now than during the Cold War, because the target audience is more accessible and bigger. Facebook has two billion active users. What are Russia's motives? A good guess would be to discredit democracy, divide Europe, weaken the transatlantic partnership, and punish governments that dare stand up to Moscow. This agenda is not ideological; it is about power, pure and simple. Russia's cyber-warriors aren't liberal or conservative; they help movements from both the far left and the far right to inflame public opinion and ignite conflict. In world affairs, this brand of cyberwarfare is the new power tool, and states across the globe are asking two questions: How can we defend ourselves? And how can we develop the same capability?

WITH COMMUNISM NO LONGER VIABLE, THE DEFAULT RALLYING CRY for an autocratic Russian leader is nationalism. Putin, with his staged military parades and frequent invocation of past heroics, sounds that trumpet repeatedly. He wants citizens to believe that only he can restore his country to its rightful position in world affairs. If that means playing a little rough, so be it. He notes sarcastically that some think the Russian bear should "start picking berries and eating honey. Maybe then he will be left alone. But no, he won't be! Because someone will always try to chain him up. As soon as he's chained, they will tear out his teeth and claws."

During the winter of 2013–14, anti-government demonstrations caused Ukraine's elected president, Viktor Yanukovych, to flee. He left behind in his compound fifty luxury cars, twenty aircraft, several speedboats, a giant wooden pirate ship complete with dining area, a painting of one of his top advisers dressed up like Julius Caesar, a karaoke station, a gold toilet seat, and a petting zoo with ostriches and ten different breeds of pheasant. The protesters had accused Yanukovych of corruption, an allegation he indignantly denied.

Putin's decision to capitalize on the turbulence in Ukraine flowed in part from his conviction, shared by most Russians, that Crimea rightly belongs to Russia. Back in 1991, when the USSR was falling apart, Yeltsin's foreign minister warned U.S. Secretary of State James Baker, "If Ukraine does secede, this will give rise to highly unpredictable consequences: the problem of relations between Russia and Ukraine, the status of Crimea, and the Donbass region. Eastern Ukraine would also be an issue."

Until 2014, Russia had to live with the hand it had been dealt, but that winter, with Ukraine in an uproar and the world distracted by events in Syria and Iraq, Putin made his move.

There ensued a farce during which Russia conceded nothing while manipulating events, then rapidly annexing Crimea with the aid of weapons and troops that were supposedly never there. The Kremlin proceeded to send more supplies and soldiers to support ethnic Russian separatists in eastern Ukraine. This, too, officials swore they hadn't done, even though the weapons were photographed by Western intelligence agencies and the bodies of very real Russian soldiers had to be trucked back across the border for burial. In July 2014, a Malaysia Airlines plane was blasted out of the sky in Ukrainian airspace, killing 298, including eighty children. Dutch investigators produced clear evidence that the plane had been shot down by a Russian-made missile from territory controlled by Moscow-backed separatists. Putin claimed that the investigation was political and pinned blame for the tragedy on Ukraine. In his telling, the entire crisis had been caused by Ukrainian Nazis. All of this reminds me of the opening quotation from an episode of *The Wire*: "A lie ain't a side of the story; it's just a lie."

In recent years, the Russian bear has also been on the prowl in Central Asia, the Caucasus, the Balkans, and Syria, where it put its considerable weight down on the side of Bashar al-Assad, a tyrant with the blood of many thousands on his hands. These aggressive moves, in combination with the troubles in Ukraine, Russian cyberhacks, and flagrant meddling in elections, have injected a dose of hysteria into relations between Washington and Moscow. Putin is, I think, sincere in believing that the United States wants to prevent his country from projecting military power well beyond its borders, because that happens to be true. However, he is wrong to think that America desires a Russia that is marginalized and weak. All we want—and what most of the world would like to see—is a Russia willing to treat others with the respect it demands for itself. That shouldn't be too much to ask.

In our first meeting, back in 2000, Putin told me, "Sure, I like Chinese food, it's fun to use chopsticks, and I've been doing judo for a long time, but this is just trivial stuff. It's not our mentality, which is European. Russia has to be firmly part of the West." Such comments are meant to be disarming, but Russia has ample cause to value access to Western markets and to be on cordial terms with the principal nations of Europe. So it is a debit for Putin, and for Russia, that few international leaders trust him. When, on May 9, 2017, the country celebrated Victory Day, the pinnacle of the patriotic calendar, Putin's high-level foreign guest list consisted, in its entirety, of the president of Moldova.

Russian foreign minister Sergey Lavrov likes to gloat that we are now in a "post-West world order." Whether that's true—and, if so, what it means—is unclear. What's curious is why Lavrov thinks Russia would benefit from a future dominated by the East. China is a more natural antagonist for Russia than either Europe or the United States. At any rate, how the world order is described matters less than how well and on what basis it functions. Putin's vision, which seems predicated on the principles of every nation for itself and every leader for himself, can be described as realistic or, as I prefer, cynical.

Earlier, I cited Oswald Spengler's chilling century-old prophecy that "the era of individualism, liberalism and democracy, of humanitarianism and freedom, is nearing its end. The masses will accept with resignation the victory of the Caesars, the strong men, and will obey them." This is the real danger posed by Putin: that he will be a model for other national leaders who want to retain their grip on power indefinitely, despite political and legal constraints.

Since the Cold War's conclusion, pro-democracy groups have emphasized the value of countries learning from the experiences of others. States like Argentina and Chile graduated from military to civilian rule in the 1980s and had much to teach Central Americans in the following decades. The Philippines got rid of Marcos in 1986 and later helped Indonesia, which moved on from its dictator, Suharto, in 1998. Today, those who have been building democracy are seeing their techniques mimed by people who are out to destroy democracy. Repressive governments from across the globe are learning from one another. If this were a college for despots, we could imagine the course names: How to Rig a Constitutional Referendum; How to Intimidate the Media; How to Destroy Political Rivals Through Phony Investigations and Fake News; How to Create a Human Rights Commission That Will Cover Up Violations of Human Rights; How to Co-Opt a Legislature; and How to Divide, Repress, and Demoralize Opponents So That No One Believes You Will Ever Be Defeated.

In 1933, shortly after Hitler took power, Mussolini told a member of his staff, "The idea of Fascism conquers the world. I have already given Hitler many good ideas. Now he will follow me."

Putin has feet of clay. The Russian economy, so robust in his first decade of rule, remains smaller than Italy's or Canada's and shows no promise of further improvement. Free enterprise is withering as foreign investors abandon the country due to sanctions, opaque rules for doing business, and an unwillingness to pay bribes. Wealth is distributed less equally than in any other major nation—a throwback to the time of the czars. The country's population is aging. Politically, there are signs (such as lower voter turnout) that Russians are growing weary of Putinism, even if most are not yet ready to rebel against the man himself. Internationally, Putin's deceptions are no longer fooling so many. Yet he has already succeeded in giving men of ambition elsewhere "many good ideas." And it is ironic and disturbing that among those watching him most reverently is a leader in Central Europe who—when the Berlin Wall fell—celebrated what the KGB mourned.

THIRTEEN

"WE ARE WHO WE WERE"

I N BUDAPEST ON JUNE 16, 1989, HUNGARIANS HONORED—BY reburying—a man who had been dead for more than three decades. A quarter of a million citizens gathered in Heroes' Square around a towering monument commemorating the thousand-year history of the Magyar people. All eyes were on the flower-draped casket holding the remains of Imre Nagy, leader of a nationalist revolt crushed by the Soviets in 1956. Fearing its own population, the quisling Hungarian government had secretly tried and hanged Nagy, then consigned his remains to an unmarked grave in a remote corner of an obscure cemetery. In the summer of 1989, under intense pressure from a burgeoning democratic movement, authorities consented to Nagy's exhumation and public reinterment, but warned against any attempt to inject politics into the solemn event. With that caution in mind, speakers were restrained throughout the day, as if fearing to acknowledge the revolutionary significance of the ceremony. Hours passed and the audience grew restless. Then the final speaker rose to his feet. He was a tall man with tousled black hair and a short beard; he gazed at his anxious countrymen through twenty-six-year-old eyes.

"We young people," he began, "fail to understand a lot of things about the older generation. . . . We do not understand that the very same party and government leaders who told us to learn from books falsifying history . . . now vie with each other to touch these coffins as if they were lucky charms. We do not think there is any reason to be grateful for being allowed to bury our martyred dead."

The crowd, coming alive, began to cheer.

"We do not owe thanks to anyone for the fact that our political organization exists and is operating today."

More cheers.

"If we can trust our souls and our strength, we can put an end to the Communist dictatorship."

Loud applause.

"And if we do not lose sight of the ideals of 1956, we will elect a government and start immediate negotiations for the swift withdrawal of Russian troops."

By now the crowd was in an uproar. The spirit of Hungarian freedom was reborn, and it was Communism instead in the coffin. Less than four months later, the reformers proclaimed a democratic republic.

IN POLAND, THE MOST EFFECTIVE VOICE FOR FREEDOM AT THE Cold War's end was that of Lech Wałęsa, the fiery yet amiable dockworker with the walrus mustache; in Czechoslovakia, it had been the mischievous, music-loving playwright Václav Havel; in Hungary, it was the youthful football enthusiast with the raven-colored beard, Viktor Orbán. Of this trio, the first two remain internationally celebrated; the third, Orbán, is more controver-

sial. He still has admirers in his home country, but to many outside observers he is "a xenophobic, anti-democratic nationalist
with a cruel anti-refugee agenda."

Who has changed more—the idealist of 1989 or those who
judge him?

In its first fifteen years, the new Hungary lived up to its bill-
ing. Elections were competitive and fair, courts independent, the
media diverse, and basic liberties respected. As secretary of state,
I was delighted when, in 1999, I joined in welcoming Hungary
into NATO. Five years on, the country was admitted to the EU.
Among its prominent personalities was the now clean-shaven
Orbán, whose Fidesz party occupied space on the center right of
the political spectrum and dueled repeatedly with the party of
the left, the Socialists. This rivalry was hard fought and would
likely have remained so had Orbán not been handed a priceless
gift. In 2006, the Socialist prime minister offered remarks to a
party conference in which he admitted to lying "morning, evening
and night," acknowledged that "we screwed up. Not a little, a lot,"
and referred to Hungary—using a polite translation—as "this
maggoty country." The profanity-laced confessional was intended
to be private. Instead it was recorded secretly (no one is sure by
whom) and broadcast nationwide. The gaffe let all the air out of
the Socialist balloon and helped lift Orbán's party to victory in
the next election, held in 2010.

On reaching office, the new head of government set to work.
His agenda was a nationalist one, patriotic in tone, and wrapped in
the red, white, and green of the Hungarian flag. Orbán's European
colleagues found him irritating—a showboat playing to the home
crowd and no help in addressing the continent's broader problems.
Every time the prime minister denounced the bureaucrats in Brussels, their distress deepened, while applause rang out in Hungary
everywhere from the high-tech entrepreneurs of Debrecen to the
sausage makers and paprika producers of Szeged.

For Orbán, Hungarian unity is a dominant theme about which he talks all the time. However, the togetherness he envisions is defined by bloodlines, not borderlines. To him, a person of Magyar ancestry living in Serbia or Romania is more authentically Hungarian than a Roma or Turk born and raised on Hungarian soil. The prime minister exploits national grievances dating back to the Ottomans, but he gives special attention to the 1920 treaty—imposed by the victors after World War I—that cost Hungary two-thirds of its territory. He urges citizens to protect themselves from threats to their collective identity, and appeals unceasingly to ethnic pride based on shared history, values, religion, and tongue. For inspiration, he turns not to multiethnic America or to the big tent that Europe has become. His ideal is what he calls "illiberal democracy," and the models of governance he acclaims are those of Putin in Russia and Erdoğan in Turkey.

An illiberal democracy is centered on the supposed needs of the community rather than the inalienable rights of the individual. It is democratic because it respects the will of the majority; illiberal because it disregards the concerns of minorities. Orbán has made clear that the aspirations of the majority correspond precisely to the program of his own movement: Fidesz. In his calculation, the people and the party are in exquisite balance, and their opponents are aliens—the enemies of Hungary. This thinking is indeed illiberal, and an echo of the jingoistic nationalism that carried Mussolini to power a century ago.

Mussolini was an ideological chameleon, and the same may be said of Orbán. This famed anti-Communist had, when a teenager, been secretary of a Communist youth organization. Now the unapologetic champion of illiberal democracy, he served, early in his career, as vice-chair of Liberal International, a federation dedicated to free enterprise and social justice. A skeptic today toward all things European, Orbán had once been among those impatiently lobbying for Hungary to join the EU. As a party leader, he has pursued conservative economic policies but also advocated tax and welfare initiatives that benefit the poor. Since he entered public life, his tactics have been flexible, his ambitions constant. He is a thin-skinned opportunist who likes to command. It would be an exaggeration to suggest that he has forced Hungary into a Fascist straitjacket, but he is encouraging his country to feel comfortable in a loose-fitting ultranationalist shirt.

Since 2010, Fidesz has used its executive and legislative clout to rewrite the constitution in a way that expands the powers of the prime minister while diminishing those of parliament. To widen the circle of conservative votes, the government extended citizenship privileges to ethnic Hungarians living outside the country. Party loyalists have taken control of the constitutional court, the National Election Commission, and much of the judiciary. The administration has replaced public radio and television channels with state-sponsored media, sapped the strength of labor unions, reshaped educational curricula, and attempted to dictate the content of movies and plays. Coziness between public ministries and a new generation of oligarchs has given Fidesz a rich source of financial backing—and abundant opportunities for corruption.

Orbán plays the soundtrack for all this by harping on the epic moments of Hungarian history, urging Magyar women to have more babies, and decrying at length the supposed meddling of foreign-funded NGOs. He singles out especially the Open Society initiatives bankrolled by Hungarian expatriate George Soros. The Hungarian leader accuses Soros of paying liberals to criticize Fidesz and of providing money to journalists who write unflattering stories. There appears to be something about the stubborn, idealistic, and deep-pocketed Soros that drives Orbán nuts. Perhaps it is because, in his twenties, the future prime minister accepted a Soros Foundation scholarship to attend Oxford; or maybe it is because Soros accuses him of turning Hungary into a "mafia state."

The prime minister is clearly unafraid to provoke Europe. In the past, Hungarian heroes have preached liberation from Austrian monarchs, aggressive neighbors, and Communist dictators. Orbán elicits cheers by promising to liberate Hungary yet again, this time from an even more insidious adversary: bureaucrats in Brussels. The EU, which sends a lot more money to Budapest than it gets back, isn't amused by the LET'S STOP BRUSSELS posters that compete for space with anti-Soros placards on Hungarian billboards and buses.

Orbán has been on the receiving end of a cascade of international criticism, which has done little to affect his approach. He does, after all, have friends nearby.

THE POPULATION OF HUNGARY IS JUST UNDER TEN MILLION, THAT of Poland thirty-eight million. Geographically, Poland is more than three times as large and its citizens prefer bigos—a stew of cabbage and meat—to Hungarian goulash, which also boasts meat, but more peppers. The countries are separated by Slovakia and have many differences, but they also have much in common—including, recently, their politics.

In 2015, Poland's Law and Justice Party (PiS) assumed the presidency and parliamentary leadership in Warsaw, and, ever since, opponents have warned that democracy is in peril. The alarmism is healthy and a good reason to hope such anxieties will ultimately prove unfounded. Party chair Jarosław Kaczyński, whose rigid conservatism prompts the fears, has a deft political touch, but his attempts to expand power at the expense of constitutional checks have met with only partial success.

Kaczyński derives charisma from his oddness. He is cerebral, dour, a lifelong bachelor, and a devout Roman Catholic more attached to his cats than he is comfortable with computers or crowds. Yet he is by far the country's most prominent public figure.

Jarosław and his younger (by forty-five minutes) twin brother,

Lech, gained fame at age twelve by starring in a movie about a pair of lazy boys who long to become rich and avoid work, only to find themselves in a city where everything is made of gold but people have nothing to eat. Film careers behind them, the round-faced twins studied law, became active in labor politics, and participated prominently in the 1980s pro-democracy movement. That eruption of defiance by freedom-loving Poles ultimately wore down the Soviet-backed government, cleared the way for elections, and helped topple the Berlin Wall.

In the process, the movement split between those, such as Solidarity leader Wałęsa, who were willing to work with Communist officials to ensure a peaceful transition, and others, including the Kaczyńskis, who sought a complete break. From that time forward, the brothers insisted that the Communists had retained too much influence in banks, corporations, the media, and the police. Disgruntled, they gradually separated themselves from their old democratic allies and formed the PiS. In 2002, Lech—the more socially congenial of the siblings—was elected mayor of Warsaw, on an anti-crime platform, and three years later he ascended to the presidency, with Jarosław joining the government as prime minister in 2006.

On April 10, 2010, Lech was killed when the air force jet he was aboard crashed while attempting to land in Russia. Although professional investigators attributed the incident to human error in foggy conditions, Jarosław never let go of his suspicion that the Russians had found a way to sabotage the plane.

One month after the tragedy, Poles cast ballots to pick the fallen president's successor. The surviving twin ran, but finished a disappointing second. Five years later, in 2015, he led a comeback. Instead of running himself, he designated more conventional politicians to stand for president and prime minister. The stratagem worked and the PiS won a decisive victory based on the nationalist slogan "Rising from our knees." Ever since, Jarosław

Kaczyński has acted behind the scenes to energize a socially conservative constituency by railing against former Communists, European politicians, and refugees who are responsible, in his words, for spreading "disease and parasites."

To a small "d" democrat, process matters more than ideology. The fairness of an election is more important than who wins. There is not, on most questions of policy, a single democratic answer. Concerns arise only when leaders try to augment their power through means that could cause permanent damage to democratic institutions. That appears to be exactly what Kaczyński is attempting to do. While Hungary's Orbán points to Russia and Turkey as models for his brand of "illiberal democracy," Kaczyński looks for guidance to Hungary, vowing to "bring Budapest to Warsaw."

The Law and Justice Party's first step upon returning to office was to subvert the independence of the country's constitutional tribunal, reducing it to a rubber stamp. The parliament then approved legislation increasing the state's hold over public broadcasters. A new civil service law made it easier to purge the bureaucracy, and the administration has replaced almost every senior military officer. The party's next move was to assume control of the National Judiciary Council (which appoints judges) and to force almost half the supreme court to retire. Along the way, the government has rarely passed up the chance to annoy officials in Brussels, even casting the lone vote against the 2017 reelection of a Pole, Donald Tusk, to the presidency of the European Council. Kaczyński insists that Tusk, Poland's prime minister in 2010, did not do enough to investigate the plane crash that killed his brother.

Nationalism is deeply entrenched in the hearts and minds of its citizens, but Poland—easily the largest net recipient of EU funds—also needs Europe; and without question, the people take democratic values very seriously. When the regime sought to ban all abortions, it had to back down in the face of nationwide protests. Similarly, an effort to restrict access by journalists to parliament was abandoned. Early in 2018, several of the more extreme cabinet officials were replaced—an apparent attempt to mollify Europe. The Law and Justice Party is still in the driver's seat, but it is neither strong nor united enough to fully dictate Poland's direction. Ultimately, the party's fate may depend on its ability to harness the energy Kaczyński provides without being consumed by his anger.

The former prime minister is still bitter toward Russia because of the death of his brother. He resents Germany for historical reasons and for having greater weight than Poland in European councils. He is furious with Lech Wałęsa for not despising Communists with sufficient vigor. He becomes enraged with anyone who suggests, as did one parliamentarian, that his twin, if still alive, would be pursuing a more moderate agenda. "Do not wipe your traitorous mugs with the name of my late brother," he fumed during parliamentary debate. "You are scoundrels. . . . You murdered him!" Finally, he denounces those who disagree with him as "haters" and calls anti-government demonstrators "the worst sort of Poles."

Kaczyński claims to speak for "true Poles," and that is the basis of his party's appeal. Since the end of the Cold War, per capita income has risen by more than 600 percent, but, because of corruption, political infighting, and administrative incompetence, those gains have not translated into satisfaction with governing institutions. The challenge for current leaders will be to deliver what their predecessors could not. However, it is easier to oppose than propose, and Kaczyński's brief term as prime minister, in 2006 and 2007, ended poorly. Poles are divided between those who look at Kaczyński unfavorably and say they "are terrified of not living in a free country" and those who view him and his party as the defenders of Polish identity in a polyglot world.

THE WAR OF WILLS BETWEEN HUNGARY AND POLAND ON ONE SIDE and the EU on the other is an important test of where extreme nationalism will lead. Despite the best efforts of EU cheerleaders, there is nothing preordained about the answer. Fear that Fascism might return to the continent where it was born is what spurred the drive for European integration, but the origins of that sentiment are now more than seventy years old, and anxieties, like human beings, eventually show their age.

Virtually every state in Europe is the product of a nationalist movement that flowered in the nineteenth century or earlier. Wilson's doctrine of self-determination gave a boost to the idea that wherever there dwelled a people, there should be a state—however impractical that concept would be to implement in a region where the movement of people and the wondrous spontaneity of romance have conspired to link some very different family trees. The whole notion of pure blood is laughable, but that does not stop tribal instincts and their accompanying national mythologies from exercising a powerful sway over behavior, as World War II so tragically demonstrated. It took the shock of that war to create a reaction strong enough for countries to embrace regional integration, but that choice has always been more compelling logically than emotionally. World War II was still under way when French financier Jean Monnet, often described as the father of Europe, told the French Committee of National Liberation:

> There will be no peace in Europe if the States rebuild themselves on the basis of national sovereignty, with its implications of prestige politics and economic protection. . . . The countries of Europe are not strong enough individually to be able to guarantee prosperity and social development for their peoples. The States of Europe must therefore form a federation or a European entity that would make them into a common economic unit.

That pragmatic vision has been validated. The EU and its predecessors were advertised as generators of prosperity, a means for combining markets, reducing the cost of doing business, and fending off a destructive struggle for competitive advantage among neighbors. Up to a point, the regional institutions have delivered. After the United States, the EU is now the world's largest economy. Fourteen of the thirty wealthiest countries are in Europe. Within the continent, the gap between the richest and poorest nations has narrowed as new investments begin to pay dividends in less wealthy states such as Romania, Bulgaria, and Slovakia. Still, gains have not fully kept pace with hopes. Back in the 1950s and '60s, unemployment in much of Western Europe was below 2 percent, while annual economic growth was at 6 or 7 percent. Such figures seem a pipe dream in today's era of larger populations, tighter budgets, and chronic joblessness.

The EU's advantage is that disentangling Europe from the single currency and a shared regulatory structure would be extraordinarily disruptive and expensive. Those nostalgic for the region's good old days are not remembering; they're daydreaming. Should Europe return to thirty borders, thirty currencies, thirty rule books, and twenty or more languages, the result would be more red tape, not less, and less money, not more, in the pockets of the average worker, farmer, or professional.

The Achilles' heel of the European project is that it has always been a top-down enterprise; a lot of people never warmed to it. In 1992, French voters gave the Maastricht Treaty—which created the framework for the EU—a tepid endorsement, with barely 50 percent voting in favor. In Denmark, voters initially rejected the pact, only to reconsider when certain "Danish exceptions" sweetened the deal. Year after year, the continent's pro-European politicians have had to plead with their constituencies to support integration, generating in their audiences—at best—a wave of mild enthusiasm.

In the 1990s, Central Europeans lined up to join the EU because they saw membership as the surest way to make their independence from Moscow irreversible. To have a home in Brussels meant being part of the West and becoming a full shareholder in Europe's prosperity and freedom. They were not expecting the fine print to include rules that would regulate so much of daily life—from the size of cucumbers to the definition of chocolate to the right of poultry farmers to kill and eat their own ducks. The EU marriage between region and state still makes economic sense, but the passion has cooled. European Commission president Jean-Claude Juncker admits, "One of the reasons European citizens are stepping away from the European project is that we are interfering in too many domains of their private lives."

For me, the continent's fate is a frequent topic of discussion with old friends, many of whom once headed foreign ministries in such countries as the UK, France, Germany, Italy, Spain, Sweden, and Portugal. Our biggest regret is that leaders underestimated the resentment men and women would feel at being told what to do by officials whose judgment they question and for whom they have never directly voted. Within our well-traveled group, the overall value of integration is understood, but for those working on a farm in Poland or at a factory in Bratislava, allegiance to Brussels does not come naturally, if at all. Our fear is that alienation from the European project will continue to grow.

One reason for the worry is that, although too much bureaucracy can be annoying, there is an even larger threat to intra-European solidarity. That danger comes from the outside, from the dread that immigration—whether legal or illegal—will swamp countries, drown them economically, and further dilute people's sense of who they are. The premise of the EU is that individuals should conceive of themselves less as French, Czech, Slovenian, or whatever their ethnicity might be and instead subscribe to the idea that they are just plain European. That exhortation is losing appeal as time passes and the faces peering back from European mirrors become more diverse.

In the 1960s, when the concept of regional unity was picking up steam, unemployment in Western Europe was much lower, and immigrants were routinely sought to fill positions in fields, on factory floors, and in shops. Beginning in the 1970s, labor shortages became surpluses, and the welcome wagon broke down. It didn't help that many of the more recent migrants were transparently "non-European" in race or creed. Since 1975, Europe's Muslim population has more than tripled; France alone has nearly six million—9 percent of its people—and for years, critics on the right have insisted that Muslims are not capable of "becoming French." Meanwhile, as the birth rate of Europe's indigenous population remains stagnant, the newcomers are fruitful and multiplying. Over time, resentment toward them has grown, along with complaints about crime, clashing values, welfare costs, and competition for jobs. Today, nearly two-thirds of the citizens in EU countries believe immigration has a harmful impact on their societies. Cosmopolitanism, once considered a virtue, is less in vogue than nativism.

In 2015, immigration became the paramount political issue in Europe, due to a huge spike in arrivals from Syria and North Africa at precisely the moment terrorist incidents seized center stage, with ISIS-inspired zealots blowing up nightclubs and slamming trucks into pedestrians in some of the continent's biggest cities. The impact of the crisis was felt in the United Kingdom, where wariness toward migrants almost certainly spelled the difference between success and failure for the 2016 Brexit referendum, an exercise in economic masochism that Britons will long regret. Grumbling about their marriage to the EU and threatening to leave gave the British leverage at the bargaining table; calling their own bluff and filing for divorce has left them with none.

In Germany, which opened its borders to more than a million asylum seekers in 2015 alone, immigration worries helped the nationalist Alternative for Germany (AfD) secure an eighth of the vote in the September 2017 election and thus enter parliament and occupy influential posts as the third-largest party. This outcome was a blow to Chancellor Angela Merkel, the country's respected but battle-scarred leader, who had at first welcomed the migrants before adopting a more neutral stance.

Fiscal conservatives founded the AfD to protest the use of German funds to help Greece avoid bankruptcy. The immigration crisis enabled it to peel off support from Merkel and convince tens of thousands of people to vote who would not ordinarily have bothered to go to the polls. Party chief Alexander Gauland captured their motivation: "I see Islam as a foreign body which will gradually, through the birth rate, come to dominate this country." That feeling, exaggerated though it clearly is, explains the rise of AfD. Ironically, the party did best in regions where the foreign-born population is relatively low. AfD supporters are responding, then, not to what *is* but to what they fear *might be*. That gives party spokesmen every incentive to go on talking about the dangers posed by immigrants and to propagate stereotypes that keep those anxieties alive.

The German election brought an emphatically nationalist perspective into the Bundestag for the first time since World War II. In so doing, it gave renewed hope to movements of a roughly similar ilk in all parts of Europe, including France's National Front in the west, the Sweden Democrats and True Finns in the north, Greece's Golden Dawn in the south, and, in the center, Austria's Freedom Party. "In the programs and statements of these parties," observes Columbia University's Robert Paxton, "one hears echoes of classical fascist themes: fears of decadence and decline; assertion of national and cultural identity; a threat by unassimilable foreigners to national identity and good social order; and the need for greater authority to deal with these problems." Beyond the formal political parties, there is a vast and growing collection of hyper-nationalist entities that make their presence known in marches and rallies, hoisting banners that advertise such sentiments as "White Europe" and "Refugees Out."

Though some of the organizations are transparently neo-Nazi, others take pains to distance themselves from Fascism's lingering odor. As they strive to make further inroads, they regularly compare notes, sound similar themes, and cheer one another on—to the point that British, French, and Polish extremists warmly congratulated the AfD on its success. One can imagine what the World War II generation might think of their countrymen celebrating the rebirth of German triumphalism. The European parties also receive financial help from external sources, notably Russia and sympathetic circles in the United States. In 2015, the largest single donation in Dutch politics was given by a right-wing American group to that country's Party for Freedom, whose leader, Geert Wilders, calls for shuttering mosques and who campaigns on the slogan "Make the Netherlands Great Again."

My native Czech Republic has not been immune to the turbulence. In January 2018, voters narrowly re-elected Milos Zeman to a second term as president. Zeman, who refers to himself as "the Czech Trump," has echoed Orbán in warning of a Muslim invasion even though the Republic has accepted barely a dozen of the twenty-six hundred asylum seekers required by EU policy. Zeman is also overtly pro-Russia and pro-Putin, which may explain the flood of lies slandering his pro-EU opponent that appeared on social media in the runup to the balloting. In parliamentary elections three months earlier, the big winner was a new party, founded in 2012, called ANO. Its leader, Andrej Babiš, is a billionaire political novice who campaigned on his experience as a businessman and who pledged to fight corruption, though he is under investigation for precisely that. Many voters apparently believe that because the wealthy have no need to steal, they don't. We'll see. A couple of years ago, I met Babiš when he was on a visit to the United States. I told friends at the time that I had not encountered any Czech (or Slovak) quite like him—cold, detached, uncommunicative, remote. Zeman and Babiš are allies. I wish my homeland well.

In Hungary, the refugee crisis has given Prime Minister Orbán yet another supposedly existential threat against which to rally his people. Instead of working constructively with regional and global institutions to stabilize the flow of migrants and meet humanitarian needs, Orbán has chosen to foment paranoia. Ignoring the fact that relatively few migrants are clamoring to enter Hungary, the prime minister declared, "The masses arriving from other civilizations endanger our way of life, our culture, our customs and our Christian traditions." He said the migrants would bring "crime and terror . . . mass disorder . . . riots . . . [and] gangs hunting down our women and daughters."

Orbán pays little heed to the wrenching humanitarian disaster in the Middle East that launched the exodus, or to the plight of the hundreds of thousands of very young and very old whose lives are in jeopardy through no fault of their own. Instead he describes the crisis as "a preplanned and orchestrated" EU scheme to "transport foreigners here as quickly as possible and settle them among us," with the goal of reshaping "the religious and cultural landscape of Europe, and to reengineer its ethnic foundations."

Orbán's strategy has been to pin responsibility for this imaginary plot on George Soros. Late in 2017, the government sent a questionnaire to every household asking whether it supported the "Soros Plan" to force Hungary to accept migrants, pay them welfare, and assure them lenient sentences for any crimes they might commit. This approach to consulting with the people takes what would ordinarily be considered a democratic tool—the plebiscite—and uses it to spread and validate a falsehood. By asking questions based on a lie, it makes the lie a central part of national conversation. Like other vile tactics, the misuse of plebiscites was perfected by the Third Reich, which employed it often to attach a small thread of legality to Hitler's rule. "The most effective form of persuasion," said Goebbels, "is when you are not aware of being persuaded."

Orbán has added to his demagoguery with a crowd-pleasing project to build border walls and by incarcerating some migrants in shipping containers surrounded by high fences topped by razor wire. Perhaps he should be reminded of his long-ago speech about Imre Nagy and the events of 1956, when tens of thousands of Hungarian freedom fighters were welcomed by the international community as they sought safety from Soviet tanks.

I AM A REFUGEE, BUT A LUCKY ONE. MY FATHER WOULD SURELY have been arrested had we not left Czechoslovakia when we did, but no one threatened to put us in shipping containers, and we arrived in our new homeland on an ocean liner, not an overcrowded raft. When people ask me to sum up my life, I always begin with "gratitude"—to my parents and to the American citizens who allowed my family to make a fresh start. So I find it impossible to be coldly analytical on the subject of migrants and refugees, and I cannot respect politicians who try to win votes by kindling hatred.

The complexity of immigration as an issue begins with a basic human trait: we are reluctant to share. In Rome in 125 B.C., officials debated whether to allow Italians from outside the city gates to enjoy the benefits of Roman citizenship. Arguing against it, a cautious legislator urged his neighbors to consider the implications: "Once you have given citizenship to the Latins, . . . do you think there will be any space for you, like there is now . . . at games or festivals? Don't you realise they'll take over everything?"

The world has long since agreed on norms that give states the authority to regulate their borders and yet respect, as well, the right of people to seek a haven from political persecution and war. In normal conditions, this is a workable balance. Men and women who are driven from their homes by repression or strife are entitled to protection, whether temporary or permanent. The broader and less clear-cut question is how to treat people who move from their native countries not because they must, but because they hope to attain a higher standard of living. The right to act on that understandable desire is not absolute; there are legal and illegal ways to go about it.

In general, the movement of people from their homes—the leaving behind of possessions, familiar sights, memories, and ancestral graveyards—does not occur without good cause. Most of us would prefer to remain in places where our names are known, our customs accepted, and our languages spoken. However, hope is another basic human trait, and so millions of people each year do try to migrate illegally, and, once they are on the road or at sea, Europe is for many the destination of choice. Human traffickers aggravate the dilemma by using social media and word of mouth to persuade potential migrants to pay fees they can't afford so that they can undertake journeys that rarely deliver on the dreams that inspired them.

The scope and pace of migration are a fair topic for debate, and, indeed, an unavoidable one. While it is morally repulsive to vilify newcomers as a group, countries have legitimate grounds to worry about their capacity to absorb large numbers of immigrants. This is particularly the case when most of the visitors are unlikely to return home soon and many already have family members lined up to join them. European leaders have reason to worry about the ability of recent arrivals to integrate themselves successfully into their adopted countries, qualify for jobs, and contribute to their communities. Uncontrolled migration produces social friction not because many refugees are criminals and terrorists (they aren't), but because living side by side with strangers requires two precious commodities: goodwill and time.

Both are necessary to build trust; neither is as widely available as we would like.

Ultimately, illegal immigration is a symptom of failures that extend well beyond Europe and that will not be solved either by welcoming newcomers or by keeping them out. Humanitarian emergencies demand a generous response, but a sound policy will concentrate on preventing crises from arising. Such an approach would separate genuine political refugees from economic migrants, allow high levels of legal migration, share intelligence to prevent infiltration by terrorists, and strive to put human traffickers out of business.

More broadly, it is vital for leaders to work across international boundaries to minimize the number of people who feel the need to leave their home countries in the first place. That requires building healthy democracies, fostering peace, and generating prosperity from the ground up. However, success in that endeavor demands a way of looking at the world that recognizes the humanity we share with one another, and the interests that nations have in common. Those who are content to look inward, and who see no higher purpose than to shield themselves from the different, the new, and the unknown, will be of no help.

Seeking to salve the worries of his constituency, Viktor Orbán assures them: "We are who we were, and we shall be what we are." That message of exclusivity and changelessness is meant to be a source of comfort, but it is also tinged with prejudice and utterly devoid of ambition. There is no hint of gaining new insights, no hunger for innovation, no curiosity or concern about others, and no desire to look forward to anything except what has already been. Too bad. The history of Europe—and indeed the world—is stained by the blood of nations convinced that the path to glory can be found by disparaging others and going it alone.

FOURTEEN

"THE LEADER WILL ALWAYS BE WITH US"

FOR NATIONS, THE REMEMBRANCE OF THINGS PAST IS MEA-sured in eras separated, sadly and most often, by war. So it is with Korea. For nearly thirteen hundred years, until the twentieth century, the country was administered from a central capital and its people were held together by shared religious and social customs, a common tongue, a distinctive cuisine, and art. Korea was never an aggressive power, but it had to endure external attacks and periods of occupation, including, most ignominiously, in the sixteenth century, by Japan. After repelling the warriors of the Rising Sun, Korea fortified itself, excluded most foreigners, and became known as the Hermit Kingdom. Then, about 150 years ago, imperial powers cracked open its shell. Deals were made and, in 1905, Japan pushed its way back in. For almost four decades the invaders exploited Korea for their own purposes, exiting only after their empire's defeat in World War II.

Following the Axis surrender, Korea's fate, like that of Central

Europe, was still to be worked out. Officially, the victorious Allies were committed to a free, united, and independent Korea. Then, in the war's last week, Stalin's Red Army penetrated far into the country's northern half. American diplomats, their inboxes overflowing, shifted their focus from what *should* be done to what could be achieved most easily. In Washington, late one night, they met with their Soviet counterparts and, tracing lines on a map from *National Geographic* magazine, consented to the peninsula's "temporary" division along the 38th parallel. The people who lived there were not consulted.

In 1948, with the Cold War well under way, the U.S.-supported Republic of Korea (ROK) and the USSR-backed Democratic People's Republic of Korea (DPRK) officially declared their existence—the former in Seoul, the latter in Pyongyang. North Korea's head of government, hand-selected by the Soviets, was Kim Il-sung, a thirty-six-year-old military officer who had spent the bulk of his life in exile and possessed little formal education. He did, however, have big ideas. Determined to reunify the Korean Peninsula on his terms, Kim persuaded the Soviets to underwrite an invasion of the South, boasting to Stalin that he would win easily. He almost did prevail, but the United States surprised the DPRK by intervening, under a UN umbrella, prompting China to counter by also entering the fray. In 1953, an armistice was signed to end the fighting, but with no victor, no formal peace, no significant change in borders, and a death toll that included more than a million and a half Koreans, 900,000 Chinese, and 54,000 Americans.

The war was a colossal waste of lives and treasure, so it matters that the DPRK has been built on a lie about who started it. The worldview of any North Korean begins with the conviction that, in 1950, their country was attacked by sadistic murderers from America and the ROK. If not for Kim Il-sung's brave leadership and the pluck of DPRK fighters, their homeland would have been laid waste and their ancestors enslaved. Worse still, the story continues, Americans are evil and do not learn from their mistakes. Given a chance, the savages will return and wreak more havoc. Out of this sham narrative come the fear, the anger, and the yearning for revenge that Kim Il-sung harnessed to justify the world's most totalitarian regime.

Kim was above all a military man. Unlike most of the leaders cited in this book, he was neither a writer nor a theorist, nor inclined to read literature or study history. He did, however, possess the ardor of a committed nationalist, knew how to command, kept the Soviets on his side, and had a true Fascist's appetite for power. He also looked good in a uniform. With Moscow's backing, he met little resistance imposing a centralized economy and single-party rule on his fledgling country.

In the wake of the Korean War, the government set out to manufacture public enthusiasm for itself as the defender of the nation against hated enemies—the South, Japan, and the United States. The DPRK built a million-man army, the world's fourth largest, and pulled together a formidable arsenal of rocket launchers and missiles. To instill patriotic spirit, national leaders developed a doctrine they called "Juche," or self-reliance, conveniently ignoring the country's dependence on aid from other Communist states. To ensure discipline, girls and boys were removed from their families at an early age so their heads could be filled with party dogma and their minds and bodies trained to obey. Every citizen was taught to be civil to neighbors, but also to inform on them should they exhibit any sign of dissent or independent thought. Children, too, were encouraged to tattle, even if that meant signing the equivalent of a death warrant for their parents. Like Fascism in Italy and Germany, the North Korean dictatorship was an outgrowth of war and the quest for order taken too far. But in North Korea, unlike those countries, power came quickly when the conflict concluded because there was no incumbent political establishment to outmaneuver or overthrow.

As years passed, the legends surrounding the life and accomplishments of Kim Il-sung were polished to a fine sheen. Supposedly, he had spent World War II leading a guerrilla band from a clandestine mountain base inside Korea where he struck blow after blow against the Japanese occupiers. In reality, he had watched the war from Russia while under the supervision of the Red Army—but the fictional account was more exciting and North Koreans believed it.

To them, Kim was the embodiment of virtue—daring, kind, wise. It was he who invented the new agricultural methods that they used to grow food, the more comfortable chairs in which they sat while studying, the ingenious machines they operated while at work, and the modern weapons they relied on to defend the motherland. Countless anecdotes were told of his visits to classrooms, factories, barracks, and farms where he dispensed Hallmark-style advice with a gentle touch and a warm smile. North Koreans were told that the outside world was depraved and that they were fortunate to have a protector to set high moral standards and to keep them safe. The cult of Kim's personality was on display daily in national ceremonies and parades, against the backdrop of an oversize bronze statue, worshipful billboards, monuments, and museums. He never claimed divine status, but to his people he might just as well have slipped into the shoes of God.

And this god had a son. North Korean Fascism is a family enterprise. For all their headaches, Western diplomats have never had to match wits with Benito Mussolini Jr., Adolf Hitler III, or Joseph Stalin IV. But since the DPRK was founded, power in that country has been transferred without interruption from one generation (the Great Leader, Kim Il-sung) to the next (the Dear Leader, Kim Jong-il) and the next (the Great Successor, Kim Jong-un).

Mussolini taught Italians to believe again in their identity and destiny. Kim Il-sung urged North Koreans to trust in their ability to reunify their peninsula, vanquish powerful foes, and maintain the unique virtues of their race. Through most of his tenure, the DPRK was more prosperous than the South. Until 1990, the leaders in Pyongyang were confident of their prominent place within the Communist solar system, but then one day the red star set and never came back up, forcing the disciples of Juche to find an orbit all their own.

WITH THE COLD WAR OVER, THE CERTAINTIES OF THE DPRK'S UNI-verse vanished. China, trusted friend and ideological soul mate, embarked on an ambitious program of economic opening and reform. The disintegrating USSR started to demand full market price for its oil. Eastern European trading partners turned their backs, the better to wrap their arms around the West. Moscow and Beijing normalized diplomatic ties with the enemy, the ROK. And with most of its foreign assistance cut off, Pyongyang lacked funds to import the food it did not have enough fertilizer and arable land to grow on its own.

Seeing all this, much of the world expected North Korea either to collapse in misery or to acknowledge the inevitable, follow China's lead, and open its economy. Kim, however, was determined to pursue a third option. In 1993, he announced plans to withdraw his country from the Nuclear Nonproliferation Treaty, then prepared to extract weapons-grade plutonium from the spent fuel rods in the DPRK's one operational nuclear reactor. Kim's intention was clear and ominous: he planned to build nuclear bombs.

This show of aggression heightened tensions throughout East Asia and led to a face-off with the Clinton administration. In Washington, our national security team took seriously the possibility of war. We developed a plan to destroy the nuclear reactor and rushed antimissile systems and attack helicopters to the region. Pentagon officials told the president to expect that thousands of U.S. soldiers and half a million South Koreans would be killed or injured in the first ninety days of fighting. Urgently, we pressed North Korea to think carefully about its options and to give diplomacy a chance. Ultimately, passions were cooled through a deal—the Agreed Framework—under which the DPRK shut down its reactor and sealed its fuel rods in return for the promise of better relations and help in meeting energy needs.

The Agreed Framework was imperfect, and implementation fell short on both sides, but the arrangement ended the immediate crisis and kept the DPRK nuclear program from breaking out. Had the framework not been in place, experts believe North Korea would have had enough fuel for fifty to one hundred nuclear weapons by decade's end; instead it had none, but North Korea's isolation continued, and so did its animus toward outsiders.

The year the framework was negotiated, 1994, Kim Il-sung died. North Koreans had lost their guiding light, but that was not all. Their new leader, Kim Jong-il, came to office at a time of terrible suffering. Massive rains led to floods that washed away soil, ruined harvests, and destroyed underground grain reserves. People who had long been hungry now starved. Pregnant women could not find nourishment, and many of their infants had no chance. Citizens were urged to supplement their diets with tree bark, leaves, and grass. Protocol within the army broke down as renegade soldiers ransacked warehouses in search of food. An estimated 5 percent of the population died. The government, desperate for a scapegoat, accused the minister of agriculture of treason, then shot him. The hardships, though extreme, did not dissuade the DPRK from pursuing its audacious military strategy.

In 1998, with the famine nearing its end, North Korea tested a three-stage rocket of a type able—with further development—to reach American soil. This was doubly alarming because, even though the DPRK was no longer producing plutonium, it still had the potential to build a nuclear weapon. So North Korea had again grabbed the world's attention, and it was in our interest—and that of South Korea and Japan—to prevent further missile tests. Once more, we decided to find out what diplomacy could accomplish. After two years of preparatory wrangling, I did what no sitting secretary of state had done before or has done since: boarded a plane for Pyongyang.

ARRIVING IN THE DPRK TOWARD THE END OF OCTOBER 2000, I found a capital city like no other. From airport to guesthouse, our motorcade encountered not a single car. Civilians walking alongside the spacious freeway didn't bother, or didn't dare, to look up as we sped by. The trees had color, leaves turning with the season, but the brownish fields appeared thirsty for rain and the sagging barns looked desperate for paint. Our state-run accommodations were on the city's eastern fringes, guarded by a large pond on which a lone duck swam in circles. The guesthouse was standard for its type, with fresh flowers on the tables, drab green carpets on the floor, a worn terry-cloth robe in the closet, and hidden in the walls and bathrooms: listening devices and cameras. Outside, there were no streetlights, so, driving downtown in the evening, we were directed to the right road by a pair of bone-like fluorescent sticks held by a policeman (or -woman) whose body was made invisible by the surrounding blackness.

In daylight, the Pyongyang I saw was a metropolis of bustling sterility, with uniformed children trekking dutifully to school, and ant-like columns of workers and bureaucrats walking or pedaling away on battered bicycles occasionally making room for Cold War–era Russian Volgas, small jeep-like trucks, and the government's multihued fleet of sedans. The city center was crowded with apartment dwellings, graced by parks, and tranquilized by the relative absence of hotels, restaurants, and shops. The modest skyline's star attraction was (and still is) the 560-foot Juche Tower, a structure erected to honor the seventieth anniversary of Kim Il-sung's birth, situated directly across from Kim Il-sung Square and containing a granite block for each day of Kim Il-sung's life.

Over two days, I spent about twelve hours with the Great Leader's dear son, Kim Jong-il. Shaking hands and posing for cameras, I found that we were about the same height, in part because we wore the same size heels. We devoted half our time to formal meetings, sitting on opposite sides of a slender wooden table with water glasses in front of us, flanked by interpreters and a small number of aides.

I had come to Pyongyang with two goals. I wanted to know what it would take to persuade our hosts to freeze their development of longer-range missiles, the type that might eventually be used to deliver a nuclear warhead. I also hoped to get a more acute sense of Kim Jong-il as a leader and a person. Was he truly in charge? Did he have a strategy? Or was he, as our intelligence services indicated might be the case, a painfully shy dilettante with a fascination for movies and little grasp of world affairs?

During our time together, I found Kim pretty normal for someone whose father's birth date is celebrated each year as the "Day of the Sun." He was cordial, in full control of his emotions, and dressed comfortably—in khaki warm-ups, leisure suits, and, at dinner the second day, a Mao jacket. His inch-long hair was dyed black, and each strand, like a little soldier, stood up straight. In our meetings, Kim listened patiently and didn't try to lecture me on history the way Milošević had done or the Turks tended to do. He didn't wander off on random subjects, a habit of the Chinese foreign minister. Instead he allowed me to have my say, and when I paused out of courtesy, urged me to go on and complete my thoughts, something that almost never happened with my male colleagues back in Washington. Kim and I began by talking generally about security in East Asia, then turned to the DPRK's missile program. On that topic, he was disingenuous but not discouraging.

He said he took the issue seriously because the United States did, but that we were wrong to think that his country would ever attack anyone. He insisted that the DPRK had begun building more powerful missiles solely for scientific reasons—out of a desire to launch communications satellites. If another nation would agree to send the satellites into orbit "for us free of charge, we would not do it ourselves." As for the revenue that the DPRK collected by selling technology to Syria and Iran, he would forgo that, too, in exchange for compensation. Pausing, he added that should his government refrain from developing longer-range missiles, he would insist that South Korea adhere to a similar restriction. Clearly, the question of how to verify all this would require further discussion.

Kim's description of himself as a virtual pacifist was not credible, but his general tone was positive and I wondered why. I asked him to clarify his feelings about the continued presence of some 37,000 American troops in South Korea. With a shrug, he said it didn't bother him, then pointed out, "Look, we are surrounded by powers, especially China and Japan, that are competing for hegemony in the Asia-Pacific. We don't want to be the target of their rivalry. The Soviet Union fell apart and our military alliance has ended. Our relationship with China is poor. We think the United States can serve as a check on these other powers. This is one reason we want to do business with you. What we need is a balance. I tried to convey this message before, through the South Koreans, but Americans always respond with suspicion, like a jilted girl."

Kim smiled slightly for a second, then grew stern. "We don't mind that the South trains its military; we do the same. But we do object to the exercises conducted jointly with the U.S. My military finds these threatening." The solution, he felt, was for the United States and the DPRK to normalize diplomatic ties, a move that he said would "give hope to our people and bring about epoch-making progress in DPRK-U.S. relations." To illustrate what this new era of good feeling might be like, he conceded that his government had not been educating its young correctly. "Our children are taught to call people from your country 'American bastards,'" he said. Then he turned to his interpreter. "Is there a translation for 'American bastards'?" Yes, came the reply: "Yankees.'"*

During our more relaxed moments, Kim was an intriguing host, plainly trying to convey confidence and yet also quick to admit his country's economic problems, including shortages of fertilizer and coal. He was well informed about world events, and we chatted easily about computers, environmental issues, and agriculture—he blamed the Russians for convincing the DPRK to grow corn, which he said had proved suitable only for livestock. On the subject of what life was like in the United States, he indicated no interest, perhaps thinking he had learned all he needed courtesy of Hollywood. I was relieved that Kim didn't drink with the gusto shown by some of his generals, for during our dinners he shielded me from the demand to raise glass after glass in toasts.

On the first day, toward the end of our meeting, he invited me to what he called a "show." This turned out to be an Olympic-scale gymnastics extravaganza held in an indoor stadium and featuring about 100,000 precisely choreographed dancing, cartwheeling, and bayonet-thrusting participants aged five to fifty-five. The gala was an amazing demonstration of discipline, if nothing else, as the athletes swirled about in perfect harmony to the accompaniment of an orchestra playing "The Leader Will Always Be with Us," "Let Us Hold High the Red Flag," and similar foot-tapping tunes. In

---

* Kim's sincerity is belied by a children's poem, written with the government's support four years later, that includes the verse *"I am going to join the army / I will take two guns, three guns / and shoot down all the American bastards / Ah, to grow up quickly / to grow up quickly, quickly."*

the far grandstand, a large contingent of people held cards that, when flashed rapidly and precisely, took the shape of intricate murals or spelled out chants. Kim, who was sitting alongside me, confided that he had designed the exhibition himself. Of course, I thought, who else? Near the conclusion of the gaudy event, the card section showed a three-stage missile blasting off into the East Asian sky, an image greeted with rapturous cheers by the robot-like crowd. Kim leaned over and said, "That was in honor of our first missile launch—it could also be our last."

The North Koreans wanted my visit to be a prelude to a climactic follow-up with President Clinton, and we hoped so, too, but there were complications. The president wasn't going to travel all the way to Pyongyang until we were certain of a deal to stop the DPRK from building and marketing its missiles. We had made enough progress in our talks to envision what such a bargain might look like, but key elements, including timing and verification, had yet to be pinned down. The calendar was against us. I had returned from Asia just a week before Election Day. A new administration would take over in less than three months.

The South Korean government urged Clinton to make the trip. The incoming president, George W. Bush, said it was Clinton's call. Many in Congress took a stand against it, suggesting that such a journey would somehow legitimize DPRK leaders. I argued that we should use the prospect of a summit to secure additional concessions, such as the on-site scrutiny of North Korean military facilities. Ultimately, the president had to choose: an all-out diplomatic effort directed toward Pyongyang (which would require side trips to consult with South Korea and Japan) or a comparable attempt to cement a peace pact between Israel and the Palestinians. Clinton did not feel he had time to pursue both and—based on personal assurances from Palestinian leader Yasser Arafat—decided that the chance for success was slightly better in the Middle East. At one of my more recent birthday parties, Clinton took me aside and said that, given Arafat's failure to keep his word, he wishes in retrospect that he had gone to North Korea.

In January 2001, when I cleared out my desk at the State Department, the DPRK had very little fissile material, no long-range ballistic missiles, and no nuclear weapons. I expected President Bush to pick up where we had left off in trying to maintain that clean scorecard. It didn't happen. Instead of negotiating with the North, factions within the Bush team fought against one another. At first, they simply refused to talk to Pyongyang; then they sent diplomats who were forbidden to say anything other than "Disarm or else"; then the president described North Korea as part of the "Axis of Evil" during his 2002 State of the Union Address. Kim Jong-il responded by kicking international weapons inspectors out of the country, removing the plutonium from eight thousand spent fuel rods, building nuclear warheads, and, on October 7, 2006, conducting a first nuclear test.

It is uncertain, in hindsight, how real an opportunity was missed in the period around 2000, but there were reasons behind our hopes. American leverage was near its peak. We had a popular president who enjoyed strong international backing. Earlier in the decade, the DPRK had been willing to make concessions on its nuclear program in return for aid. The South Koreans, who had a keener understanding of Kim's psychology than we did, told us that if Clinton went to Pyongyang, the North Koreans would make sure his trip was a success. We can never be certain, but whatever opening there might have been narrowed further in 2003 after President Bush's invasion of Iraq. For the DPRK and its military, the ouster of Saddam Hussein conveyed a powerful message: it's not enough to pretend to have weapons of mass destruction. To be secure, a nation must build them, own them, and hide them.

I TELL MY STUDENTS THAT THE FUNDAMENTAL PURPOSE OF FOR-eign policy is elementary: to convince other countries to do what we would like them to do. To that end, there are various tools at our disposal, which range from making polite requests to sending in the Marines. The incentives we can offer include everything from words of praise to boxes of seeds to shiploads of tanks. We can apply pressure on the recalcitrant by enlisting allies, friends, and international organizations to reinforce our requests. If right is clearly on our side, we can threaten to support economic and security sanctions, or go ahead and impose them, then tighten them again and again should the government in question refuse to do what we think it must. To concentrate minds, we can arrange peaceful, yet instructive, displays of military prowess in the country's front yard. We can, if circumstances allow, use covert means to disrupt its activities so that when, for example, a missile is launched, it goes sideways not up. All the while, we can stress the benefits an accord might produce: an end to isolation, a new era of prosperity, long-term security, and peace.

In 2015, the Obama administration, its European partners, Russia, and China used elements of this formula to cause Iran to mothball or ship out the most worrisome components of its dangerous nuclear program, thus making the world safer. This landmark accomplishment would never have taken place had not economic sanctions prodded the Iranian people to pressure their leaders to find a way to make life more tolerable.

Iran, though, is a modern society—historically a trading nation—and located in the heart of Southwest Asia. The DPRK is perched on a peninsula, with a heavily fortified border to its south and China to the north. It has never embraced foreigners, and its government is neither answerable to its own people nor much interested in what outsiders think.

To those of us in the West, North Korean leaders often seem irrational, but that is because the decisions they make appear to invite trouble that, in our eyes, could easily be avoided. Officials in Pyongyang see the same world we do, but differently. Their goal is not to avoid unpleasantness but to survive. For decades, they have taught their citizens to believe in the moral goodness of their society and to think that monsters dwell without. Given the pervasiveness of those teachings, the assumption that North Koreans desire more intimate engagement with the international community is a dubious one. DPRK leaders have never shown much interest in making friends. To legitimize their harsh rule, they need enemies. They also need to look as if they're winning—or at least holding their own.

That's why Kim Il-sung developed a conventional military deterrent able to fire tens of thousands of rockets and artillery shells into the ROK in the first hour of any conflict. Most of those munitions would fall short of Seoul, but many have the range to reach the capital and beyond. Since 2016, the DPRK's nuclear and missile programs have advanced with startling speed, using what appear to be Russian designs featuring more powerful rocket engines and smaller warheads. This arsenal, too, is almost surely intended as a deterrent, but a North Korea equipped with intercontinental ballistic missiles and deliverable nuclear arms is inherently an offensive threat.

"If we have to go to war, we won't hesitate to totally destroy the United States." So predicted Mun Hyok-myong, a thirty-eight-year-old North Korean teacher speaking to a reporter from the *New York Times*. Whether the North Korean military and the founder's grandson, Kim Jong-un, share that delusion is hard to know, but every expression of fear on our part is welcomed as a victory in Pyongyang. I suspect that the newest Kim would face far greater resistance from his military if he tried to strike a deal than if he did not. North Korea is a poor habitat for doves.

When they met in the Oval Office soon after the 2016 election, President Obama told his successor that the DPRK would be the gravest national security challenge he would face. Trump has responded erratically. His first instinct was to count on China for help, a well-worn tactic that has yielded few benefits because North Korea doesn't always listen to Beijing and because U.S. and Chinese interests don't fully mesh. Trump said he would be "honored" to speak directly with Kim Jong-un, then decided that "talking is not the answer." He rebuked his own secretary of state for opening the door to negotiation, then apparently thought it smart to engage in a war of taunts with the DPRK leader, referring to Kim as "Rocket Man . . . on a suicide mission" and promising to obliterate North Korea should America be attacked. He has both adamantly opposed, and warmly endorsed, direct consultations between North and South. He restored Pyongyang to the list of state sponsors of terror—not a meaningful gesture—and urged all countries to sever relations with the DPRK, which many will not do. In addition, if reports are accurate, he has given considerable thought to a preemptive military strike.

We live with the possibility that DPRK provocations, Trump's impatience, or a technological accident or human misunderstanding will lead to a violent outbreak despite the immense peril to people on both sides of the 38th parallel. We have, after all, had close calls before, when tensions were not so fraught and leaders were more experienced. A less dire eventuality, though still unsatisfactory, is continued stalemate, with the parties snapping at each other, but neither one so angry or fearful as to take the first bite.

For now, missile defense, solidarity among allies, and economic pressure must remain at the core of U.S. policy. The third of these tools, international sanctions, has a mixed record of effectiveness. On the plus side, sanctions helped to end apartheid in South Africa and to derail nuclear programs in Libya and, under the 2015 agreement, Iran. North Korea is vulnerable to such penalties due to its relative isolation, but at the same time resistant because its population has grown accustomed to improvising and, if necessary, doing without. The government has also forged alternative revenue streams that include profits from cybertheft, smuggling, and a big share of the wages earned by citizens working abroad. North Korea is poor but almost certainly not so desperate that Kim can be coerced into bargaining away the nuclear program his father and grandfather spent the past three decades assembling.

The question then arises: How great is the likelihood of disruption to the regime from within? The information revolution has not permeated the DPRK, but it has penetrated. If accounts from refugees are accurate, North Koreans no longer believe much of what they are told by the government. They doubt, for example, that their pampered young leader, Kim Jong-un, really learned how to shoot a gun at age three and ride a horse at five. Official salaries are so low that many people see no other option but to steal what they can, thus undermining the culture of obedience. Cynicism is widespread but that sentiment is more likely to translate into a desire to leave—which requires daring—than a plan for organizing internal opposition, which seems more like suicide. There have been greater surprises in history, so a sudden collapse of this house of cards cannot be ruled out, but odds are better that if the North Korean system evolves, it will do so slowly.

This doesn't mean that diplomacy is hopeless; indeed, the door to negotiations should always be kept open. The DPRK could decide to accept international inspections and freeze or slow down the development of its nuclear and missile programs, provided it receives something in return that its leaders can crow about—such as sanctions relief and a suspension or redesign of joint military exercises by the United States and South Korea. Further down the road, diplomatic tools might, if artfully employed, eventually bring about a formal end to the Korean War, the normalization of relations, and ultimately—in return for credible security guarantees—the denuclearization of the peninsula. These objectives are unrealistic at present, but circumstances never stop changing and what is unreachable today may fall within our grasp tomorrow if we are ready. We should be, because it is hard to imagine worthier goals.

THE CONFRONTATION ON THE KOREAN PENINSULA POSES A SIG-nificant risk of war, but even should that cataclysm be avoided, the cost to humanity of DPRK Fascism is beyond any scientific measure. North Koreans are born and grow up in a society where ideological loyalty to the regime determines where and how well they live, the jobs they have, and whether they will be among the 40 percent of the population that is chronically malnourished. Citizens who are detained for political reasons or common crimes alike are consigned to vast prison camps in remote areas and may be tortured, worked to death, or starved. A person accused of a crime may be executed, in public, without trial, as may his or her family. Women and girls who are abused by government officials, prison guards, and police have no recourse. Food is used to reward docility and withheld to punish any sign of an independent spirit. The practice of religion is prohibited. Possessing an electronic device with international reach is a crime. Surveillance is nonstop, as is the propaganda blasted from loudspeakers set up in apartment buildings and village squares.

Visitors to North Korea often report that the people there seem happy. Years ago, in military-run Burma, I heard the same story from the generals who ruled then with an iron fist. "Look around," I was told. "Everyone is smiling." I thought, well, sure, but people often smile out of fear. I don't know what would happen should a free and fair election ever take place in the DPRK. We do know that when the Burmese were finally given a chance to vote, the democratic opposition won more than 85 percent of the parliamentary seats at stake. We know, as well, that North Korea today has an estimated 100,000 political prisoners, more than any other country—not a symptom of contentment.

We have grown accustomed to speaking critically about the repression of civil liberties wherever such violations take place; but in North Korea, we must ask whether something can be repressed that has never been allowed. The DPRK is a secular ISIS; its existence provides further evidence of the tragedy that can result when power is concentrated in the hands of too few for too long.

FIFTEEN

PRESIDENT OF THE UNITED STATES

T HE UNITED STATES HAS BEEN A SOURCE OF HOPE TO MIL-
lions since before its founding. Writing from Paris in
1776, Benjamin Franklin assured the Continental Congress, "All Europe is for us. Tyranny is so generally established
in the rest of the world that the prospect of an asylum in America for those who love liberty gives general joy, and our cause
is esteemed the cause of all mankind." During the Civil War,
especially in the wake of the Emancipation Proclamation, ide-
alists from many corners of Europe crossed the Atlantic to join
the crusade against slavery. In New York, an international brigade named in honor of Italian general Giuseppe Garibaldi was
formed to assist the army of Lincoln. Declared Garibaldi: "The
American question is about life for the liberty of the world." A
less rosy assessment, from a very different source, came many
years later: "The beginnings of a great new social order based on
the principle of slavery were destroyed by that war," lamented

Adolf Hitler, "and with them also the embryo of a truly great America."

Hitler fantasized that the United States so fully shared his racist views that it would ultimately side with the Third Reich. Nazi writers regularly pointed to America's anti-Asian immigration quotas and bigoted Jim Crow laws to deflect foreign criticism of their own discriminatory statutes. Even the German quest for *Lebensraum* found its model in America's westward expansion, during which, as Hitler noted, U.S. soldiers and frontiersmen "gunned down . . . millions of Redskins."

Still, the story of America's birth—wrapped in the swaddling cloth of Jefferson's prose—has always been powerful enough to overcome internal contradictions. Americans have never ceased to learn from mistakes, in part because every generation has had the ideal of equality against which to measure itself. Thus, Hitler underestimated the United States, and for that error, he paid an enormous price.

When, in the spring of 1944, I was in England with my family, we had our first close-up look at U.S. troops. In their leisure hours, the soldiers strode jauntily about, trailed by children like me calling, "Hey there, Joe, got any gum, chum?" For weeks, the GIs could be seen in their olive-green uniforms, driving camouflaged jeeps, lorries, and the peculiar-looking amphibious vehicles known as Ducks. When the time came to fight, they were ready. In the early-morning hours of June 6, Operation Overlord, the Normandy invasion, established five beachheads along a fiercely contested fifty-mile stretch of the French coast. Despite a chilly northwest wind, 160,000 troops moved across the Channel in a flotilla so thick with ships and boats that it seemed possible almost to walk from England to France. In the sky, more than eleven thousand allied warplanes weakened enemy defenses and guarded against attacks from above.

It is in such testing moments that a country discovers its own purpose and carves out a singular identity in the eyes of the world. That is also when expectations of ongoing leadership are forged. From "Give me liberty or give me death" to "Mr. Gorbachev, tear down this wall!" the United States has been counted on to speak as John Quincy Adams said early on, "though often to heedless and often to disdainful ears, the language of equal liberty, of equal justice, and of equal rights."

Such is the grand tradition and grave responsibility that every U.S. president inherits upon taking the oath of office. Each answers that call in a way reflecting that particular leader's character, integrity, and seriousness of purpose.

Donald Trump is fond of reciting a poem about a foolish but tenderhearted woman who goes for a walk one winter's day and comes across a half-frozen snake. She kindly brings the reptile into her home, lays it beside the fire, feeds it milk and honey, and restores it to health. Pleased to see the snake doing well, she picks it up and is bitten on the chest. Dying, she asks her patient why he has been ungrateful, and is told, "Shut up, silly woman, you knew damn well I was a snake before you took me in." Basking in laughter and applause, the president asks his audience, "Does that explain it, folks? Does that explain it?" Then, he adds, "We'll build the wall, folks. Don't even worry about it. Go to sleep. Go home, go to sleep."

Decades ago, George Orwell suggested that the best one-word description of a Fascist was "bully," and on the day of the Normandy invasion, Franklin Roosevelt prayed to the Almighty for a "peace invulnerable to the schemings of unworthy men." By contrast, President Trump's eyes light up when strongmen steamroll opposition, brush aside legal constraints, ignore criticism, and do whatever it takes to get their way.

Since June 2016, Rodrigo Duterte has been the head of government in the Philippines. In that time, he has gained global notoriety for his reliance on police and civilian vigilantes to kill suspected drug dealers. He insists that his shoot-first policy is tough on crime, but the knife-edge of that toughness falls on what is already the most disadvantaged portion of his country's population. Per news reports, the number of Filipinos slain by police during Duterte's presidency exceeds ten thousand. We don't know, and neither does he, how many of the dead carried weapons, how many were guilty of peddling drugs, and how many were gunned down by mistake or for no reason at all. We do know that Duterte has concentrated his fire on the streets and that the people who profit most from the drug trade live in penthouses or in walled estates. We know as well that the police solicit bribes to remove names from their kill lists, that many families of the victims are so poor they must rely on charity to buy coffins, and that Duterte plays the whole sad issue for laughs, urging the public to invest in funeral parlors and bragging, "I'll supply the dead bodies." Duterte has told police officers who are on trial for abusing their authority to go ahead and plead guilty so he can pardon and promote them. Early in his presidency, Donald Trump phoned Duterte to congratulate him for doing an "unbelievable job."

In 2013, Egyptian general Abdel Fattah el-Sisi seized power in a military coup. As president, he turned the clock back on the Arab Spring and installed precisely the kind of politically airless regime that Tahrir Square demonstrators thought they had rid themselves of two years earlier. Today, once more, an Egyptian government is censoring public debate, using lethal force against protesters, harassing journalists, outlawing political opposition, and filling its jails with tens of thousands of dissidents—some secular, some religious. There is no more reliable formula for generating future terrorists. In Donald Trump's view, el-Sisi is "fantastic."

The Kingdom of Bahrain systematically discriminates against its Shiite Muslim majority, robs dissidents of their citizenship, maintains a tight lid on civil society, and refuses to tolerate serious political opposition. The United States and Bahrain share important strategic interests but the relationship has been strained, in the past, by disagreements over human rights. In 2017, President Trump assured the country's monarch that "there won't be strain with this administration."

In April of that same year, President Erdoğan narrowly won a popular referendum to amend the Turkish constitution, add to his powers, and enable him to remain in office, potentially, until 2029. Most democratic leaders found this outcome regrettable. Trump's response was to reach for the phone and laud Erdoğan on his win.

The president's admiration for autocrats is so ingrained that it extends to men even less worthy of respect than these. To Trump, Saddam Hussein "was a bad guy, a really bad guy. But you know what he did well? He killed terrorists. He did that so good. They didn't read them the rights. They didn't talk. They were a terrorist, it was over." As for Kim Jong-un: "You have to give him credit. How many young guys—he was like 26 or 25 when his father died—take over these tough generals, and all of a sudden . . . he's the boss. It's incredible. He wiped out the uncle. He wiped out this one, that one. I mean, this guy doesn't play games." Finally, there's Vladimir Putin: "a man so highly respected within his own country and beyond."

There is nothing unusual about one national leader speaking well of another. A spoonful of sugar can be as helpful in dealing with foreign diplomats as it is in child psychology, for these are not unrelated fields. Trump, then, cannot be faulted for trying to develop cordial relations with his counterparts overseas; indeed, that is a key element of his job. Two aspects of his approach, however, are troubling. First, he often endorses actions by foreign leaders that weaken democratic institutions. Second, while he may think it rude to criticize a country such as China or Russia on human rights, he hasn't hesitated to pick fights on immigration policy with our ally Australia, or with British leaders on anti-Muslim tweets, or on trade with such valued commercial partners as Mexico, Canada, "bad, very bad" Germany, or—with horrendous timing—a nuclear-threatened South Korea.

When Ambassador Nikki Haley claims, oddly, that her boss "slaps the right people [and] hugs the right people," she speaks the truth upside down.

TRUMP'S VIEW OF THE UNITED STATES IS DARK. AMONG HIS FA-vorite mantras are that U.S. courts are biased, the FBI is corrupt, the press almost always lies, and elections are rigged. The domestic impact of these condemnations is to demoralize and divide. Americans have never heard a president speak with such persistent scorn about U.S. institutions. But Trump's audience is a global one. Instead of encouraging others to respect and follow the example of the United States, he invites the opposite. That reversal has a harmful effect, particularly in countries where there are few practical checks on executive power. In such places, the lives of investigative reporters, independent jurists, and others who pursue truth are at risk under the best of circumstances. The danger intensifies when the occupant of the White House ridicules the credibility of their professions. This is not to say that journalists and judges should be beyond criticism, but Trump's allegations are so thoughtless and broad that they can be—and are—used to discredit entire callings that are essential to democracy.

During his first month in office, Trump excluded some prominent reporters from a press briefing. Almost immediately, the government of Cambodia threatened to kick a contingent of American journalists out of its country. Spokesmen in Phnom Penh said they perceived a "clear message" from Trump that "news broadcast by those media outlets does not reflect the truth," adding that "Freedom of expression . . . must respect the state's power."

Cambodia's was the first of many governments—others include those of Hungary, Libya, Poland, Russia, Somalia, and Thailand—to insist that negative stories about them are false for no reason except that the press cannot be trusted. According to the *People's Daily*, the house organ of the Chinese Communist Party: "If the president of the United States claims that his nation's media outlets are a stain on America, then negative stories about China should be taken with a grain of salt, since it is likely that the bias and political agenda are distorting the real picture." The ability of a free and independent press to hold political leaders accountable is what makes open government possible—it is the heartbeat of democracy. Trump is intent on stilling, or slowing down, that heartbeat. This is a gift to dictators, and coming from a chief executive of the United States, cause for shame.

In Washington and overseas, the president has met with numerous leaders who ignore the civil and political rights of their citizens. Instead of urging them to reform, he changes the subject. When his administration does take a stand on human rights, it is to lob criticisms at the easiest of targets, such as Cuba, Venezuela, and Iran.

During his campaign, candidate Trump was asked about the importance of due process. He answered, "When the world looks at how bad the United States is, and then we go and talk about civil liberties, I don't think we're a very good messenger." For a person so quick to think the best of himself, it is peculiar that the president seems blind to what is most important about America—and so reluctant to speak out on behalf of principles that are more intimately associated with the United States than any other country.

As UN ambassador and secretary of state, I sought meetings with literally hundreds of foreign officials to urge, for example, freedom for a political prisoner, the release of a jailed journalist, support for religious liberty, or respect for a fair and open electoral process. These were not, as a rule, pleasant encounters—my hosts would offer me tea and a cookie; I'd say, "Thank you," then start

complaining. The Chinese were particularly vehement in arguing that such matters are not anybody's business but their own.

Ordinarily, this isn't the sort of discussion during which either
side will concede a point, but that doesn't mean that the give-and-
take is without value. At a minimum, raising human rights cases
can put violators on the defensive and force them to cope with
inquiries from the media. It can also save lives. Jimmy Carter and
Ronald Reagan were very different presidents, but the transition
between the two early in 1981 was marked by a historic bit of col-
laboration. Convinced that the firmly anti-Communist Reagan
wouldn't object, the South Korean dictatorship prepared to ex-
ecute the country's best-known liberal dissident, Kim Dae-jung.
At Carter's request, Reagan sent his top national security aide
to Seoul with the message that he *did* object—firmly. Kim Dae-
jung's life was spared, and eighteen years later, I had the pleasure
of meeting with him following his election as Korea's president.

As to America's standing to argue on behalf of human rights, my
reply is that "standing" is beside the point. The real question is: who
has the *responsibility* to uphold human rights? The answer to that is:
everyone. If a blemished record were enough to disqualify a country from speaking out, governments could murder, torture, and
otherwise brutalize their citizens without the least fear of criticism
or sanctions. Such a world would be less stable and filled with more
suffering than the one we have. Why would we want that? To the
extent that the United States lives in a glass house, we need to repair
it; but there is no excuse for a "see no evil, hear no evil" approach
to the clash between democracy and dictatorship. Being accused of
having double standards is preferable to being convicted—due to
our own refusal to act—of honoring no standards at all.

For decades our country has lived through the greatest jobs
theft in the history of the world. You people know it better

than anybody in Pennsylvania. Our factories were shut-
tered, our steel mills closed down, and our jobs were stolen
away and shipped far away to other countries, some of which
you've never even heard of. Politicians sent troops to pro-
tect the borders of foreign nations, but left America's borders
wide open for all to violate.

We've spent billions and billions of dollars on one global
project after another, and yet, as gangs flooded into our
country, we couldn't even provide safety for our own people.

Our government rushed to join international agreements
where the United States pays the costs and bears the bur-
dens, while other countries get the benefit and pay nothing.

These remarks, delivered to an appreciative crowd in Harrisburg, Pennsylvania, in April 2017, are typical of Trump's rhetoric.
Here again, the picture they paint is bleak. The president claims
that the United States has "been disrespected, mocked and ripped
off for many, many years by people that were smarter, shrewder,
tougher." He wants his countrymen to see themselves as the victims of negotiators who have given handouts to foreigners in return for nothing and who gullibly sign on to blatantly unfair trade
and climate deals. This gloomy assessment is greeted with whis-
tles and handclaps by the many Americans who, for one reason or
another, feel aggrieved. The sources of that ill feeling may include
economic hardship, discomfort with social and cultural changes,
or a skeptic's conviction that most public servants are incompe-
tent, crooked, or both.

Trump has been voicing similar opinions for decades so his
sincerity cannot reasonably be questioned, but his approach is
that of a demagogue. His analysis is filled with full-throated as-
sertions that are riddled with bunkum and his arguments are
designed to exploit insecurities and stir up resentment. A speaker
with a more objective approach might have noted the decline in

Pennsylvania's unemployment to below 5 percent, from 8 percent a few years earlier, and the more than 200,000 jobs in the state that are supported by exports, largely to Canada, Mexico, and China. Nationally, between 2009 and 2016, inflation remained low, the jobless rate declined by more than half, and the U.S. workforce grew by twelve million. Trump inherited an economy that, among countries larger than Switzerland, was the world's most competitive. There is always room for improvement, but the picture the president paints of an America that has been losing in negotiation after negotiation is simply false. His apparent intention, therefore, is not to address and alleviate anger, but to inflame it.

THE ARCHITECTS OF THE TRUMP ADMINISTRATION'S FOREIGN policy use two labels to describe the structure they have built: "Principled Realism" and "Putting America First." Principled Realism is merely a slogan; America First is a slogan with a past. Founded in 1940, the America First Committee (AFC) brought together pacifists, isolationists, and Nazi sympathizers to fight against the country's prospective entry into World War II. The AFC opposed creation of the Selective Service and also a Roosevelt initiative, known as Lend-Lease, to keep the British in food and arms as they struggled to survive the German onslaught. Within twelve months of its founding, the committee had built a membership of more than 800,000 and attracted support from across the political spectrum—corporate tycoons and Socialists alike. Contributing mightily to its popularity was the famed aviator Charles Lindbergh, who worried that Jewish influence was pushing the country into a conflict it did not, in his view, have reason to fight.

Four days after the Japanese attack on Pearl Harbor, Hitler declared war on the United States. The AFC soon disbanded and, in the intervening decades, its name has carried the stigma of naïveté and moral blindness. Now "America First" is back—but what does it mean?

The president says that "every decision on trade, on taxes, on immigration, on foreign affairs, will be made to benefit American workers and American families." At the UN, he declared, "I will always put America first, just like you, as the leaders of your countries, will always and should always put your countries first." This premise—that every nation can be expected to look out for its own interests—is hardly a revelation. Who would assume anything different? What the assertion ignores is the stake that all countries have in the fates of others. Lindbergh was willing to live with a Nazi-dominated Europe because he saw that as preferable to the risks and costs of war. What if his view had prevailed and the Third Reich still ruled? Would that really have served America's interests?

Trump's top advisers have praised him for his "clear-eyed outlook that the world is not a 'global community' but an arena where nations, nongovernmental actors and businesses engage and compete for advantage." This formulation puzzles because, although it's fair to say the world isn't exactly Sesame Street, it *is* a place where people from all countries must live. To reduce the sum of our existence to a competitive struggle for advantage among more than two hundred nations is not clear-eyed but myopic. People and nations compete, but that is not all that they do. Imagine a small town in America or a village in Africa or a city in Asia where there is no sense of community, no sharing of responsibility, no looking out for the other guy—just a grim daily fight to "win" at the expense of neighbors. Whose interests would that put first?

Globally, there is hardly an economic, security, technological, environmental, or health-related challenge that any country can better address alone than through a joint effort with neighbors. It is the duty of diplomats to foster that cooperation. Trump's view of life as a wilderness of Darwinian dogfights doesn't correspond to the intricately interdependent world in which we must frequently join forces if we are to make the best of our lot.

Responsible governments understand this, but responsible governments aren't the ones that cause the most pain. Designating "(Fill in the blank) First" as the golden rule of international relations provides an all-purpose justification for tyrants to do as they like. What is Pyongyang's rationale for building nuclear weapons if not to put North Korean interests first? By annexing Crimea, Putin placed Russian desires above international law. Why, if not for its own benefit, does Iran intervene in the affairs of its neighbors? For centuries, imperial powers perpetrated physical and economic atrocities against colonial populations to exalt their own countries and monarchs. Hitler invaded Czechoslovakia to help the Fatherland "compete for advantage." Underlying Fascism is the theory that nations are entitled to take what they want for no other reason than that they want it. There are better golden rules.

A second source of blurriness in Trump's vision is that it offers no incentive for friendship. If every nation is focused entirely on gaining an edge over every other, there can be no trust, no special relationships, no reward for helpfulness, and no penalty for cynicism—because cynicism is all we promise and all we expect. This attitude explains the president's peculiar view of NATO as a protection scheme in which the United States is "owed" billions of dollars for supposedly hiring out its armed forces to provide security for others. Personally, I have never conceived of NATO as a business proposition; it is something far more valuable. The Alliance is a unique political and military arrangement that for more than seven decades has allowed Europe and the United States to prepare, train, share intelligence, and fight against common dangers. It's the cornerstone of world peace and a living testament to our collective will; you can't put a price on that.

The course I teach at Georgetown is about the tools of foreign policy and how to use them. From what I've seen, the president would have a hard time passing it. He considers himself a master at bluster and bluff, which can be an effective tactic, when applied sparingly. During the Cold War, Henry Kissinger tried to pry concessions out of the Soviets by suggesting that Nixon was a little crazy and that there was no telling what he might do if he didn't get his way. Given Trump's undisciplined style, a similar strategy now would certainly have the advantage of credibility. Trump can seem unhinged. But unpredictability is a trait, not a strategy. The question is whether the president's penchant for insults and off-the-wall threats is linked to a plan for making progress toward specific national security objectives.

If so, how well is that plan working? Are key foreign leaders seeking to mollify Trump by becoming more supportive of U.S. goals, or are they tuning him out and negotiating their own agreements? Is the president persuading others to follow him, or is he being manipulated into echoing the agendas of others, as, for example, Saudi Arabia in the Middle East? In a craft requiring experience, sound judgment, and the vision to understand the impact of today's decisions on tomorrow's world, how well is Trump measuring up when compared to his peers?

As in most arenas, foreign policy perceptions help to shape foreign policy outcomes. I, for one, do not foreclose the possibility that the president's brash disregard for diplomatic convention might, in some cases, be exactly what's needed to awaken people to new possibilities. No one who has been in a position of trust, including myself, can look back at their time in office without regret at the many problems left unsolved. Maybe Trump does have the answer, as he has claimed, to forging better trade agreements, securing Arab-Israeli peace, ending North Korea's nuclear program, and combatting violent extremism. I hope he does.

There are those who consider Trump to be an unintelligent man. I make no such accusation. I do, however, confess to concern about his steadiness and the transparent brittleness of his ego. Publicly, to date, his record of achievement is sparse, but the president admits to no doubts about how well he is doing. His comment to the *New York Times*: "So I go to Poland and make a speech. Enemies of mine in the media, enemies of mine are saying it was the greatest speech ever made on foreign soil by a president." To Fox News regarding the record number of high-level vacancies in the State Department: "I'm the only one that matters." To *Time* magazine: "I'm a very instinctual person, but my instinct turns out to be right." To the whole world on Twitter, I'm "a very stable genius."

Genius or not, this presidency has often been painful to observe. I find it shocking to cross the Atlantic and hear America described as a threat to democratic institutions and values. A month after Trump's inauguration, the head of the European Council listed four dangers to the EU: Russia, terrorism, China, and the United States. In the wake of one Trump visit, an exasperated Angela Merkel said, "The times in which we can fully count on others are somewhat over." Since early 2017, surveys show a marked decline in respect for the United States. In Germany, belief that the American president can be counted on to do the right thing shrank from 86 percent under his predecessor to 11 percent under Trump. In France, the fall was from 84 percent to 14; in Japan, 74 to 24; in South Korea, 84 to 17.

It is true that Trump has learned while in office. At times, he has shown real awareness of the gravity of his responsibilities. He deserves credit for preserving Crimea-related sanctions against Russia, sending arms to a beleaguered Ukraine, and managing an effective military campaign against ISIS. In December 2017, he implemented a law, the Global Magnitsky Act, that imposes penalties on individuals and entities accused of corruption and human rights violations. Beneath the headlines, many U.S. positions on other important issues have gone unaltered. Too often, however,

Trump has attempted to fulfill campaign promises that he should never have made. The list is a long one and includes: renunciation of the Paris Climate Agreement; putting at risk the benefits of the North America Free Trade Agreement; badmouthing the Iran nuclear pact; squandering resources on the Mexico wall; trying to ban Muslim immigrants; and proposing to slash our budget for diplomacy, development, and environmental health. These and other actions have raised widespread questions about America's willingness to assist—let alone lead—in solving global problems. If greatness is the objective, we are headed the wrong way.

I am often asked whether I am an optimist or a pessimist. My reply is, "I am an optimist who worries a lot." I continue to believe that the United States banked enough international goodwill in the interval between George Washington and Barack Obama to recover from the present embarrassment—but I am not sure how extensive or lasting the harm will be, hence the worries.

The potential damage may be of several types. Trump's election alone cast doubt in international circles on the judgment of the American people and on the reliability of the democratic system to produce defensible outcomes. That is disheartening for pro-freedom activists worldwide and welcome news for autocrats and for other leaders who have major disagreements with the United States.

The commander in chief's swaggering disregard for how his words are perceived has at times stunned the world, including allies of long standing in Europe and Asia. Our shared interests are so deep that I expect alliance members to continue working with America when possible. However, many of them fear—as I do—that the unilateralist mind-set espoused by Trump will endure in the United States even after the man himself has retired.

The president's penchant for denigrating other countries has cost America an immense amount of goodwill while boosting the electoral prospects of foreign politicians who express hostility toward Washington and its policies. His animus directed at Muslims is even more harmful because it reinforces the narrative fostered by terrorist leaders that the United States is at war with Islam and wants to hold Muslims down. Early in his term, the president went to the Arabian Peninsula, denounced Iran, sold the Arab establishment some weapons, and called it a historic victory in the fight against violent extremism. It wasn't. Late in 2017, he recognized Jerusalem as Israel's capital and said the decision would bring closer the prospect of peace between Israel and the Palestinians. I wish that were the case, but the more likely outcome is a complete loss of credibility for U.S. diplomats as honest brokers within the region.

There is a cost attached as well to Trump's antiquated ideas on trade. The president is obsessed with correcting imbalances between exports and imports that have little effect on overall prosperity or the creation of well-paying jobs. Instead of focusing on the modernization of commercial agreements, raising labor and environmental standards, and enforcing rules already on the books, the president tosses around insults and ultimatums. His withdrawal from the previous administration's proposed Trans-Pacific Partnership has contributed to a loss of American prestige in the world's most dynamic region at a time when President Xi Jinping of China has emerged as the most powerful leader of his country since the apogee of the Qing Dynasty in the eighteenth century. Historically, the United States has served to balance Chinese presence in the Asia-Pacific, but Trump's scattershot approach to relationships has tarnished America's image. All the while Beijing has been systematically expanding its economic clout in the Pacific region and also in Central and South Asia, Europe, the Middle East, North Africa, and Latin America—pretty much everywhere. Because of Trump's "America First" fixation, China can portray itself as a champion of free trade despite having substantially higher tariffs, more rigorous market restrictions, and more onerous barriers to foreign investment than the United States. Because influence in one arena often overlaps into others, I fear that the next U.S. president will inherit a world more inclined to follow Beijing's lead not only on economic matters but also on lowering norms in such key areas as labor standards, media freedom, religious liberty, and human rights.

It is important to remember that actions taken today depend largely on expectations about the future. If a country feels abandoned by the United States, or uncertain about its leadership, that nation may see a need to act more forcefully—and perhaps unwisely—on its own. At a minimum, the country may see no choice but to invest in what amounts to foreign policy insurance by strengthening ties to others, leaving America on the outside looking in. There is also the chance that intemperate words and ill-conceived threats will ramp up tensions suddenly, induce panic on the part of some, and lead everyone over the cliff to war. There are certainly enough trouble spots—beginning with the Middle East and the Korean Peninsula—to merit anxiety. During the Cold War, we installed hotlines so the U.S. president could allay any misunderstandings by talking directly to a foreign leader. I'm not sure how much faith we would invest in that option today.

Finally, and even more seriously, I fear a return to the international climate that prevailed in the 1920s and '30s, when the United States withdrew from the global stage and countries everywhere pursued what they perceived to be their own interests without regard to larger and more enduring goals. When arguing that every age has its own Fascism, Italian writer and Holocaust survivor Primo Levi added that the critical point can be reached "not just through the terror of police intimidation, but by denying and distorting information, by undermining systems of justice, by paralyzing the education system, and by spreading in a myriad subtle ways nostalgia for a world where order reigned." If he is right (and I think he is), we have reason to be concerned by the gathering array of political and social currents buffeting us today—currents propelled by the dark underside of the technological revolution, the corroding effects of power, the American president's disrespect for truth, and the widening acceptance of dehumanizing insults, Islamophobia, and anti-Semitism as being within the bounds of normal public debate. We are not there yet, but these feel like signposts on the road back to an era when Fascism found nourishment and individual tragedies were multiplied millions-fold.

SIXTEEN

BAD DREAMS

S ET IN THE VEGETABLE MARKETS OF CHICAGO, *THE RESIST-ible Rise of Arturo Ui* is a parable of how Fascists can ascend to the top in any community. In Bertolt Brecht's play, an ambitious gangster, egged on by unscrupulous aides, blackmails a politician into appointing him to a position of power. From there, a few acts of betrayal, some finely targeted violence, a little instruction in public speaking, and a couple of threats are enough to crush all rivals. By the final curtain, the gangster has seduced the public, silenced the press, cowed the courts, and eliminated all opposition, even while admitting to "not being loved."

Written in 1941, the script parodies Hitler's rise and shows Fascism to be a vicious predator, quick to exploit—among other human frailties—timidity and greed. Brecht stresses a further point: that for Fascism to extend its reach from the streets to the high offices of state, it must secure backing from multiple sectors of society. This insight has value today because of the growing tendency in the media to portray Fascism as a logical outgrowth of populism and to attribute both allegiances to an unhappy lower middle class, as if anti-democratic sentiments were the exclusive property of one economic tier. They're not, and there is nothing inherently biased or intolerant about being a populist, which Merriam-Webster defines as "a believer in the rights, wisdom, or virtues of the common people." Were I to be given the choice of sitting inside or outside that large circle of believers, my response would be, "Include me in."

In the United States, *populism* was first associated with the American People's Party, founded in 1890. The movement attracted workers from coast to coast, including farmers angry at railroads for charging too much to transport crops. Its presidential candidate, James B. Weaver, promised to raise taxes on the wealthy, nationalize telephone and telegraph lines, and resist the "haughty millionaires who are gathering up the riches of the new world." In the 1892 election, Weaver carried five states.

Four decades on, in the 1930s, Louisiana senator Huey Long needled Franklin Roosevelt from the left. Flying the banner "Every Man a King," Long claimed to speak for families denied their fair share of the American Dream. His rousing call for income guarantees, property limits, and old-age pensions inspired the formation of more than 27,000 "Share Our Wealth" clubs. With the Great Depression as a backdrop, Long could have made a formidable candidate for the White House had he not, in 1935, been assassinated by one of his many political enemies.*

In the late 1960s, Alabama's George Wallace weighed in from the anti-Washington right, hurling calculated gibes at the rich, welfare queens, hippies, civil rights advocates, and "pointy-headed college professors who can't even park a bicycle straight." Like

---

* Long is thought to be the model for Senator Berzelius "Buzz" Windrip, the Fascist elected president in Sinclair Lewis's cautionary novel *It Can't Happen Here* (1935).

Long, he was often called a Fascist, to which Wallace, an Army Air Corps sergeant in the latter stages of World War II, replied, "I was killing Fascists when you punks were in diapers." In 1972, he was shot while campaigning in Maryland and spent the remainder of his life in a wheelchair, apologizing for his racist past, and getting reelected as governor.

Twenty years later, Texas oil billionaire Ross Perot attacked the entire political establishment from the vantage point of a folksy, fed-up, libertarian, penny-pinching nationalist. Matched against Bill Clinton and the senior George Bush, he captured 19 percent of the 1992 presidential vote by campaigning against corruption, budget deficits, and the "giant sucking sound" of U.S. companies and jobs moving to Mexico. Perot blamed both parties for a big-government "propaganda machine in Washington that . . . Goebbels would have just envied."

These examples barely scratch the surface.

From the Republic's earliest days, candidates for office in the United States have affirmed a deeply rooted belief "in the rights, wisdom, and virtues" of the common people. Why? Because common people are the majority, and having the majority on one's side is a pretty good strategy for winning elections. No wonder, then, that American presidential campaigns have been enlivened by an array of folksy nicknames, from "Old Hickory" Andrew Jackson, "Young Hickory" James Polk, and "Old Rough and Ready" Zachary Taylor to "the Rail-Splitter" Abraham Lincoln, "Unconditional Surrender" Grant, "Boatman Jim" Garfield, "the Great Commoner" William Jennings Bryan, "Fighting Bob" La Follette, "Give 'Em Hell" Harry Truman, and "the Gipper" Ronald Reagan. In addition, Ivy Leaguers such as Barack Obama, George W. Bush, and both Roosevelts struck populist chords whenever they could, and even Richard Nixon claimed to champion a neglected constituency: the "silent majority."

Historically, populism has wielded a broad brush, but a lot of people now seem determined to paint it into a corner. The 2017 annual report of Human Rights Watch bears the title *The Dangerous Rise of Populism*, as if populism were inherently a threat to civil liberties. Headline writers often refer to Vladimir Putin as a standard-bearer for global populism, even though his inner circle is dominated by former KGB agents and nothing irritates him more than a demonstrator with a bullhorn. Donald Trump is routinely described as a populist despite his country-club lifestyle, a cabinet stocked with billionaires, and a penchant for hiring foreigners to make the beds in his hotels and to stitch together clothes stamped with his brand. In Europe, right-wing political movements have been called populist because of their "illiberal" tendencies, but by that measure, military dictatorships would be among the most populist states on earth.

Consider that, though street protests are rightly taken as signs of populism, fighting corruption is the most frequent theme of such demonstrations, and as we have witnessed in—among other countries—South Korea, Brazil, Romania, Peru, and Guatemala, there is nothing illiberal about exposing crooks. Opposition to immigration is often assumed to be a populist trait, and yet in the United States it is the "Dreamer" movement that displays the traditional earmarks of populism: a community-level effort to empower voices not previously heeded. Similarly, racial bias is regularly associated with populists, and fairly so in some cases; but it was the Reverend Dr. Martin Luther King Jr. who got more Americans into the streets with linked arms and signs demanding change than any other. In Europe today, right-wing protesters are often confronted by left-wing protesters—who speaks for the common people then?

This doesn't make sense. If populists are, as some suggest, the bad guys in an epic debate about the future of democracy, who exactly are the good guys? Elitists? I don't think so. In fact, elitists pose a more lethal threat to freedom than populists, but neither term is precise, and both have been so thoroughly abused as to be almost meaningless. We need to do a better job of describing the reality we confront.

There are two kinds of Fascists: those who give orders and those who take them. A popular base gives Fascism the legs it needs to march, the lungs it uses to proclaim, and the muscle it relies on to menace—but that's Fascism from the neck down. To create tyranny out of the fears and hopes of average people, money is required, and so, too, ambition and twisted ideas. It is the combination that kills. In the absence of wealthy backers, we likely would never have heard of Corporal Mussolini or Corporal Hitler. In the absence of their compulsion to dominate at all costs, neither would have caused the harm he did.

Most political movements of appreciable size are populist to one degree or another, but that doesn't make them Fascist, or even intolerant. Whether they seek to limit immigration or expand it, criticize Islam or defend it, lobby for peace or agitate for war, all are democratic, provided they pursue their goals by democratic means. What makes a movement Fascist is not ideology but the willingness to do whatever is necessary—including the use of force and trampling on the rights of others—to achieve victory and command obedience.

It is worth remembering, too, that Fascism rarely makes a dramatic entrance. Typically, it begins with a seemingly minor character—Mussolini in a crowded cellar, Hitler on a street corner—who steps forward only as dramatic events unfold. The story advances when the opportunity to act comes and Fascists alone are prepared to strike. That is when small aggressions, if unopposed, grow into larger ones, when what was objectionable is accepted, and when contrarian voices are drowned out.

Soon enough, the government that silences a media outlet finds muffling a second easier. The parliament that outlaws one political party has a precedent for banning the next. The majority that strips a particular minority of its rights doesn't stop there. The security force that beats protesters and gets away with it doesn't hesitate before doing so again, and when repression helps a dictator in country A to extend his hold on power, the rulers in country B embark on a parallel road. Before too long, Mussolini's prescription has been followed and once again, feather by feather, the chicken is plucked.

Consider the testimony of a well-educated but not politically minded German who experienced the rise of the Third Reich:

> *To live in this process is absolutely not to be able to notice it—please try to believe me. . . . Each step was so small, so inconsequential, so well explained or, on occasion, "regretted," that, unless one were detached from the whole process from the beginning, unless one understood what . . . all these "little measures" that no "patriotic German" could resent must some day lead to, one no more saw it developing from day to day than a farmer in his field sees the corn growing. . . .*
>
> *And one day, too late, your principles, if you were ever sensible of them, all rush in upon you. The burden of self-deception has grown too heavy, and some minor incident, in my case my little boy, hardly more than a baby, saying "Jew swine," collapses it all at once, and you see that everything, everything, has changed and changed completely under your nose.*

GIVEN THAT FASCISM TENDS TO TAKE HOLD IN A STEP-BY-STEP manner rather than by making one giant leap, could it ever proceed very far in America before being stopped? Is the United States immune to this malady—or susceptible?

Before addressing those questions, I ask you to envision Uncle Sam in his long white nightshirt, tossing and turning, his sleep disturbed by three very bad dreams.

In the first, reactionary billionaires conspire to monopolize media platforms and pour their riches into the campaigns of favored candidates who, when in office, ensure the selection of compliant judges. Laws are enacted to ban Muslim immigrants, criminalize abortions, unfairly restrict voting, divert funding for public education to private schools, and drill for oil here, there, and everywhere. The president is given full authority to issue or revoke broadcasting licenses, expand Guantánamo to include domestic criminal suspects, and bar investigations of himself. From cradle to grave, an increasing number of citizens spend their lives within a conservative echo chamber, where they watch nothing but Fox News, memorize the Breitbart catechism, and learn only what goose-stepping right-wingers want them to know. Finally, as climate change advances and epic floods inundate our cities, heavily armed civilian militias are organized to protect private property, made bold by the promise of presidential pardons should anyone pull a trigger in "self-defense."

Nightmare number two: Wealthy liberals from Hollywood and New York invest their money in favored candidates who, when elected, conspire to enforce rigid standards of political correctness across all the major institutions of society—government, police, media, sports, theater, universities, and kindergarten classrooms. Anyone who violates these vague and unwritten norms, or is accused of having done so, is labeled a bigot and fired. Right-wing speakers are barred from public gatherings because their exercise of free speech might injure the sensitivities of club-wielding anti-Fascists. Gender-specific bathrooms are banned as discriminatory, and terrorists pour across our borders because to stop them would require racial profiling. The Second Amendment is repealed, fossil fuels are prohibited, and an increasing number of citizens spend their entire lives within a Socialist echo chamber, learning only what Fascist liberals want them to know.

Nightmare number three: The United States is hit by multiple terror attacks, killing thousands, with responsibility claimed by U.S.-based Muslim radicals. A shaken president begs Americans to trust their government and not take the law into their own hands. Although acknowledging the need for toughness, the White House refuses to round up Muslims or shut mosques down. In the wake of yet another terrorist assault, and another, and another, a mesmerizing young orator appears on television—and Twitter—to accuse leaders from both major parties of cowardice. He calls for a revolution that will free the country from the lies that have been sapping its will and shackling its might. He vows to smash and destroy the terrorists just as they have done to the innocent men, women, and children slain in their loathsome strikes. He pledges a baptism by fire that will bring about a great awakening, the rebirth of America as it used to be—independent, proud, brave, pure, and worthy of God's blessing. He beseeches listeners to prepare their minds and bodies for the struggles to come—not only against the terrorists but also against their apologists and enablers. He warns them that their enemies are already preparing to attack, so their only chance is to strike first. "We must not hesitate," he shouts. "They will say we are barbarians, and they are right. We want to be barbarians. It is an honorable title. Let us harden our hearts and take America back!"

I PUT THE QUESTION TO MY CLASS OF GRADUATE STUDENTS AT Georgetown: "Can a Fascist movement establish a significant foothold in the United States?" Immediately, one young man responded, "Yes, it can. Why? Because we're so sure it can't." His argument is that Americans have so much faith in the resilience of our democratic institutions that we will ignore for too long the incremental erosion that is taking place in them. Instead of mobilizing, we will proceed merrily along, expecting all to turn out for the best, until one morning we open our eyes, draw back the curtains, and find ourselves in a quasi-Fascist state.

The student explained that, in his view, neither Democratic nor Republican leaders know what to do about Trump. They still haven't grasped how he could have been nominated and elected while ignoring every piece of high-priced strategic advice he received and doing or saying enough offensive things to doom any other candidate a dozen times over. Party leaders don't understand why, through the many tribulations of his unfolding presidency, Trump's political base has remained combative and firm—and what politicians can't comprehend, they won't be able to cure.

The president's poll numbers are mediocre, it's true, but they are still more robust than those of the congressional leaders who have been forced to cross sabers with him. Yet those leaders continue to engage in the kind of partisan spats that opened the door to Trump in the first place. The Republicans appear gutless because few have dared complain even while their party is taken over by people who despise them; the Democrats seem unaware that something similar might happen to them. The vital center, which in the past has saved the country from divisions over a host of contentious issues, has become a lonely place—historically an augury of more extreme problems in the offing.

What the country needs is a plainspoken commitment by responsible leaders from both parties to address national needs together, accompanied by a general plan of action for doing so. Instead, Republicans are guarding their right flank and Democrats their left, leaving a gaping hole in the only place in the ideological spectrum where lasting agreements on behalf of the common good can be forged. Years from now, we may look back on Trump as a onetime oddity who taught us a lesson we will not forget about the quirks of democracy. We may also look back on him as the agent of a political fracturing from which it will take decades to recover, during which every president will fail because the only càndidates elected are those who make promises impossible to keep. Much depends on the lesson politicians draw from recent experience—whether it is better to reject Trumpism, or copy it.

That's one reason for concern. There are others.

We have learned from history that Fascists can reach high office via elections. When they do, the first step they attempt is to undermine the authority of competing power centers, including parliament or, in America, Congress. As another of my students noted, the United States has been at war since 2001 based on a sixty-word-long congressional authorization to use force against those who "planned, authorized, committed, or aided" the September 11 terror attacks. That straightforward phrase has since been relied on by Presidents Bush, Obama, and Trump to justify anti-terror operations not only in Afghanistan and Pakistan but also Cameroon, Djibouti, Eritrea, Ethiopia, Georgia, Iraq, Kenya, Libya, Niger, the Philippines, Somalia, Syria, Uganda, and Yemen. Much of this activity has been directed at groups that did not even exist in 2001. The connection between the original authorization and the subsequent actions has stretched to a thinness no longer visible.

One might think that members of Congress would be eager to reassert their constitutional right to declare war and to set boundaries on the use of force. Some are, but the majorities of both parties have chosen to duck the responsibility. Hawks fear that a second resolution would tie the president's hands; doves are wary of giving the commander in chief what might amount to a blank check. So year after year they do nothing. As a result, three presidents have ordered thousands of military strikes over a period of years based solely on their own judgment of effectiveness and need. It's hard to imagine an authority more susceptible to future abuse. Aware of this, President Obama urged Congress to approve new legislation—to no avail. Congress isn't doing its job in this arena, just as it has become über-politicized and undereffective in so many others—approving a budget, scrutinizing nominations, conducting objective investigations, overseeing government agencies, and holding serious hearings before trying to rush through laws.

My students point to additional troubling developments. Fascism feeds on social and economic grievances, including the belief that *the people over there are receiving better treatment than they deserve while I'm not getting what I'm owed.* It seems today that almost everyone has a grievance: the unemployed steelworker, the low-wage fast-food employee, the student up to her ears in debt, the businessperson who feels harassed by government regulations, the veteran waiting too long for a doctor's appointment, the fundamentalist who thinks war is being waged against Christmas, the professional with her head brushing against a glass ceiling, the Wall Street broker who feels unfairly maligned, the tycoon who still thinks he is being overtaxed.

Obviously, personal gripes—legitimate or not—have been part of the human condition ever since Cain decided to work out his jealousy on his brother. What is an added concern now is the lack of effective mechanisms for assuaging anger. As described above, we all tend to live in media and information bubbles that reinforce our grievances instead of causing us to look at difficult questions from many sides. Rather than think critically, we seek out people who share our opinions and who encourage us to ridicule the ideas of those whose convictions and perspectives clash with our own. At many levels, contempt has become a defining characteristic of American politics. It makes us unwilling to listen to what others say—unwilling, in some cases, even to allow them to speak. This stops the learning process cold and creates a ready-made audience for demagogues who know how to bring diverse groups of the aggrieved together in righteous opposition to everyone else. Consider this summons: "The time has come for a movement that takes the best of the left and the right, forging a new unity amongst the various peoples who make up America, molding them into a single people, a united nation." Such is the benign rallying cry of a group calling itself the American Blackshirts.

At this juncture in the discussion, my students brought up the issue of trust. How is it built? Are there any individuals or institutions who will be listened to by all sides? These are harder questions to answer than they should be. In the political realm, broadly respected leaders are rare precisely because, in trying to establish a middle ground, they leave themselves open to attack from the extremes. Candidates with the best chance to win general elections can't get past their primaries. Legislators who try to work across the aisle are unappreciated by one side and castigated for disloyalty by the other. In a recent *Reader's Digest* survey, the four people most trusted by Americans were all fictional role players—movie actors—with Tom Hanks heading the list. Evidently the individuals we most believe in aren't real.

What about the press? My generation came of age watching three nightly news shows, staying up late for Johnny Carson, and pondering the thoughts of such eminent columnists as James Reston, Flora Lewis, Mary McGrory, William Raspberry, and William Buckley. The information they provided served as a mighty unifying force in American society.

We did not all subscribe to the same beliefs. On the contrary, there were substantial divisions between the major parties, and at the margin there was competition for space among Nazis, Communists, Black Panthers, the John Birch Society, Yippies, and the Klan. But the media played a huge role in preserving our equilibrium. People actually read the editorial pages of major newspapers. Most everyone knew who was on the latest cover of *Life, Time, Newsweek,* and *Rolling Stone.* Together, we sat in our living rooms and watched our country bury a president, then his brother, and, in between, Dr. King. We witnessed the first televised war, the first lunar landing, and the first resignation by a president. We disagreed frequently, but at least we started from the same general base of information. That's no longer true. Today citizens get their news from a kaleidoscope of sources, some reliable, many not—and we're pretty sure it's the other guy, not us, who is being taken in by partisan propaganda and fake news.

MY CLASS IS FAR FROM UNIFORMLY GLOOMY IN ASSESSING THE future. One student offered as a hopeful sign the nonmilitary aspects of George W. Bush's response to the 9/11 terror attacks. Bush cautioned Americans not to blame Islam or its practitioners for the actions of a small group of terrorists. On this principle, he was consistent and courageous throughout his presidency. Not once did he seek to win cheap applause at the expense of American Muslims, nor did he spread lies about them, nor fail to speak out when some were targeted by hate crimes. The example he set in the face of the most serious attack on American soil since Pearl Harbor is worth remembering.

Another student seconded her classmate's earlier warning about complacency but saw a possible remedy in the response to Trump's election. Among her peers, she was seeing an eruption of interest in public affairs and a greater willingness to organize and participate in protests and to sign up for campaigns. She was excited about the number of smart women who have announced plans to run for office. Trump, she hoped, might be the wake-up call that American democracy needs.

I share that hope, but we must remember that the nerve-shattering forces at work in the United States and the world today were hardly set in motion by one man. The currents will still be felt long after Trump exits the public stage. In the past, I have always believed that time was on our side—as a healer, a teacher, a creator of space for innovation and break-the-mold ideas. Now I'm not so sure. My yearning to be upbeat is as powerful as ever, but a lot of what I see I don't like. On the economy, I'm reminded of the *Sgt. Pepper* tune where Paul sings, "I've got to admit it's getting better," and John taunts him, "It can't get no worse." Perspective is everything. Stock markets may soar, but living standards for the majority haven't improved in a long time, and large numbers of young people are convinced they will never do as well as their parents.

If so many didn't feel they were being left behind, they would be more upbeat and less inclined to ignite little fires on the Internet and in the voting booth. Expectations matter. The jumps in family income that took place in the United States after World War II may have seemed normal then, but they were, in fact, unprecedented—a product of recovery from Depression and war in a country that controlled an outsize portion of global wealth. If people are now willing to settle for steady, modest gains, and if tax and budget policies are reformed to ensure that benefits are more widely distributed, prospects will brighten. However, we may be in for a long wait.

More generally, I fear that we are becoming disconnected from the ideals that have long inspired and united us. When we laugh, it is more often at each other than with each other. The list of topics that can't be discussed without blowing up a family or college reunion is lengthening. We don't just disagree; we are astonished at the views that others hold to be self-evident. We seem to be living in the same country but different galaxies—and most of us lack the patience to explore the space between. This weakens us and does, indeed, make us susceptible.

The trio of nightmares cited earlier are exaggerated, as dreamscapes tend to be. However, the emotions and attitudes they reflect are real and part of a waxing hostility toward one another that we seem unable to reverse. It doesn't take much imagination to conceive of circumstances—another major recession, a corruption scandal, racial unrest, more terror incidents, assassinations, a series of natural disasters, or an overnight plunge into an unexpected war—that might cause a split too wide for our constitution, democracy's needle and thread, to mend.

SEVENTEEN

THE RIGHT QUESTIONS

Whoever fights with monsters should see to it that in
the process he does not himself become a monster.

—NIETZSCHE

WITHIN EACH OF US, THERE IS AN INEXHAUSTIBLE
yearning for liberty, or so we democrats like to believe. However, that desire often seems in competition with the longing to be told what to do. We are of two minds.
In classrooms, we search constantly for the right balance between instilling discipline in our students and allowing their
curiosity and creativity to run free. In religious circles, rote
memorization is the means of learning favored by some, but for
others the search for wisdom, though beginning with scripture,
opens itself to the full range of human experience and imagin-
ings. When rabbis are accused of answering every question with
a question, they typically reply: "And why do you think that is?"
In the Gospels, Jesus asks forty questions for every declarative
statement he makes. In business, too, and in the armed forces,
there are commandments that must be obeyed, mixed with ex-

hortations to reject the stale conventions of dogma in search of fresh insights.

We all value the right to push against boundaries and go boldly where none has preceded us; however, that is not all we value. Especially when we are afraid, angry, or confused, we may be tempted to give away bits of our freedom—or, less painfully, somebody else's freedom—in the quest for direction and order. Bill Clinton observed that when people are uncertain, they'd rather have leaders who are strong and wrong than right and weak. Throughout history, demagogues have often outperformed democrats in generating popular fervor, and it is almost always because they are perceived to be more decisive and sure in their judgments.

In times of relative tranquillity, we feel we can afford to be patient. We understand that policy questions are complicated and merit careful thought. We want our leaders to consult experts, gather as much information as possible, test assumptions, and give us a chance to voice our opinions on the available options. We see long-term planning as necessary and deliberation as a virtue, but when we decide that action is urgently needed, our tolerance for delay disappears.

In those moments, many of us no longer want to be asked, "What do you think?" We want to be told where to march. That is when Fascism gets its start: other options don't seem enough. There is a reason that vigilante movies are popular. We all know the scenarios: a law-abiding citizen is hurt—a loved one slain, a daughter kidnapped, a rape unprosecuted—and the police have no answer. Suddenly we feel ourselves identifying with an agent of vengeance such as those portrayed on-screen by Liam Neeson, Bruce Lee, Jodie Foster, or Batman, and all that pent-up fury goes in search of its target, due process be damned. When the villains are annihilated, we cheer. It is our nature—or at least part of it.

In the lives of nations, the origins of anger do not have to be deeply personal to awaken the desire for instant solutions. Mussolini and Hitler drew on the anguish of their citizens following the carnage of World War I. Kim Il-sung played guardian and guide in a country scarred by four decades of strife. Milošević and Putin tapped into deep wells of nationalist outrage in the aftermath of the Cold War. Chávez and Erdoğan rose to power amid political and economic crises that were knocking members of the middle class off their financial ladders and into poverty. Orbán and his fellow travelers on the European right promise to shield voters from the psychological demands that stem from religious, cultural, and racial diversity. Going much further back, the ancient Israelites—surrounded by enemies—pleaded with Samuel to give them a king, so that "we will be like all the other nations, with a king to lead us and to go out before us and to fight our battles." The prophet cautions the Israelites to think twice, warning that the monarch they are demanding will certainly take their sons to be warriors, their daughters to be cooks, and their vineyards, fields, cattle, sheep, and servants to satisfy his own needs. Still the people persist, and their prayer is answered. A century later, their kingdom is split and careens toward destruction.

THERE IS NOTHING OBJECTIONABLE ABOUT WANTING A STRONG leader—few yearn for a weak one—but the list of national leaders who were thought virtuous before revealing one or more disastrous defects of character begins with history itself and is still lengthening. In 1980, Robert Mugabe was hailed as a hero of Africa for his role in freeing Rhodesia (now Zimbabwe) from white colonial rule. He proceeded to mismanage the country's economy, foster corruption, run roughshod over human rights, suppress political dissent, and refuse to leave until finally forced out, in November 2017, at the age of ninety-three. In 1985, Hun Sen seemed the right man to lead Cambodia, still in recovery from the genocidal Khmer Rouge, but that was more than three decades ago, long enough for him to become a dictator. Uganda's Yoweri Museveni promised full democracy when, in 1986, he took the helm of his country following a brutal civil war. Many considered him to be the herald of a new and enlightened generation of African leaders; but while others in his cohort have moved on, he has stayed and stayed, growing more autocratic with each term.

Sadly, many more names could be added to this list, from Nicaragua's Daniel Ortega to Rwanda's Paul Kagame to Azerbaijan's Ilham Aliyev to the longest name of all, Gurbanguly Berdimuhamedow, self-described "protector" of Turkmenistan. Power is, as we know, an addiction prone to abuse. Even those who enter public life with the best of intentions are susceptible to its pull. We ought, therefore, to be mindful of our own bad habit—which is to look for and expect easy answers when the most serious problems we face are anything but. We might want to remember the explanation that Hitler gave, in 1936, for his popularity: "I will tell you what has carried me to the position I have reached. Our political problems appeared complicated. The German people could make nothing of them. . . . I, on the other hand, . . . reduced them to the simplest terms. The masses realized this and followed me."

ON THE NINETEENTH OF OCTOBER 2017, I TOOK THE TRAIN TO NEW York for an event convened by George W. Bush in celebration of the "Spirit of Liberty." Years ago—when Bush was president and I had just set out on my new career as a former somebody—we disagreed often about matters of policy. However, I have always admired the man's easygoing optimism and his personal decency, qualities that have become far less common in public life than they should be.

On this occasion, he had an important message to convey. Speaking quietly but firmly, the ex–commander in chief warned against the degradation of political conversation in the United

States and overseas. He found fault with relentless partisanship, the revival of isolationist and protectionist sentiments, the twisting of national pride into nativist bigotry, and the witless acceptance by some of conspiracy theories and outright fabrications. "We know, deep down," he said, "that repression is not the wave of the future. . . . We know that free governments are the only way to ensure that the strong are just and the weak are valued. And we know that when we lose sight of our ideals, it is not democracy that has failed. It is the failure of those charged with preserving and protecting democracy."

During my opportunity to speak, I expressed alarm—as I often do—at those now in office who think the United States can get by without help from its friends. In my view, we need to work well with others, whether we are trying to stop terrorists, halt the spread of nuclear arms, raise living standards, preserve the environment, prevent epidemic disease, put international drug dealers in jail, or—yes—safeguard our borders. There's no reason on earth why we should be afraid or unwilling to engage constructively. The idea that the United States is a nation of chumps that has spent the past fifty years getting ripped off by wily foreigners is absurd. The suggestion that our country can back away from its responsibilities in an era at least as dangerous as any other is just plain sad. That's not the America I recognize.

As secretary of state, I was proud to join presidents George H. W. Bush and Bill Clinton in calling the United States "the indispensable nation." I worry today that the country is, by its own choice, becoming less admired and less relevant in shaping world affairs. Partly for this reason, I believe that Fascism and Fascist policies pose a more virulent threat to international freedom, prosperity, and peace than at any time since World War II. I am drawn again to my conclusion that a Fascist is someone who claims to speak for a whole nation or group, is utterly unconcerned with the rights of others, and is willing to use violence and whatever other means are necessary to achieve the goals he or she might have. Throughout my adult life, I have felt that America could be counted on to put obstacles in the way of any such leader, party, or movement. I never thought that, at age eighty, I would begin to have doubts.

THE SHADOW LOOMING OVER THESE PAGES IS, OF COURSE, THAT of Donald Trump. He is president because he convinced enough voters in the right states that he was a teller of blunt truths, a masterful negotiator, and an effective champion of American interests. That he is none of those things should put us on edge, but there is a larger cause for unease. Trump is the first antidemocratic president in modern U.S. history. On too many days, beginning in the early hours, he flaunts his disdain for democratic institutions, the ideals of equality and social justice, civil discourse, civic virtues, and America itself. If transplanted to a country with fewer democratic safeguards, he would audition for dictator, because that is where his instincts lead. This frightening fact has consequences. The herd mentality is powerful in international affairs. Leaders around the globe observe, learn from, and mimic one another. They see where their peers are heading, what they can get away with, and how they can augment and perpetuate their power. They walk in one another's footsteps, as Hitler did with Mussolini—and today the herd is moving in a Fascist direction.

For all their differences, there are also links that connect figures like Maduro, Erdoğan, Putin, Orbán, Duterte, and—the sole example among them of a true Fascist—Kim Jong-un. Each has tried to nudge followers away from the consensus of support for democratic norms that required decades of struggle and sacrifice to build. These willful men see access to high office not as a temporary privilege but as a means of imposing their own desires for as long as they can. In public statements, they display no interest in cooperation outside the specific groups they purport to speak for and represent. They all claim for themselves the mantle of "strong leader"; they all say they speak for "the people"; and they look to one another for help in further enlarging their ranks.

If this circle of despots hadn't come into being, Trump's dispiriting influence would likely be temporary and manageable, a minor malady from which a healthy body could rapidly recover; but when the law-based international order is already fighting off a variety of illnesses, the immune system is weakened. That is the peril we confront.

ONE OF MY PASTIMES IN RECENT YEARS HAS BEEN TO PARTICIPATE in think tank projects that assess, for example, the outlook for democracy in the Middle East and threats to political and social pluralism in the United States and abroad. Most often the process—which, God help me, I enjoy—entails getting smart, highly caffeinated people to sit together around a table, talk, nibble on cold cuts, and write recommendations that are circulated internally, revised, and published. Some might imagine that this is how elitists come up with Machiavellian plans for running the world. To those involved, however, it is an exercise in abject humility. Only very rarely do our painstakingly composed and earnestly argued reports have an impact, though I, for one, think the globe might profit should more people be willing to read, mark, and learn their contents.

Because the reports are out there and in need of consumers, I am not going to ask readers of this book to wade through a long list of proposals about purging excess money from politics, improving civic education, defending journalistic independence, adjusting to the changing nature of the workplace, enhancing inter-religious dialogue, and putting a saddle on the bucking bronco we call the Internet. We should do all these things and more; but would that be enough?

President Obama spent eight years trying to push the United States forward in most of these areas, with some success. His administration's tax and spending policies were aimed directly at lifting wages for low- and middle-income people. The Department of Education promoted lifelong learning, vocational training, and reduced tuition costs while taking on a handful of high-profile for-profit universities that were ripping off students. The president tried hard to bring a healing presence—even a touch of "Amazing Grace"—to the racial divide. More than any of his predecessors, he was attuned to social media and the complex realities of the cyberworld. He was as zealous in enforcing immigration laws as he was creative in trying to find a legal path for the deserving to become citizens. He inherited an economic meltdown and left office following the longest sustained expansion of private sector employment in U.S. history.

So here's what doesn't make sense. In November 2016, Obama's favorability rating was the highest of his presidency—and yet the American Electoral College rewarded a candidate who insisted that the United States was going to hell.

The puzzle is not limited to 2016 or to one country. In Russia, the rise of Putin can perhaps be explained by the disasters of the 1990s. In 2002, when Erdoğan first ran for president, he seemed a savior compared to the weary old misfits who had run Turkey into the ground.

More recently, however, the sources of discontent are less evident or less weighty. Countries such as Hungary, Poland, and the Philippines are not in unusually dire economic straits, nor have they suffered a recent historical trauma. Further, the world is by many measures in better shape now than it has ever been. Infants born today are more likely to begin life healthy, more likely to receive the necessary vaccines, more likely to have access to an education, and more likely to reach old age than those in any prior generation. World Bank figures show that the global rate for extreme poverty has dipped below 10 percent for the first time. Partnerships between aid agencies and the private sector have yielded immense dividends by broadening the availability of medicine, tackling malaria and HIV/AIDS, and increasing access to electricity and modern communications. The international system has an abundance of flaws, and the Syrian refugee crisis stretched its humanitarian capacity beyond the breaking point, but professionals in the fields of development, public health, and refugee care have never done more good in as many places or for as large a number of people.

Yes, salaries remain too flat, and we have much work ahead to provide jobs for the next generation and the next. There is no cause to be satisfied, but neither should we fall under the spell of believing that authoritarianism is somehow a more practical option. One might ask: Well, what about China? Its rise has contributed much to global gains, but that is because three decades ago, the leaders in Beijing decided to open their economy and embrace many of the principles of free enterprise. China is a major player not because it's the master of its own game but because its people are so adept at capitalism.

CONSIDER ALL THE DEMANDS THAT ARE PLACED ON GOVERNMENT, then factor in the gargantuan changes that have taken place in the past seven decades: the end of colonialism, the lifting of the Iron Curtain, the narrowing of the North–South divide, the revolution in technology, and the increased mobility of people. By any objective standard, democracy—though everywhere tested—has not failed and is not failing. Why, then, do we feel so often that it has and is?

In my twenty-plus years as a professor, I have learned to ask myself, when I am not getting good answers, whether it is because I haven't been looking in the right places. I wonder now whether we, as democratic citizens, have been remiss in forming the right questions. Maybe we have grown so accustomed to receiving immediate satisfaction from our devices that we have lost patience with democracy's sluggish pace. Possibly, we have allowed ourselves to be manipulated by hucksters who pledge to deliver the world on a silver platter but have no clue how to make good on their promises. Perhaps we have been letting appearances—the illusion of decisiveness, the breathless reporting of trivia, the faux drama of reality TV—deceive and confuse us to the point that we can't recognize what is true, and instead believe with certainty what is not. The moment may be right to take a time-out and consider more carefully what we really mean when we talk about such concepts as greatness and strength.

FEW INCOMING AMERICAN PRESIDENTS WERE MORE WIDELY scorned than Abraham Lincoln. Critics in the southern states were predictably abusive, but leading northern politicians—even from his own party—called him "vacillating & inefficient," "weak as water," and "an admitted failure [who] has no will, no courage, no executive capacity." The chorus grew louder when, for security reasons, he wore a low-crowned hat and capacious overcoat to avoid being recognized while changing trains en route to Washington for his inauguration. Apparently the new president was not only—among the other epithets directed at him—a bumpkin, yahoo, gorilla, and idiot; he was also a coward. Four years later, when leaping from the balcony at Ford's Theatre, John Wilkes Booth called him a tyrant.

In his impact on the times during which he served, no U.S. chief executive was more divisive than Lincoln, yet today he is one of the handful of presidents revered by Republicans, Democrats, historians, and everyday citizens in all parts of the country and by many millions across the globe. History long ago judged him a strong leader, but not because he professed to be. While the object of much ridicule himself, Lincoln never mocked the downtrodden, nor bragged of his own accomplishments, nor exhibited personal cruelty. He was a savvy politician who could play rough and whose wartime policies compromised civil liberties, but his true aim—to save a nation from the ugliness of its own worst passions and policies—never wavered.

As a communicator, he was an original who demanded more from the American people and spoke to them with greater frankness than any president before or since. His plea when the war began was directed toward the "better angels of our nature" and, when the conflict was winding down, to the principles of "malice toward none" and "charity for all." He told a nation burdened by sorrow to consider the possibility that it had—by tolerating slavery for so long—invited its own Armageddon. He urged those with a thirst for vengeance to concentrate instead on binding up the nation's wounds and caring "for him who shall have borne the battle, and for his widow and his orphan."

A century later, and across an ocean to the east, Nelson Mandela began serving twenty-seven years, the prime of his life, in prison. His crime was to oppose the racist oppressors who had secured a monopoly on power and privilege in his country. The courageous dissident had a profound cause for grievance, a legitimate reason for bitterness, and thousands of days behind bars to cultivate hate. Instead he chose to spend time learning about the people who had put him in jail—the Afrikaners. He studied their language, history, resentments, and fears. When the long-awaited day came and he was finally released, Mandela not only understood those who had thrown him into prison; he was able to communicate with them, find common ground with them, forgive them, and—most astonishingly—lead them. As president,

Mandela pushed back against the many in his party who wanted immediate justice for the multitude of wrongs done to members of the anti-apartheid movement. He appointed a Truth and Reconciliation Commission that received testimony from all sides. Unlike so many, he found the trappings of high office eminently resistible and refused to stand for a second term. In his valedictory address to the United Nations, he said:

> *As I sit in Qunu and grow as ancient as its hills, I will continue to entertain the hope that there has emerged a cadre of leaders in my own country and region, on my continent and in the world, which will not allow that any should be denied their freedom as we were; that any should be turned into refugees as we were; that any should be condemned to go hungry as we were; that any should be stripped of their human dignity as we were.*

Lincoln and Mandela each fought with monsters; neither became one.

SOME MAY VIEW THIS BOOK AND ITS TITLE AS ALARMIST. GOOD. We should be awake to the assault on democratic values that has gathered strength in many countries abroad and that is dividing America at home. The temptation is powerful to close our eyes and wait for the worst to pass, but history tells us that for freedom to survive, it must be defended, and that if lies are to stop, they must be exposed.

Had Donald Trump not been elected president, I would still have embarked on this work, for it is a project I conceived with the thought of lending momentum to democracy during Hillary Clinton's first term. Trump's election just added to my sense of urgency. We cannot, of course, expect every leader to possess the wisdom of Lincoln or Mandela's largeness of soul, but when we think about what questions might be most useful to ask, perhaps we should begin by discerning what our prospective leaders believe it worthwhile for us to hear.

Do they cater to our prejudices by suggesting that we treat people outside our ethnicity, race, creed, or party as unworthy of dignity and respect?

Do they want us to nurture our anger toward those who we believe have done us wrong, rub raw our grievances, and set our sights on revenge?

Do they encourage us to have contempt for our governing institutions and the electoral process?

Do they seek to destroy our faith in essential contributors to democracy such as an independent press and a professional judiciary?

Do they exploit the symbols of patriotism—the flag, the pledge—in a conscious effort to turn us against one another?

If defeated at the polls, will they accept the verdict or insist without evidence that they have won?

Do they go beyond asking for our votes to brag about their ability to solve all problems, put to rest all anxieties, and satisfy every desire?

Do they solicit our cheers by speaking casually and with pumped-up machismo about using violence to blow enemies away?

Do they echo the attitude of Mussolini: "The crowd doesn't have to know," all it has to do is believe and "submit to being shaped"?

Or do they invite us to join with them in building and maintaining a healthy center for our societies, a place where rights and duties are apportioned fairly, the social contract is honored, and all have room to dream and grow?

The answers to these questions will not tell us whether a prospective leader is left- or right-wing, conservative or liberal, or—in the American context—a Democrat or a Republican. However, they will tell us much that we need to know about those wanting to lead us and much, also, about ourselves. For those who cherish freedom, the answers will provide grounds for reassurance or a warning we dare not ignore.

ACKNOWLEDGMENTS

I N JANUARY 2001, WHEN I COMPLETED MY SERVICE AS U.S. SEC-
retary of state, I looked forward to telling my story in the pages
of a book. My memoir, *Madam Secretary*, was published two
and a half years later. Having already arrived at the conventional
age of retirement, I figured that my career as an author was over.
I was wrong. *Fascism: A Warning* is book number six. Either I
don't know when to stop, or events have dictated that I continue to
speak my mind—I think the latter. This effort, more than others,
is tied to recent and ongoing developments in the public arena
and may therefore be overtaken, in some of its details, by what
happens next. However, I suspect (and fear) that the larger themes
will remain relevant because they are intimately connected to human nature and to how people of differing backgrounds find, or
fail to find, peaceful ways to live together.

Every book is the product of a team and, now that we have had
so much practice, our squad is a seasoned one. As always, I appreciate deeply the help and support of my family: my sister, Kathy
Silva; my brother and sister-in-law, John and Pamela Korbel; my
three daughters, Anne, Alice, and Katie; my sons-in-law; and
my six grandchildren. There is little I could do, and nothing I love
doing, without them.

The phenomenon we call Fascism played a central role in my life, as it has in that of so many others, and in the history of our times. Knowing this, however, is not the same as understanding Fascism's origins and methods; for that, research is indispensable. I thank my longtime writing partner, Bill Woodward, for his exploration of the past, his many ideas, and his hard work. Elaine Shocas, another colleague of long standing, provided essential help in reviewing drafts and offering sage advice. Richard Cohen has edited every book I have written—even the one on pins—and, each time, improves everything from the core themes to the use of commas. He is a delight to work with, and forbidden to retire.

An author needs a publisher, and it is a lucky writer indeed who finds the best in the business. I am indebted to the all-star lineup at HarperCollins—beginning with Jonathan Burnham and Jonathan Jao, but also including Sofia Groopman, who has devoted many hours to this project—and to the entire Harper team, including Brian Murray, Michael Morrison, Tina Andreadis, Kate D'Esmond, and Juliette Shapland; I am thankful for their ongoing faith and guidance.

Bob Barnett and Deneen Howell, my counselors, set the standard of excellence in their profession. There are none smarter and none more pleasant. I value their help and treasure their friendship.

The reason for my pleased expression on the book's back cover is that the photographer, Timothy Greenfield-Sanders, is among the world's most skilled. I don't give him much to work with, but he always finds a way to capture something deeper than the surface impression. I am honored that another of his portraits of me has been made part of the Smithsonian National Portrait Gallery's permanent collection.

Like most books, this one went through numerous drafts. I thank all those who took the time to review various chapters, including my colleagues Wendy Sherman, Jim O'Brien, Jacob Freedman, and Fariba Yassaee, and especially Ken Wollack, the longtime president of the National Democratic Institute. Ken had many important insights, and I also appreciate the help of NDI's Scott Hubli on the relationship between information technology and democracy.

An effort of this type demands a large investment of time, something that can distract from other obligations. Fortunately, I am privileged to work every day alongside an understanding and talented crew at the Albright Stonebridge Group. Jan Stewart and Liza Romanow have been at my side throughout this process and I could not have made it in the absence of their assistance, patience, and skill. There are too many others to cite everyone by name, but special thanks are also due to Melissa Estok, Mica Carmio, Lauren Cotter, and Nancy Sefko.

Anna Stolk devoted many hours to research and fact-checking. Her sound judgment and careful eye were valuable contributors to this project. Will Palmer did a superb job as copy editor and I commend him for it.

One of the joys of my life is that when I travel and spend time with old friends, it is often with a public purpose in mind. Back in 2003, I came up with an idea for staying in touch with some of the former foreign ministers with whom I had worked when serving as secretary of state. Our original name for the group, "Madeleine and her Exes," has stuck, but the formal appellation is The Aspen Ministers Forum. We meet once or twice a year, continue to add more recent retirees, and often issue statements or write articles to summarize our thoughts. Lately, we have been discussing the situation in Europe, the political environment in the United States, and the implications of both for the rest of the world. Naturally, the subject of this book came up and several of the "ex-mins" allowed me to pick their brains. For their time and thoughts, I particularly want to thank my friends Lloyd Axworthy (Canada), Lamberto Dini (Italy), Erik Derycke (Belgium), Jan Eliasson (Sweden), Joschka Fischer (Germany), Jaime Gama (Portugal), Susana Malcorra (Argentina), David Miliband and Malcolm Rifkind (United Kingdom), Ana Palacio (Spain), George Andreas Papandreou (Greece), Hubert Védrine (France), and Knut Vollebæk (Norway). To be clear, though, the opinions expressed in this book are solely my responsibility, not theirs.

Finally, I am profoundly grateful to the students of my graduate class at Georgetown for their provocative thoughts on Fascism and for cheerfully agreeing to act as guinea pigs for this book. The lasagna was not payment enough. Sound the roll call: teaching assistants Friederike Kaiser, Shannon Mizzi, and Kirby Neuner; students Hadeil Abdelraouf, Bassima Alghussein, Katherine Ayanian, Daniel Bishop, Dainis Butners, Yanique Campbell, Samuel Denney, Shane Feifer, Anthony Johnson, Melissa Karakash, Ted Kenyon, Annie Kowalewski, Jennifer Lincoln, Amelie Lohmann, James Lowe, Gayle Martin, Alexandra Memmott, Sarah Oldham, Yusuke Saito, Sonny Santistevan, Samta Savla, Sally Scudder, Amanat Thind, Amanda Thoet, and Patrick Zimet. Thanks to each and every one.

NOTES

CHAPTER ONE: A DOCTRINE OF ANGER AND FEAR

2 "The Force which is born": Mohandas K. Gandhi, quoted in Surendra Bhana and Bridglal Pachai, eds., *A Documentary History of Indian South Africans* (Cape Town: D. Philip, 1984), as quoted in "Gandhi Explains 'Satyagraha,'" South African History Online, www.sahistory.org.za/archive/44-gandhi-explains-satyagraha.

4 "the end of the Cold War has been a victory": George H. W. Bush, 1991 State of the Union Address to the 102nd U.S. Congress, Washington, D.C., January 29, 1991.

4 "Europe is attempting to create": Václav Havel, Address to the Nation, Prague, Czechoslovakia, January 1, 1994.

4 "under assault and in retreat": *Freedom in the World 2018: Democracy in Crisis* (Washington, DC: Freedom House, 2018), 1.

5 "the enemy of the American people": Donald J. Trump, quoted in "Trump Calls the News Media the 'Enemy of the American People,'" *New York Times*, February 17, 2017.

5 "laughingstock": Trump, quoted in Ruth Marcus, "Our Criminal Justice System Is Not a 'Joke,' Yet," *Washington Post*, November 3, 2017.

11 "Fascism was the major political innovation": Robert O. Paxton, *The Anatomy of Fascism* (New York: Vintage, 2004), 3.

13 "every people has a right": Woodrow Wilson, Address Delivered at the First Annual Assemblage of the League to Enforce Peace, May 27, 1916, American Presidency Project, www.presidency.ucsb.edu/ws/?pid=65391.

CHAPTER TWO: THE GREATEST SHOW ON EARTH

15 "genius of the modern age": Thomas Edison, quoted in Richard Collier, *Duce! A Biography of Benito Mussolini* (New York: Viking, 1971), 93.

15 "superman": Gandhi, quoted ibid., 93.

15 "struggle against the bestial appetites of Leninism": Winston Churchill, quoted ibid., 93.

21 "to break the bones of the democrats": Benito Mussolini, quoted in Paxton, *Anatomy of Fascism*, 17.

21 "Either we are allowed to govern": Mussolini, quoted in Denis Mack Smith, *Mussolini* (London: Phoenix Press, 1981), 51.

22 attracted a mixed group: Description of marchers from Collier, *Duce!*, 25–26.

23 "I could have turned this drab grey hall": Mussolini, quoted in Collier, *Duce!*, 66.

25 "I want to make a mark on my era": Ibid.

25 "Never before . . . have the peoples thirsted": Mussolini, "*La dottrina del fascismo*" ("The Doctrine of Fascism"), in *Enciclopedia italiana di scienze, lettere ed arti* (Rome: Treccani, 1932).

25 "Live dangerously": Mussolini, quoted in Smith, *Mussolini*, 112.

25 "the greatest colonial war in all history": Ibid., 201.

25 "raise up your banners": Mussolini, quoted in Collier, *Duce!*, 130.

26 "when Signor Mussolini stepped out": Herbert Matthews, "Mussolini Declares War Unnecessary; Present Problems Do Not 'Justify It,'" *New York Times*, May 15, 1939.

26 IF I ADVANCE, FOLLOW ME: slogan on banner cited in Collier, *Duce!*, 91. The saying may have originated with French general Henri de La Rochejaquelein (1772–94).

28 "Only one person in Italy is infallible": Mussolini, quoted in Smith, *Mussolini*, 180.

28 "Often, I would like to be wrong": Mussolini, quoted ibid., 110.

CHAPTER THREE: "WE WANT TO BE BARBARIANS"

29 "That night at the Inn": Patrick Leigh Fermor, *A Time of Gifts* (New York: New York Review Books, 1977), 77.

31 "I do not want your votes": Adolf Hitler, quoted in Alan Bullock, *Hitler: A Study in Tyranny* (London: Penguin, 1990), 270.

31 "cantankerous, willful, arrogant": Dr. Eduard Hüner, quoted ibid., 27.

33   "colossal untruths": Hitler, quoted ibid., 70.

33   "of those who feel cheated": Friedrich Nietzsche, quoted in Karl Dietrich Bracher, *The German Dictatorship: The Origins, Structure and Effects of National Socialism* (New York: Praeger, 1970), 63.

34   "We National Socialists": Hitler: *Mein Kampf*, Volume Two, chapter VII, www.hitler.org/writings/mein_kampf/mkv2ch07.html.

34   "a man born to be a dictator": Hitler, quoted in Bullock, *Hitler*, 117.

35   "policy of legality": Hitler, quoted in Bracher, *The German Dictatorship*, 118.

37   "a legal revolution": Hitler, quoted ibid., 48.

37   "The reactionary forces believe": Hitler, quoted in Bullock, *Hitler*, 276.

39   "If I am to be killed": Ernst Röhm, quoted in "Night of the Long Knives," *The Triumph of Hitler*, The History Place, 2002, www.historyplace.com/worldwar2/triumph/tr-roehm.htm.

40   "Workers, . . . you must look": Hitler, quoted in Bullock, *Hitler*, 632.

41   "We studied it as a Bible": Martin Bormann Jr., quoted in Erna Paris, *Long Shadows: Truth, Lies and History* (New York: Bloomsbury, 2000), 55.

41   "Those who have met Herr Hitler": Winston Churchill, *Great Contemporaries* (New York: W.W. Norton, 1990; first published 1937), 170.

42   "grow the German Reich of which great poets": Hitler, quoted in Bullock, *Hitler*, 632.

CHAPTER FOUR: "CLOSE YOUR HEARTS TO PITY"

44   "stupid, barbarous, and unworthy": Benito Mussolini, quoted in Collier, *Duce!*, 148.

44   "the great man south of the Alps": Adolf Hitler, quoted in Robert M. Edsel, *Saving Italy: The Race to Rescue a Nation's Treasures from the Nazis* (New York: W.W. Norton, 2013), 10.

45   "Hitler talks, talks, talks": Count Galeazzo Ciano, quoted in Bullock, *Hitler*, 678.

46   "War is to a man": Mussolini, address to Italian Chamber of Deputies, April 28, 1939.

47   "love total, pitiless war": Mussolini, quoted in Peter Wyden, *The Passionate War: The Narrative History of the Spanish Civil War, 1936–1939* (New York: Simon and Schuster, 1983), 446.

47   "close your hearts to pity": Hitler, quoted in Bullock, *Hitler*, 526.

48   "Hitler always presents me with a fait accompli": Mussolini, quoted in Collier, *Duce!*, 178.

51   "It is necessary to spread an atmosphere of terror": General Emilio Mola, quoted in Wyden, *Passionate War*, 108.

53   "We three men": Hitler, quoted in Bullock, *Hitler*, 609.

53   "the greatest mistake of his life": Hitler, quoted ibid.

CHAPTER FIVE: VICTORY OF THE CAESARS

57   "The last century was the winter of the West": Oswald Spengler, *Decline of the West* (New York: Knopf, 1922).

57   "an overwhelming arrogance": Jennie Lee, quoted in John Simkin, "Oswald Mosley," Spartacus Educational, http://spartacus-educational.com /PRmosley.htm.

58   "be they Hebrew or any other form": William Joyce, quoted ibid.

60   "the people that descended, several millennia ago": Houston Stewart Chamberlain, *Aryan World-View* (Henderson, NV: Patriot Press, 2002), 11.

60   "revival of the Aryan culture": spokesman of the Hindu Party, March 25, 1939, quoted in Marzia Casolari, "Hindutva's Foreign Tie-Up in the 1930s: Archival Evidence," *Economic and Political Weekly*, January 22, 2000, 224, http:// www.sacw.net/DC/CommunalismCollection/ArticlesArchive/casolari.pdf.

62   "Just as Christ wanted little children": girl in a Nazi youth camp in Milwaukee, Wisconsin, quoted in Mark D. Van Ells, "Americans for Hitler— the Bund," *America in WWII*, August 2007.

62   "Rosenfeld" and his "Jew Deal": Fritz Kuhn, quoted ibid.

62   "The speakers started ranting": Meyer Lansky, quoted in Michael Feldberg, "But They Were Good to Their People," My Jewish Learning, www .myjewishlearning.com/article/but-they-were-good-to-their-people/2.

64   "The branch": John Kander and Fred Ebb, "Tomorrow Belongs to Me," from *Cabaret*, directed by Bob Fosse (New York: Allied Artists Pictures, 1972).

CHAPTER SIX: THE FALL

68   "The whiz of a flying bomb": Prokop Drtina, *Československo můj osud* (Prague: Melantrich, 1991), 573. Author's translation.

70   "many tens of millions of people": Hermann Göring, war directive, May 23, 1941, quoted in Bullock, *Hitler*, 642.

72   "a much better" new dad: David F. Crew, ed., *Nazism and German Society, 1933–1945* (London: Routledge, 1994), 180.

72   "emancipation from emancipation": German slogan, quoted ibid., 3.

75   "You believe you have the devotion of the people": Dino Grandi, quoted in Collier, *Duce!*, 218–19.

75   "you are the most hated man in Italy": King Victor Emmanuel, quoted ibid., 229.

76   "lose any sense of balance": Benito Mussolini, quoted ibid., 317.

78   to "men who despise you, enslave you . . .": *The Great Dictator*, directed by Charles Chaplin (Hollywood, CA: Charles Chaplin Film Corporation, 1940).

CHAPTER SEVEN: DICTATORSHIP OF DEMOCRACY

79   "the State is all-embracing": Benito Mussolini, "Doctrine of Fascism."

81   "engineers of human souls": Joseph Stalin, quoted in Michael Geyer and Sheila Fitzpatrick, eds., *Beyond Totalitarianism* (New York: Cambridge University Press, 2009), 319.

85   "I do not agree with the policy of your government": Yugoslav army office, quoted in Josef Korbel, *Tito's Communism* (Denver, CO: University of Denver Press, 1951), 124–25.

88   "*Ili Schweigen ili Gefängnis*": Russian citizen quoted in I. F. Stone, *The Haunted Fifties: 1953–1963* (Boston: Little, Brown, 1963), 80.

90   "I have in my hand a list": Joseph McCarthy, quoted in Jack Anderson and Ronald W. May, *McCarthy: The Man, the Senator, the "Ism"* (Boston, Beacon Press, 1952), 194.

91   "a conspiracy so immense": Ibid., 237.

CHAPTER EIGHT: "THERE ARE A LOT OF BODIES UP THERE"

95   "Fascism did not die with Mussolini": Harry S. Truman, remarks to founding session of the United Nations, San Francisco, California, June 26, 1945.

98   "We must secure unity in Serbia": Slobodan Milošević, quoted in Steve Engleberg, "Carving Out a Greater Serbia," *New York Times*, September 1, 1991.

CHAPTER NINE: A DIFFICULT ART

110 "The Constitution only maps": Adolf Hitler, quoted in Bracher, *The German Dictatorship*, 193.

111 "it is a difficult art": Cicero, quoted in Edith Hamilton, *The Roman Way* (New York: W.W. Norton, 1932), 58.

116 "have had enough of experts": Michael Gove, interview by Faisal Islam, *Sky News*, June 3, 2016.

118 "Democracy is not only a form of state": Tomáš Masaryk, quoted in Karel Čapek, *Talks with T. G. Masaryk*, ed. and trans. Michael Henry Heim (North Haven, CT: Catbird Press, 1995).

CHAPTER TEN: PRESIDENT FOR LIFE

121 "irresponsible populism": Brian Palmer, "Why Did Hugo Chávez Hate the United States So Much?" *Slate*, March 6, 2013.

127 "I was overwhelmed by the feeling": Gabriel García Márquez, quoted in Rory Carroll, *Comandante: Hugo Chávez's Venezuela* (New York: Penguin Press, 2013), 4–5.

129 "How can I forget the feelings": Hugo Chávez, quoted ibid., 188.

131 "Fourteen years ago, my barrio neighbors": Lisa Sullivan, "Yo Soy Chavez, Tu Eres Chavez, Todos Somos Chavez," Chicago Religious Leadership Network on Latin America, https://www.crln.org/reflection-on-the-death-of-hugo-chavez.

132 "rolling on in": Andrew Lloyd Webber and Tim Rice, "And the Money Kept Rolling In," from the musical *Evita* (1976).

135 "coup-mongering, power-grabbing": Nicolás Maduro, quoted in Mariana Zuñiga and Nick Miroff, "Venezuela's Opposition Holds Its Biggest Protests in Years. Will They Change Anything?," *Washington Post*, April 12, 2017.

CHAPTER ELEVEN: ERDOĞAN THE MAGNIFICENT

137 "The mosques are our barracks": Ziya Gökalp, "The Soldier's Prayer" (1912).

139 "For the People, In Spite of the People": political slogan, quoted in Steven Kinzer, *Crescent and Star: Turkey Between Two Worlds*, rev. ed. (New York: Farrar, Straus and Giroux, 2008), 47.

141 "Other parties have members": Necmettin Erbakan, quoted in Soner Cagaptay, *The New Sultan: Erdogan and the Crisis of Modern Turkey* (London: I.B. Taurus, 2017), 69.

142 "shining star in the darkness": Adolf Hitler, quoted in William O'Connor, "The 20th-Century Dictator Most Idolized by Hitler," *Daily Beast*, November 24, 2014.

143 "whatever issues are going on in Turkey": Madeleine Albright, press conference with Valdis Birkavs, foreign minister of Latvia, Washington, D.C., June 13, 1997.

146 "pious generation": Recep Tayyip Erdoğan, quoted in "The Decline of Turkish Schools," *The Economist*, September 30, 2017.

146 "holy path": Erdoğan, quoted in "Erdoğan Strengthens Grip with AKP Return," *Financial Times*, May 21, 2017.

146 "Turkish-style" . . . "half-people": Freedom House, "Freedom in the World 2017" report, March 2017, https://freedomhouse.org/report/freedom-world/2017/turkey.

149 "the second war of independence": Erdoğan, quoted in "Brave 'New Turkey': The Legacy of an Attempted Coup," *The Economist*, April 12, 2017.

151 "Nazism . . . risen from the dead": Erdoğan, quoted in Patrick Kingsley and Alissa J. Rubin, "Turkey's Relations with Europe Sink amid Quarrel with Netherlands," *New York Times*, March 12, 2017.

151 "If the West calls someone a dictator": Erdoğan, quoted in Steven A. Cook, "Five Myths About Turkey," *Washington Post*, March 17, 2017.

151 "I don't look at what Hans and George say": Erdoğan, quoted in Patrick Kingsley, "Erdogan and Supporters Stage Rally on Anniversary of Failed Coup," *New York Times*, July 16, 2017.

152 "surpassed Hitler in barbarism": Jack Simpson, "Turkish Prime Minister Says Israel Is 'More Barbaric Than Hitler,'" *Independent* (UK), July 20, 2014.

CHAPTER TWELVE: MAN FROM THE KGB

156 "a pure and utterly successful product": Vladimir Putin, with Nataliya Gevorkyan, Natalya Timakova, and Andrei Kolesnikov, *First Person*, trans. Catherine A. Fitzpatrick (New York: PublicAffairs, 2000), 41–42.

159 "Do not try to squeeze Russia": Putin, quoted in Madeleine Albright, *Madam Secretary: A Memoir* (New York: Talk/Miramax, 2003), 560.

162 "almost uncontained hyper use of force": Putin, address to 43rd Munich Conference on Security Policy, Munich, February 10, 2007, http://www.washingtonpost.com/wp-dyn/content/article/2007/02/12/AR2007021200555.html.

162 "We have no democracy": Nikita Orlov, quoted in Neil MacFarquhar and Ivan Nechepurenko, "Across Russia, Protesters Heed Navalny's Anti-Kremlin Rallying Cry," *New York Times*, June 12, 2017.

165 "start picking berries and eating honey": Putin, annual press conference, Moscow, December 18, 2014.

166 "If Ukraine does secede": Eduard Shevardnadze, quoted in James A. Baker III, *The Politics of Diplomacy* (New York: Putnam, 1995), 560.

166 "A lie ain't a side of the story": *The Wire*, season 5, episode 8, "Clarifications," directed by Anthony Hemingway, written by Dennis Lehane and David Simon, aired February 24, 2008, on HBO.

167 "Sure, I like Chinese food": Putin, quoted in Albright, *Madam Secretary*, 439–40.

168 "The idea of Fascism conquers the world": Benito Mussolini, quoted in Collier, *Duce!*, 114.

CHAPTER THIRTEEN: "WE ARE WHO WE WERE"

170 "We young people": Viktor Orbán, quoted in Timothy Garton Ash, *The Magic Lantern: The Revolution of '89 Witnessed in Warsaw, Budapest, Berlin, and Prague* (New York: Vintage, 1990), 51.

171 "a xenophobic, anti-democratic nationalist": Carol Giacomo, "A Democracy Road Trip Through Hungary," *New York Times*, July 1, 2017.

171 "morning, evening and night": Ferenc Gyurcsány, quoted in Pablo Gorondi, "Hungary's Prime Minister in Trouble over Leaked Recording," Associated Press, September 18, 2006.

173 "mafia state": George Soros, quoted in Palko Karasz, "George Soros Accuses Viktor Orban of Turning Hungary into 'Mafia State,'" *New York Times*, June 1, 2017.

176 "disease and parasites": Jarosław Kaczyński, quoted in Henry Foy, "Poland's Kingmaker," *Financial Times*, February 26, 2016.

176 "bring Budapest to Warsaw": Kaczyński, Polish TVN24, October 9, 2011.

177 "You are scoundrels": Kaczyński, quoted in Rick Lyman, "In Poland, an Assault on the Courts Provokes Outrage," *New York Times*, July 19, 2017.

177 "the worst sort of Poles": Kaczyński, quoted in Monika Scislowska, "Divisive Polish Party Leader Kaczynski Pulls the Strings," Associated Press, February 7, 2017.

177 "terrified of not living in a free country": Paulina Wilk, quoted in Isaac Stanley-Becker, "Led by Populist Law and Justice Party, Polish Parliament Moves to Strip Supreme Court of Independence," *Washington Post*, July 23, 2017.

178 "There will be no peace": Jean Monnet, remarks to the French Committee of National Liberation, August 5, 1943.

180 "One of the reasons European citizens are stepping away": Jean-Claude Juncker, remarks to the Parliamentary Assembly of the Council of Europe, Strasbourg, France, April 19, 2016.

182 "I see Islam as a foreign body": Alexander Gauland, quoted in Guy Chazan, "Gauland Struggles to Tame Germany's Wayward AfD," *Financial Times*, July 22, 2017.

182 "one hears echoes of classical fascist themes": Paxton, *The Anatomy of Fascism*, 185–86.

183 "Czech Trump": Milos Zeman, quoted in Griff Witte, "'Czech Trump' Wins Second Term as President," *Washington Post*, January 28, 2018.

184 "The masses arriving from other civilizations": Viktor Orbán, Address to the Nation, Budapest, Hungary, March 15, 2016.

185 "The most effective form of persuasion": Josef Goebbels, quoted in Rory Sutherland, "The Hitler Guide to Rigging a Referendum," *The Spectator*, May 11, 2013.

185 "Once you have given citizenship": Roman legislator, quoted in Mary Beard, *SPQR: A History of Ancient Rome* (London: W.W. Norton, 2015), 237.

187 "We are who we were": Orbán, speech in Budapest, March 15, 2016.

CHAPTER FOURTEEN: "THE LEADER WILL ALWAYS BE WITH US"

202 "If we have to go to war": Mun Hyok-myong, quoted in Nicholas Kristof, "War Drums Inside the North," *New York Times*, October 8, 2017.

203 "Rocket Man . . . on a suicide mission": Donald J. Trump, address to the UN General Assembly, September 19, 2017.

CHAPTER FIFTEEN: PRESIDENT OF THE UNITED STATES

207 "All Europe is for us": Benjamin Franklin, quoted in Stacy Schiff, *A Great Improvisation: Franklin, France, and the Birth of America* (New York: Henry Holt, 2005), 64.

207 "The American question": Giuseppe Garibaldi, quoted in Don H. Doyle, *The Cause of All Nations: An International History of the American Civil War* (New York: Basic Books, 2015), 299.

207 "The beginnings of a great new social order": Adolf Hitler, quoted ibid., 10.

208 "millions of Redskins": Hitler, quoted in James Whitman, "Why the Nazis Loved America," *Time*, March 21, 2017.

209 "though often to heedless": John Quincy Adams, speech before the U.S. House of Representatives, July 4, 1821.

209 "Shut up, silly woman": Donald J. Trump, remarks at Make America Great Again rally, Harrisburg, Pennsylvania, April 29, 2017. http://transcripts.cnn.com/TRANSCRIPTS/1704/29/se.02.html.

209 "peace invulnerable to the schemings": Franklin D. Roosevelt, radio address, Washington, D.C., June 6, 1944.

210 "I'll supply the dead bodies": Duterte, quoted in *The Duterte Manifesto* (Quezon City, Philippines: ABS-CBN Publishing, 2016), 40.

210 "unbelievable job": Trump quoted in Michael Gerson, "Trump's Embrace of Strongmen Is a Very Bad Strategy," *Washington Post*, June 22, 2017.

210 "fantastic": Trump, quoted ibid.

211 "there won't be strain": Trump, quoted ibid.

211 "was a bad guy": Trump, campaign rally, Raleigh, North Carolina, July 6, 2016.

211 "You have to give him credit": Trump, campaign rally, Ottumwa, Iowa, January 9, 2016.

211 "a man so highly respected": Trump, quoted in Jeremy Diamond, "Timeline: Donald Trump's Praise for Vladimir Putin," CNN, July 29, 2016.

212 "bad, very bad": Trump, quoted in Anthony Faiola, "The Germans Are 'Bad, Very Bad': Trump's Alleged Slight Generates Confusion, Backlash," *Washington Post*, May 26, 2017.

212 "slaps the right people": Nikki Haley, press briefing, White House, September 14, 2017.

212 a "clear message": Phay Siphan, quoted in Mike Ives, "Cambodian Government Cites Trump in Threatening Foreign News Outlets," *New York Times*, February 28, 2017.

213 "If the president of the United States": Chinese *People's Daily*, quoted in "Autocrats Across the Globe Echo Trump's 'Fake News' Swipes," *New York Times*, December 13, 2017.

213 "When the world looks at how bad": Trump, interviewed by David E. Sanger and Maggie Haberman, "Donald Trump on NATO, Turkey's Coup Attempt and the World," *New York Times*, July 21, 2016.

214 "For decades our country": Trump, remarks at Make America Great Again rally, Harrisburg.

215 "been disrespected, mocked and ripped off": Trump, interviewed by David E. Sanger and Maggie Haberman, "Donald Trump Expounds on His Foreign Policy Views," *New York Times*, March 26, 2016.

217 "every decision on trade": Trump, Inaugural Address, Washington, D.C., January 20, 2017.

217 "I will always put America first": Trump, address to the UN General Assembly, New York, September 19, 2017.

217 "clear-eyed outlook that the world": H. R. McMaster and Gary Cohn, "America First Doesn't Mean America Alone," *Wall Street Journal*, May 30, 2017.

220 "So I go to Poland": Trump, interviewed by Peter Baker, Michael S. Schmidt, and Maggie Haberman, "Excerpts from the Times's Interview with Trump," *New York Times*, July 19, 2017.

220 "I'm the only one": Trump, interviewed by Laura Ingraham, *The Ingraham Angle*, Fox News, November 2, 2017.

220 "I'm a very instinctual person": Trump, interviewed by Michael Scherer, *Time*, March 23, 2017.

220 "a very stable genius": Trump, quoted in David Nakamura and Karen Tumulty, "Trump Defends Fitness for Office," *Washington Post*, January 7, 2018.

220 "somewhat over": Angela Merkel, quoted in Samuel Osborne, "Angela Merkel Says Germany Can No Longer Rely on Donald Trump's America," *Independent* (UK), May 28, 2017.

223 "not just through the terror": Primo Levi, quoted in Stanislao Pugliese, "A Specter Haunting America: Trump and Italian Fascism," *La Voce di New York*, November 20, 2016.

CHAPTER SIXTEEN: BAD DREAMS

226 "haughty millionaires who are gathering up the riches": James B. Weaver, *A Call to Action* (Des Moines: Iowa Printing Co., 1892), 6.

226 "Every Man a King": Huey P. Long, "Share Our Wealth," national radio address, February 23, 1934.

226 "pointy-headed college professors": George Wallace, quoted in Ken Ringle, "The Enduring Symbol of an Era of Hate," *Washington Post*, September 15, 1998.

227 "I was killing Fascists": Wallace, quoted in Federico Finchelstein, *From Fascism to Populism in History* (Berkeley: University of California Press, 2017), 221.

227 "giant sucking sound": Ross Perot, second presidential campaign debate, Richmond, Virginia, October 15, 1992.

227 "Goebbels would have just envied": Perot, quoted in Jeff Noonan, "Lessons from History IV: Right Wing Populism in America: Too Close for Comfort," *Jeff Noonan: Interventions and Evocations* blog, www.jeffnoonan.org.

230 "To live in this process": German citizen quoted in Milton Mayer, *They Thought They Were Free: The Germans, 1933–45* (Chicago: University of Chicago Press, 1981), 166–73.

235 "The time has come for a movement": "Who We Are," American Blackshirts, https://www.americanblackshirts.com/about.

CHAPTER SEVENTEEN: THE RIGHT QUESTIONS

241 "Whoever fights with monsters": Friedrich Nietzsche, *Beyond Good and Evil*, trans. R. J. Hollingdale (London: Penguin, 1973; first published 1886), 102.

243 "we will be like all the other nations": 1 Samuel 8:20 (New International Version).

244 "I will tell you what has carried me": Adolf Hitler, quoted in Bullock, *Hitler*, 381.

245 "We know, deep down": George W. Bush, Bush Institute National Forum on Freedom, Free Markets, and Security, Lincoln Center, New York, October 19, 2017.

250 "vacillating": Senator Zachariah Chandler (R-Mich.), Senator William Fessenden (R-Maine), William M. Dickson (R-Ohio), quoted in Mark Bowden, "'Idiot,' 'Yahoo,' 'Original Gorilla': How Lincoln Was Dissed in His Day," *Atlantic*, June 2013.

252 "As I sit in Qunu": Nelson Mandela, UN General Assembly, September 21, 1998.

253 "The crowd doesn't have to know": Benito Mussolini, quoted in Smith, *Mussolini*, 126.

INDEX

ABOUT THE AUTHOR

MADELEINE ALBRIGHT served as America's sixty-fourth secretary of state from 1997 to 2001. Her distinguished career also includes positions on Capitol Hill, on the National Security Council, and as U.S. ambassador to the United Nations. She is a resident of Washington, D.C., and Virginia.

ALSO BY MADELEINE ALBRIGHT

PRAGUE WINTER
A Personal Story of Remembrance and War, 1937-1948
Available in Paperback, Large Print, eBook, and Digital Audio
Drawing on her own memory, her parents' written reflections,
interviews with contemporaries, and newly-available documents,
former US Secretary of State and *New York Times* bestselling
author Madeleine Albright recounts a tale that is by turns
harrowing and inspiring.

MADAM SECRETARY
A Memoir
Available in Paperback, eBook, and Digital Audio
"Her portraits of foreign leaders are lively and evocative. . . .
The result is a book that creates a sense of policy made by
real people." —*The New Yorker*

THE MIGHTY AND THE ALMIGHTY
Reflections on America, God, and World Affairs
Available in Paperback, eBook, and Digital Audio
A thoughtful and often surprising look at the role of religion in
shaping America's approach to the world. Drawing upon her
experiences while in office and her own deepest beliefs about
morality, the United States, and the present state of world affairs, a
woman noted for plain speaking offers her thoughts about the most
controversial topics of our time.

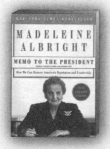

MEMO TO THE PRESIDENT
**How We Can Restore America's Reputation and
Leadership**
Available in Paperback
Madeleine Albright offers provocative ideas about how to confront
the myriad challenges facing America across the globe. Secretary
Albright's advice is candid and seasoned with humor and stories
from her years in office.

READ MY PINS
Stories from a Diplomat's Jewel Box
Available in Hardcover and eBook
"[Albright has] written a book that speaks directly to her personal
style and emerged with her brainy reputation unscathed. In the
world of politics, it is an accomplishment that requires more self-
confidence and swagger than a million tell-alls."
—*Washington Post*